Freemas

Quest for Immortality

Christopher Earnshaw PhD 33°

Written to commemorate the 300th anniversary
of the founding of the fraternity of Freemasonry
in London, 1717

Dedication

*This book is dedicated to all the Brethren worldwide for their
devotion to the labour of spreading Light.*

LVX

Chris Barnshaw 33°

First Printing, 2019   R2-8-2

ISBN: 9781673308129

1. The main category of the book: Freemasonry – Social History – 17th and 18th centuries

2. Freemasonry – Alchemy – Enlightenment

3. Title: Freemasonry: Quest for Immortality

4. Author: Christopher Earnshaw PhD

5. Publisher: Author's Proof, Tokyo

Images used in this publication are copyright-free, used under CC-BY-SA 3.0

Cover image: *A General View of the City of London, next the River Thames.* engraved by T. Bowles, 1751

R1-3-4

www.YouTube.com/c/SpiritualFreemasonry

www.chris-earnshaw.com

Contents

The Sanction

WHEREAS Worshipful Brother Christopher Earnshaw
has compiled a Book entitled "FREEMASONRY: Quest for
Immortality," and has requested our Sanction
for the publication thereof: we having perused the said
Book, and finding it to correspond with the Antient
practices of this Society, so recommend the same.

Donald K. Smith, Past Grand Master
Grand Lodge of Japan

Prologos

The Motivations of the First Three Grand Masters

After the Premier Grand Lodge was established in 1717, which later became the Grand Lodge of England, the first three Grand Masters were urged on by a moral imperative to rewrite and expand the existing two degrees of Operative Masons, and then add another, the Third Degree. However, their reasons have, until now, remained obscure, for example:

- How does the Hiramic Tragedy relate to the Kabbalistic *Tree of Life* and why?

- What important aspects suggest that Sir Francis Bacon's *New Atlantis* might have been a template for Freemasonry?

- Why did George Washington's apron have a skull and crossed-bones depicted inside the Square and Compasses?

- Were medieval mystery plays, that had been performed by guilds, the origin of Freemasonry's Third Degree?

- What does the *Scarlet Pimpernel* have to do with the Masonic emblem of the forget-me-not?

- What perfidy were Freemasons addressing, when they re-wrote the degrees of Operative Masons to add a Third Degree, that was a cause célèbre at the time and even debated on in Parliament?

- Why did Masons despise atheists, though Catholics were welcome in Lodge, whereas in England generally at the time it was the Catholics that were reviled, not atheists.

What we discover is that the Freemason's Monitor, the book that contains all the rituals and ceremonies, is in fact a puzzle. It has been purposely written to hide some secrets that indicate a far richer and more important lesson. Each of the three degrees that were created is based on a unique type of alchemy, which leads the Brother to understand the ultimate lesson - that of immortality. However, a Brother would not discover this information without a key to the puzzle. This book gives the key to understanding the puzzle, and the reason why it was thought necessary to go to such great lengths to hide the secret teachings in the first place.

The first three Grand Masters had changed the existing Operative Mason's rituals in some way, and the only way to find out what those changes were was to compare the current ritual to the bits of ritual that exist prior to the establishment of the Premier Grand Lodge in 1717, the event Masonic scholar Albert Pike calls the "Revival."[1] The allure of researching the early days of Freemasonry is that we can learn about the objectives of the first three Grand Masters, and thus answer some or all of the above questions.

First, I review in broad strokes (Ch.1) the four hundred years prior to the era of the Stuart monarchy, and the important events that changed England forever that ultimately prepared the ground for the Stuart dynasty.

Next, I scrutinize the one hundred years of the Stuarts in detail (Ch.2~3), the plots and revolutions, the religious wars and catastrophes, and the events that eventually brought down the Stuart monarchy. I also examine the religious issues (Ch.4) that had such a strong influence on the three Grand Masters who rewrote the rituals. Then, I investigate the use of the Tree of Life in the Hiramic Legend (Ch. 5) and finally the Quest for Immortality (Ch.6) and the building of a New Jerusalem in the Epilogos.

I like to tell new Masons that Freemasonry is not about the destination, it's about the journey, though Masons seem fixated on becoming Master of a Lodge or even on Grand Honours. For me, this book has been a wonderful journey, and though before I set out, I already knew my premise was strong, along the way, like a "forensic historian," I found so many other interesting details, that the book was in danger of becoming an encyclopaedia!

I also heeded the warning from the introduction to the 1738 Constitutions by James Anderson:

But the History here chiefly concerns Masonry, without Meddling with other Transactions, more than what only serves to connect the History of Masonry, the strict Subject of this Book. It is good to know WHAT NOT TO SAY!

The Third Degree, Religion and Superstition

The Third Degree was added by the first three Grand Masters sometime around 1725, for two main reasons. The first reason was that it completed the alchemical requirement of a three-step process of transformation. The second reason for its inclusion was to counter a growing challenge to Christian theology. To understand the importance of this challenge, it is important to look at the history of that time and how it influenced the first three Grand Masters to rewrite the degrees.

The Stuart era was a time of witch hunts and superstition, which church authorities railed against. Several times King James's own physician was called upon to investigate reports of magic being used. The king even believed that a coven of witches had once tried to drown him in a storm that they had conjured up. In 1605, when the Catholic King James VI of Scotland became the king of Protestant England, it started a series of problems for the country. English Catholics tried to kill the king with several plots, even though the king had tried to make things easier for Catholics in England. His son, Charles I, was executed for treason. Following this, there was the Interregnum, when Cromwell abolished the monarchy and set up a commonwealth. At the same time, he gave various freedoms to non-Anglican Protestants, the Dissenters, who flourished in the new atmosphere of religious freedom.

One of the unforeseen outcomes of this freedom was that established Christian dogma was challenged, such as the validity of the Trinity, reincarnation, predestination and immortality or, more accurately, what happen to a believer after death. This controversy included not just the ecclesiastic authorities, but also the intelligentsia of the day. The argument became so vociferous that, because of the censorship laws of the day, parliament was called on to debate the issues.

With this background of "religious turmoil," the first three Grand Masters decided to make a statement concerning immortality, and they used the Third Degree to do it. At the same time, they used the Third Degree to complete the alchemical process of the transformation of the perfect Mason.

A New Theory on the Rituals of Freemasonry*[1]

From my studies of esoterica, I realized that the "Rule of Three" tends to be true, that is, the first time something arises is a happenstance - a chance happening or event - the second time is a coincidence, and the third time shows that a pattern exists. But what is it when there are more than twenty correspondences, as in this case? I started to research these one by one, which brought me to an inevitable conclusion, which is the raison d'être of this book. With my new insight I analyzed the ritual of Speculative Freemasonry to find that there were twenty-five Signposts in the Ritual that point at a hidden teaching.

There are few books that focus on the early days of the Revival, however, one of the most useful is by American historian Margaret Jacob, *The Origins of Freemasonry: Facts and Fictions*. In it she focuses on "following the money" but I think she misses the importance of spiritual alchemy as she may not be familiar with the ritual of Freemasonry.[2] I believe that to understand the Craft properly the Reader needs several things that were natural to an early 18th gentleman; a classical education which includes Latin and Greek, an in-depth knowledge of the Bible, an understanding of alchemy, and lastly familiarity with Freemasonry. In this book I have tried to bridge any gaps in the Reader's knowledge of those subjects.

Like Jacob, I believe that to understand the objectives of the early days of the Revival, it is important that we "walk in their shoes" to appreciate not just the Freemasons' culture and environment, but also their concerns and aspirations. Understanding the realpolitik of that period, cutting through the myth, understanding the processes of power and the very real threats that Freemasons faced.

---

[1] * Sections of the Prologos that are repeated in all three books are marked with an asterisk.

The reconstruction of Freemasonry's old rituals was not the endeavour of one individual, but the efforts of the first three Grand Masters, probably together with the Grand Warden, James Anderson.

What are the Secrets of Freemasonry? *

It is important to have a definition of "the secrets of Freemasonry," because as a Mason I promised to never divulge these "secrets," and I won't. This is the import of the Past Master's sign. So, the Reader may need to be an adept at either alchemy or the Craft of Freemasonry to get the most from this book.

I believe the ritual was written in cipher for two reasons, first, that a cowan[2] (a person who attempts to pass himself off as a Freemason without having received the degrees) would not understand the text and secondly, to hide a secret teaching in the ritual.

People have said to me that it is impossible to write about Freemasonry without disclosing its secrets and making oneself liable to censure from the Grand Lodge. So here I would like to define what constitutes the secrets of Freemasonry.

If someone wants to hide a secret in some text, normally a code or cipher is used. So, parts of the ritual of Freemasonry are in "open text," some in cipher. Uniquely the ritual of both the Grand Lodge of Japan and the Grand Lodge of China in Taiwan both use only open text, probably due to the difficulty of encoding Chinese characters; but does that mean nothing in it is secret? Everything in the Monitor (the book that contains the rituals) that is in open text is either a prayer or concerns morality. In the First Degree that is the Working Tools lecture, the Description of the Lodge followed by an explanation on the Ornaments and the Four Cardinal Virtues. In the Second Degree there are the Working Tools followed by the Orders of Architecture, the Seven Liberal Arts and Sciences, and lastly a description of Geometry. In the Third Degree there is one Working Tool, a description of King Solomon's Temple followed by the twelve Emblems of the Third Degree, which all allude to a moral teaching.

---

[2] The origin of the word is a stonemason who has not served an apprenticeship.

I believe that the objective of having "open text" in the Monitor is that if it was found by a non-Mason, he would only read about moral teachings and a society with an interest in architecture, especially the construction of the symbolic King Solomon's Temple. That would reinforce the message that "*Freemasonry is a peculiar system of morality, veiled in allegory, and illustrated by symbols.*" So, the non-Mason would look no further, because what he had read in the Monitor confirmed his belief about Freemasonry. Also, he would understand Freemasonry to be a Christian organization as it used lessons or prayers taken from the Bible.

So what secrets are written in cipher? In the first two degrees, all that is written in cipher are the signs of recognition, and the oaths that the candidate takes. In the Third Degree the Hiramic Tragedy is also in cipher. So, are we to understand that the secrets of Freemasonry boil down to what is written in cipher? In other words, just six things: the modes of recognition, the signs, tokens and words, our oaths and the Hiramic Legend?

The Hiramic Legend is to be found in the First Book of Kings, chapter seven, but Hiram's death is not included. In the *Constitutions* of 1723, Anderson did not even mention the legend, but then in 1738 he did include it in the updated *Constitutions* writing, "three ruffians killing the Prince of Architects;" this indicates that the content of the Third Degree had not been decided in 1723. People have associated the death of Hiram with the deaths of Osiris or even Noah, but there is a more apt explanation, which I will explain in a later chapter. As the Hiramic Legend is found both in the Bible and *Book of Jewish Antiquities* by Flavius Josephus, it is not considered a secret by the United Grand Lodge of England (UGLE). I quote from the Report of the Board of General Purposes, adopted 10th March 1999:

> The Board considers that it may be opportune to remind Brethren of the scope of Masonic 'secrecy,' so that in explaining Freemasonry to their families and friends they may know what they may and may not discuss. Every Freemason is bound by his obligations not to reveal the traditional modes of recognition. This admits of no compromise. The ceremonial ways of proving that one is a Freemason should not normally be used outside the context of Masonic meetings. Brethren making improper

disclosure or use of the signs, tokens and words of Craft and Royal Arch Masonry render themselves liable to Masonic disciplinary sanction. The promise not to reveal the modes of recognition may also be seen as symbolic of a wider pledge by a Brother to abide by all his obligations, non-Masonic as well as Masonic.[3]

So, the secrets consist of the modes of recognition, just three things; the signs, tokens and words. In truth there are lots of hidden secrets in the Three Degrees, and once the key to the degrees is found, the secrets start to become apparent, (see *Freemasonry: Spiritual Alchemy*).

The Scope of this Book

This book is based on thirty-three lectures that I gave while Master of the Research Lodge of the Grand Lodge of Japan (2007-2010), and the translation and publication has been approved by then GM Donald K. Smith. This is important as Freemasons are not allowed to publish books or articles about the Craft without the Grand Master's approval.

The emphasis of this book is on the beginning of the Revival of Freemasonry in 1717, though I touch on Operative Masonry in passing to explain the historical roots of Freemasonry. However, I do not include what are known as "appendant bodies," or concordant bodies, such as Scottish Rite and York Rite, of which there are about thirty. There is much confusion in the public's mind about the relationship of these organizations to what is termed "*Blue Masonry*," the original Three Degrees of Freemasonry.

Initially this book was a much larger work, over 550 pages long. It was suggested by a publisher, whose judgement I respect, that the manuscript be divided into three, one for each degree. This brought about a few problems, as the themes were interwoven, for example the Twenty-five Signposts had to be separated out. However, the most important Signposts are given for each degree and this should show the Reader how to find the others. The part of the Prologue that is repeated in each book is marked with an asterisk * as not everyone will read the four books in the order they were published. I got around the above problem by repeating the last three chapters in the first three books, though the content is different; Alchemy by Degrees, Lodge Laboratory and Temple, and Immortality. The emphasis of this book is on the Third Degree. The First Degree is analyzed in *Freemasonry: Initiation by Light*, and the Second Degree in *Freemasonry: Spiritual Alchemy*.

Also, this book's objective is not to analyze a possible history of Freemasonry, but to look at the forces in play just before and just after the Revival in 1717, to understand the objectives the first three Grand Masters had when they rewrote and expanded the rituals. Though I give a possible history of the Craft, my interest is in the original objectives of "Speculative" Freemasonry.

Many people have suggested that "Speculative Freemasonry" must be akin to "speculative philosophy." The dictionary defines this as "a philosophy professing to be founded upon intuitive or a priori insight and especially insight into the nature of the Absolute or Divine; broadly: a philosophy of the transcendent or one lacking empirical basis."[4] However, this term "speculative philosophy" was first coined in 1855-60, one hundred and thirty years after the Revival.[5] I believe we can find the origin of the term "Speculative Freemasonry" in alchemy.

The present-day objectives of "making good men better" would have seemed very foreign to the first three Grand Masters who did not envision the international charitable organization that Freemasonry has now become. An example of this is that Freemasonry was intended to be a Christian organization - though not in the way of a sectarian church - for otherwise the government of the time would have closed it down very quickly. It was only later, probably in Victorian times, that Masonry became open to people of other religions joining and thus more syncretic, and secondly more moralistic. Since then, Masonry has had to change with the times, acknowledging

Women's Freemasonry and Prince Hall Lodges. As the Grand Lodge of Scotland states:

> Freemasonry is not a religion, nor is it a substitute for religion. The one essential qualification means that Freemasonry is open to men of many religions and it expects and encourages them to continue to follow their own faith. It is not permitted for Freemasons to debate these subjects at Masonic meetings, as it is not expected that an individual should have to justify their own personal religious beliefs.[6]

Education*

This book is not intended to replace a rounded Masonic education. It is a journey of discovery, and though I believe I have found a "great treasure" there are other important things to be found in Freemasonry.

More Masons are asking about education in the Craft; for example, "Masonic education is why most of our members joined in the first place, and one of the last things they'll find in many of our Lodges today."[7] Again, the Scottish Rite Journal asks in its March/April 2017 edition, "Is Freemasonry Esoteric?" This book goes at least part of the way to answer that question.

Another conundrum is whether it is possible to learn about the intentions of the first Freemasons of the Revival 300 years ago, when they left no books or journals? As James Anderson wrote in 1738:

> This Year [1720], at some private Lodges, several very valuable Manuscripts ... concerning the Fraternity, their Lodges, Regulations, Charges, Secrets, and Usages ... were too hastily burnt by some scrupulous Brothers, that those Papers might not fall into strange Hands.[8]

Grand Master George Payne had only two years previously asked Lodges in London for any old documents they had to be submitted to Grand Lodge, now these documents are now lost to us forever.

I believe the answer lies in the text of Masonic rituals called the Monitor or Cipher. By close analysis of the text, several things stand out, and point the Reader in a certain direction. That direction is what this book is about.

The subject matter of each chapter could have easily been a book in its own right. I had to leave out many subjects, such as military campaigns, not because they were not worthy of pursuit, but just so that I could focus on my main objective.

Does this book change the accepted definition of Freemasonry: "*A peculiar system of morality, veiled in allegory, and illustrated by symbols*"? In part, yes it does. I believe as Mackey states, that Freemasonry was never intended to be a moral education:

> Freemasonry is not a system of morality, either in its Speculative form or as it was in its Operative form, and it was never intended to be, but is a fraternity or brotherhood of men of which the grand idea is work. It has never been an ethical culture society, nor one devoted to moral reform; on the contrary it requires that any work of moral reform shall have been completed (if needed) in the Petitioner as a qualification for his Candidacy. [9]

This then begs the question, what *work* are Speculative Masons engaged in? This becomes apparent in later chapters.

For the Brethren*

For a long time, I deliberated whether to disclose this information or not. There were many pros and cons; on the negative side, problems such as what I could say without breaking my oath to the Craft or laying myself open to criticism such as "Earnshaw's crazed, he's been sniffing the mercury himself!"[3] However, on the positive side, this book is a stimulating adventure that I believe needs a wider audience.

Having now been a Freemason for more than thirty years, I have seen many people join the Lodge but only stay for a year or so. The reason for this is multifold, but it has to do with the Lodge not meeting the expectations of the new member. People join for three main reasons; to learn some esoteric truths that cannot be found in books or the Church, to join a charitable community and lastly, to network.

---

[3] Which is true, but not real mercury but its spiritual counterpart!

The networking potential is low, as often the members of many Lodges are nearing the end of their careers. As for esoteric truths, these are thin on the ground too. After a while the new member will say something along the lines that Freemasonry is just a factory to make "good men better," and the Brethren are merely workers on an assembly line, doing the same things week in week out. Add to that the considerable amount of time needed to learn large chunks of ritual and the shine soon wears off Freemasonry, as new members feel they are getting little out of membership.

Then there are the Brethren who stay and become the backbone of the Lodge, the ones who are always filling in for absent members, the ones that can be counted on to help out. Why do these Brothers continue coming, especially as they do not learn much in the way of esoterica? A Brother told me the answer; "it is like Christian priests or Buddhist monks who repeat the same services every week, year on year; it is a spiritual connection that holds them and enthralls them."[10] It is the same with Freemasonry. It is the spiritual Brothers who continue year after year, they feel something special in the ritual and the Lodge in which it is enacted. This book helps explain the reason for this, and I hope it will make the Brethren's experience much richer, serving to rekindle the "light" for them to continue their studies. In this book they will discover that one of the objectives of their journey in Freemasonry is to discover the Philosophers' Stone!

References*

It is not my intention that this book become an academic study, but I want to give detailed references so that if the Reader finds something controversial, he/she can go to the source that I used to check it for him/herself. Wherever possible I have used the source nearest to the date of the event. Where there are square brackets, that indicates that I have added a word or phrase to make the original text easier to understand.

I always have at the back of my mind a warning that my research might be due to apophenia, "the human tendency to perceive meaningful patterns within random data," so I have used the most dependable scholarly references I could find.

The Ritual*

Though I have access to the modern rituals as used by the Grand Lodges of England, Scotland, Massachusetts and Japan, as I am a member of a Lodge of each constitution, I decided to use Duncan's *Masonic Ritual and Monitor;*[11] the reason being that this book is available online for the general public, should they wish to compare it to my book. Secondly *Duncan's* was written in 1866 and so retains a classic feel to the ritual which has been edited out of some other newer rituals. Though, in places, I have used the Massachusetts' ritual for comparison as well.

One difficulty Brethren may find reading this book is that the ritual may differ slightly from Grand Lodge to Grand Lodge, such as that of New York or the Grande Loge Nationale Française. In the early days the ritual was not written down, but rather it was passed from Brother to Brother orally. This was known as the Emulation, Brethren emulating or copying each other. This led to variations creeping into the ritual.

We can see from the exposé *A Mason's Examination* of 1723, that a catechism was being used, though it differs from both the ritual and catechism currently employed. By 1730, however, Samuel Pritchard's *Masonry Dissected* gives a ritual that is very similar to the one currently performed. As the Premier Grand Lodge (the first Grand Lodge in England) did not publish an "authorized" ritual, other rituals started to appear. In 1732 and in 1763, more Christianized rituals were written by Martin Clare, Thomas Manningham and William Hutchinson.[12] Then a rival Grand Lodge, the Antients, published their own official ritual in 1763, drawn up by William Preston. In 1775 Preston published *Illustrations of Masonry* and gave lectures on his system, which are continued to this day as the *Prestonian Lecture*, the only system of education (apart from Quatuor Coronati Lodge) authorized by the United Grand Lodge of England, UGLE.

It seems that a combined Hutchinson-Preston ritual was used until the Union in 1813.[13] Initially, the Moderns set up a Lodge of Promulgation in 1809 to consolidate the Landmarks, as well as to consider the new roles of Deacons and Stewards. After the Union, a Lodge of Reconciliation was established consisting of nine expert Master Masons from each Grand Lodge, which worked from 1813 to 1816 trying to produce a "uniform work." Eventually a compromise was reached, and much of the Preston ritual was discarded and a ritual proposed by Dr. Samuel Hemming, the Senior Grand Warden, was adopted which is similar to the authoritative standard of English Freemasonry now used by UGLE.[14]

In America the situation was slightly different. Prior to the Union of 1813, many Lodges were either set up by colonists or had formerly been travelling military Lodges, warranted during the American War of Independence (1775–1783), known by the British as the American Revolutionary War. According to Mackey, the Grand Lodge of the Antients was particularly active in warranting military Lodges and by the end of 1789 it had approved forty-nine military warrants. The first Monitor to be published in North America is believed to have been the *Preston Ritual* published by a printer named Hanmer in 1797,[15] or the *Freemason's Monitor*, based on Preston's ritual, published the same year, in Albany New York.[16]

The *Preston Ritual*, which was based on an Operative ritual, was then elaborated on by another printer, Thomas Webb, in Boston, Massachusetts. In 1806 the *Webb Ritual* was adopted as the standard for the Grand Lodges of Massachusetts and New Hampshire. The current ritual of the Grand Lodge of Pennsylvania is said to be closest to the *Preston Ritual*. Webb is believed to have simplified Preston's "distribution of the first lecture into six, the second into four and the third in twelve sections, not being agreeable to the mode of working in America."

Malcolm Duncan states "No three States in the Union work alike. Each Grand Lodge has a work of its own, which is taught the subordinate Lodges annually by its Grand Lecturer," however, as Duncan uses the Webb Ritual in his *Masonic Ritual and Monitor*, and for the above reasons, I have mainly used *Duncan's Ritual* in this book, with some illustrations from the ritual of the Grand Lodge of Massachusetts.

The Bible*

In the latter part of the book the Reader will find that there are many references to the Bible, this is because Freemasonry's ritual is closely associated with the Bible, and the people of those times were very religious and knew their Bibles very well. Nearly 20% of the references in this book are from the Bible. That is an indication of how important the Bible was to people of that time. They discussed, and often fought over, the meaning and implications of small details in the Bible, such as the Black Rubric, and some arguments were continued on through generations, and others even raised in Parliament. I have included chapter and verse so that, if the Reader is so inclined, the Bible can be checked to see if he or she agrees with the arguments. The Bible quoted in this book is the King James Version as it is appropriate to the day and age.

Consistency*

For the sake of consistency, I use the term Fellow Craft, rather than Fellowcraft or Fellow-Craft. This is for two reasons, first, other grades within Freemasonry are written in two words, Entered Apprentice, Master Mason and Grand Master; and secondly, in the Constitutions of the UGLE, Fellow Craft is used in preference to Fellowcraft. Lastly, I have used "square and compasses" in place of the popular "square and compass," the compass is used to find direction, and compasses to draw and measure.

Four-dimensional Chess*

Writing this book has been like playing four-dimensional chess! The first dimension is the history - the wars, the calamities and plots - that lead to the Revival of Freemasonry. The second dimension, which was very important to people at that time, was the religious aspect, the Protestant-Catholic question, the spread of new denominations and the fight against superstition and atheism. On top of these there is a third dimension, that of a flood of innovative ideas and experimentation, and *the birth of science and the death of alchemy*. These three dimensions are inside a fourth, the timeframe, and between these four dimensions the pieces move effortlessly; pieces such as the bishop, John Desaguliers, the knight, Sir Christopher Wren, the castle, George Payne and the king, Sir Isaac Newton.

The bottom line is that many things had to be deduced as I wasn't there! However, by reading the narrative, the Reader will intuitively understand:

> Do not believe in anything simply because you have heard it. Do not believe simply because it has been handed down for many generations. Do not believe in anything simply because it is spoken and rumoured by many. Do not believe in anything simply because it is written in Holy Scriptures. Do not believe in anything merely on the authority of Teachers, elders or wise men. Believe only after careful observation and analysis, when you find that it agrees with reason and is conducive to the good and benefit of one and all. Then accept it and live up to it.[17]

Finally, as Albert Pike said concerning his book Morals and Dogma written in 1871, the caution also applies to this book:

> Everyone is entirely free to reject or dissent from whatsoever herein may seem to him to be untrue or unsound. It is only required of him that he shall weigh what is taught and give it fair hearing and unprejudiced judgment.

Ch. 1   Guilds and the Dissolution of Monasteries

After many in England believed that Operative Freemasonry had died out, the "Revival" of Freemasonry was made possible by five significant events that changed the course of English history during the preceding five hundred years: the persecution of the Knights Templar, the dissolution of monasteries, the suppression of guilds, the Reconquista and finally the Act of Supremacy.[4]

The English Reformation

The period from the 11th century to the 13th century in Europe is known as the High Middle Ages. Knights in armour were now outmoded as new methods of warfare had been adopted. The feudal system was coming to an end, and the kings of England worked to regain dominion over their subjects that had been usurped, first by French barons, who had settled in England after the Norman Conquests of 1066 and 1071, and later by the Catholic Church.

The population increased rapidly during the 11th and 13th centuries and there was an exodus from rural areas to major cities. Initially this led to growth in the economy, but wars brought economic stagnation, which was compounded by the Great Famine of 1315–17 and especially following the Black Death of 1348. The result was social unrest and civil disobedience such as the Peasants' Revolt of 1381. The Catholic Church was also facing its own problems with the Western Schism that threatened its unity.

The Protestant Reformation was initiated by Martin Luther in 1517 when he nailed Ninety-five Theses [complaints] to the door of All Saints' church and other churches in Wittenberg. There was a continuing struggle throughout Europe until the Peace of Westphalia in 1648 ended the Thirty Years' War between Catholics and Protestants. In

---

[4] The Knights Templar and the Reconquista were reviewed in *Freemasonry: Spiritual Alchemy*

England the reformation was accelerated by the decline of feudalism, the adoption of common law, the spread of printing presses and the resultant availability of the Bible, which led to challenges to the status quo, together with the growth of religious dissension.

In 1527 King Henry VIII asked Pope Clement VII to annul his marriage to Catherine of Aragon, but was denied. In England this started a groundswell against what the people perceived as "popery." The subsequent English Reformation became a political dispute, rather than a theological one based on Luther's complaints. Henry was displeased that the Vatican was directly taxing English citizens by imposing *Peter's Pence*, a donation made in church after the service, attendance being compulsory by law. Secondly, the king had no say in how the Catholic Church in England governed itself, as bishops were appointed by the Vatican. So, the pope's refusal to recognize Henry's divorce was unconscionable as far as Henry was concerned. He petitioned Parliament to break with Rome, and this was finally effected by a series of acts of Parliament starting in 1532 and ending with the Act of Supremacy of 1534. Henry then declared himself the Supreme Head of the Church of England, reasserting the power of the kings of England as the final authority in both legal and theological matters, and initiating the English Reformation.

In Tudor times, the maintenance of the feudal order was of prime importance. The king ruled through "Divine Right" as God's vice-regent on Earth, [18] and this authority extended to the courtiers who served him, part of the "Great Chain of Being"(see detail on p. 46). This also applied to the king inheriting land, for example, as it was said to have been given him by God. To emphasize the king's God-given authority, a homily named "Against Disobedience and Wilful Rebellion" was required to be read in church on nine Sundays in a year, starting in 1571. During the Early Middle Ages in England the Church and common Law were supreme, but King Henry VIII changed this, giving himself absolute authority. This led the Protestant reformer William Tyndale (1494-

1536) to comment that "If the King sin he must be reserved unto the judgement and vengeance of God."[19]

Dissolution of the Monasteries

Pilgrimages were an important part of life for Christians in the Early Middle Ages, and as the Arab Rashidun Caliphate had taken Jerusalem in 637 AD, pilgrims would often travel to the great cathedrals in England instead. Many would travel hundreds of miles just to see a beautiful picture of the Madonna displayed in a cathedral, and some were recorded as fainting in awe in front of the paintings.

After the crusaders retook Jerusalem in 1099, pilgrimages to the Holy Land restarted. However, in 1348 plague swept across Europe, and it was generally believed that the disease had been carried along trade routes from China.[20] Panic gripped England, rich people built walls around their property to keep the sick out, and the diseased poor were often bricked up in walls to prevent the spread of the disease. One of the consequences was that as European countries did not want pilgrims passing through their land on the way to Jerusalem, they either turned them back or incarcerated them.

King Richard II's grandfather, Edward III of the House of Plantagenet, had started a war against the French House of Valois in 1337, which ended in 1453, later known as The Hundred Years' War. Richard had a difficult relationship with Parliament as he was seen to patronize, in an extravagant manner, some of his favourite courtiers. For two months in 1386, Parliament sat to audit the king, in what is now known as the Wonderful Parliament. It resulted in fourteen commissioners being appointed to oversee the Royal purse. This was the start of a struggle between King Richard and five nobles, a duke and four earls, known as the Lords Appellant.

The Lords Appellant, who wished to convict five of Richard's courtiers and charge them with treason, held power in place of the king for one year. During the following Parliament in 1388, now known as the Merciless Parliament, many of Richard's favourites were exiled, imprisoned or executed. [21] Initially, the Lords Appellate had the support of the House of Commons, having raised expectations of "reform at home and a more vigorous foreign policy," but by May 1389 they had lost that authority and fell from power, and in the following years the five lords were either executed or exiled.[22] This is important because the wealthy monasteries were then an easy target for Richard who was short of funds to continue the war against France. He had not paid the English garrisons in France, and the soldiers there were on the point of deserting. Richard had already pawned the crown jewels, and they were about to be forfeited.[23]

Act of Dissolution

The movement that promoted the idea of confiscating the lands of Catholic monasteries started with John Wycliffe. He had campaigned against Catholic abuses such as the luxurious life of bishops and the pomp of Catholic ceremonies, and addressed Parliament recommending the abolition of not just the entire hierarchy of Church officials but also the papacy.

In the *Domesday Book* there is an indication of the wealth of monasteries and nunneries in England in the twelfth century. Seven of the forty-five institutions listed had an income between £500 and £900 a year, the modern-day equivalent of £150~£270 million. Nearly one-sixth of the landed wealth of England was in the hands of monastic orders, worth £3.5 billion at today's values.[24] By King Henry VIII's time there were over 620 monasteries in England, run by Benedictine, Cluniac and Cistercian orders, including preceptories run by the Knights Hospitaller in Leicestershire and Derbyshire.

Many of these religious houses had been founded by Celts or Anglo-Saxons from before the Norman Conquest, followed by a growth in "monastic enthusiasm" in the early medieval era. The monasteries were wealthy because they had two incomes, a "spiritual" income from local churches in the form of tithes, and a "temporal" income from the land they owned and worked, as well as that rented out. It was said in jest that if the Abbess of Shaftesbury married the Abbott of Glastonbury, they would jointly have more land than the king of England.[25]

In 1536, following the Act of Supremacy of 1534, King Henry VIII introduced the Suppression Act, also known as the Dissolution of Monasteries Act, which allowed him to seize the property and assets of all Catholic orders. According to Professor George Bernard, it was one of the most revolutionary acts of English history; one person in fifty was in a religious order, at a time when England's population was just 2.7 million people.[26]

The first act of 1536 allowed King Henry to dissolve monasteries with incomes of less than £200 a year, on the basis that they had wasted their endowments by being inefficient, so the king took them over "to prevent further waste." A "Pilgrimage of Grace" by priests and monks seeking restitution convinced Henry that he had not gone far enough. So, in 1539 Parliament, at Henry's bidding, extended the dissolution to cover all monasteries, and Henry's income suddenly quadrupled, not counting all the gold and silver plate, bullion and jewels he confiscated. [27]

Historians have conjectured that the nursery rhyme *Little Jack Horner* is based on Thomas Horner, the steward of the Abbey of Glastonbury, who was given the task of taking a pie that had many valuable deeds baked inside to the king as a present/bribe to convince him not to seize the abbey. En route, Horner took a couple of the deeds for himself, one of which had some lead mines on the property, and thus the reference in the rhyme to "pulling out a plumb" - plumb being a pun on the Latin for lead, "plumbum."

> Little Jack Horner
> Sat in the corner
> Eating a Christmas pie;
> He put in his thumb,
> And pulled out a plum,
> And said, 'What a good boy am I!'

Guilds in England

Guilds were organized labour that had monopolies in certain industries or geographical areas. The word "guild" comes from the Saxon word "gilden," meaning money or "to pay." Each guild had leaders, experts in their field, and rates for work were set, often in agreement with city aldermen. New members had to complete a seven-year apprenticeship before they could receive a wage. The guilds were very pious, and yearly they would perform plays in remembrance of their patron saint.

The plays that were staged by guilds are the most obvious place to look for influences on the evolution of the Third Degree of Freemasonry. This is especially pertinent as Freemasons claim that three old manuscripts from this era, the Regius Manuscript written around 1390, the Matthew Cooke Manuscript of 1450 and the Dowland Manuscript dated 1550, all purport to show the mediaeval origins of Freemasonry.

In England more than 110 guilds survive today, mainly in the City of London, where they are now called "livery companies." The oldest, the Worshipful Company of Weavers, was established in 1130 and received a Royal Charter in 1155. Though it is the oldest, it only ranks forty-second in precedence; the precedence was decided in 1515 based on each guild's economic or political power, and some guilds still today dispute their ranking. Most of the livery companies are run by Masters, but the Goldsmiths have "Prime Wardens" and the Weavers an "Upper Bailiff." The Worshipful Society of Apothecaries, established in 1617, has a Master as well as Senior and Junior Wardens.

We can get a good insight into the life of a guild from the writings of Geoffrey Chaucer (1343-1400), especially in *The Canterbury Tales*. The story begins at a tavern just outside of London, circa 1390, where a group of pilgrims have gathered in preparation for their journey to visit the shrine of St. Thomas à Becket in Canterbury. The pilgrims go to dinner, during which the owner of the tavern, the host, makes a proposal to the group: he challenges the pilgrims to tell two stories on the way to Canterbury, and two on the way back. The host would accompany the group and judge the merit of their stories, the pilgrim who told the best story would win a free dinner at the tavern at the end of the journey. Chaucer had planned 120 stories, but *The Canterbury Tales* ends after only 24 of them. We do not know if the pilgrims ever reached Canterbury, nor who won the challenge.

Section 9 of the Prologue concerning guildsmen reads:

> An HABERDASSHERE and a CARPENTER,
> A WEBBE, a DYERE, and a TAPYCER,
> Were with us eek, clothed alle in o lyveree,
> Of a solemne and greet fraternitee.

The haberdasher, who sold hats and gloves, a carpenter, a weaver, a clothing dyer, and a tapestry maker were members of guilds and, according to the story, wore very fine clothes. Their accessories, such as purses, belts, and even small knives were expensive, their handles made from silver rather than brass, as would have been common. They refer to their fraternity as "solemn and great." Chaucer mentions that their wives were proud to be married to such prestigious men, so besides being wealthy, they may have had some position of power in the community, not only as heads of guildhalls, but possibly serving as aldermen, leaders in the community. The other portraits in the prologue were of individuals, but in this tale, Chaucer chose to group these five tradesmen together in one portrait. He showed that trades-men, by forming guilds, the medieval equivalent of a trade union, aspired to move to a higher social class and a position of increased status during this period.

Originally the guild was a pious institution, which followed the strict orthodox religious doctrines set down by Plantagenet kings, but in Chaucer's time tradesmen would join a guild for mutual aid, self-improvement and social success. However, guilds were unable to adapt to the changing religious and political climate and they were suppressed following the Dissolution of Monasteries 1536-1547, their numbers were greatly reduced and strictly controlled.

Our understanding of the structure and daily workings of guilds comes mainly from the lawyer and historian, Joshua Toulmin Smith, who researched the guild returns of 1389.[28] Smith recorded thirty-two guilds in Yorkshire alone and nearly 500 in the whole country; which seems a lot of guilds for such a small population. Based on the *Domesday Book* written in 1086, the population of England was about 1½ to 2 million people. Comparing tax returns of the 1380s - the first national census wasn't until 1801- the population had not changed that much. The population of London was under 25,000 people in the 1300s.

In 1388 sheriffs had been instructed to collect a report from every guild within their bailiwick, listing the year of their founding, their oaths, feasts, privileges and customs. This was done to assess whether the guilds constituted a threat to law and order, at a time when King Richard was trying to assert himself. The Cambridge Parliament was considering suppressing a large number of guilds as the king viewed them with suspicion and he also wanted to confiscate their large wealth in order to fund his wars with France.[29] Evidence suggests that, despite the guild returns, a large portion of the guilds' assets was hidden. It should be remembered that in February of the same year, the Lords Appellant in the Merciless Parliament, convicted King Richard's entire court for treason and they were all either executed or, the lucky ones, exiled.

King Henry II in 1179 and King Edward I in 1306, found many illegal guilds that had not been chartered and so had them disbanded, also by the late 1300s many guilds had become politicized and they were also shut down. After the Peasants' Revolt of 1381, landowners and Parliament were concerned about the guilds' domination of trade, so they tried to control the guilds' power and influence, but at the same time supported the guilds' focus on public piety, believing that they "promoted harmony in society."[30]

In 1547, a large number of guilds and chantry chapels were closed by Henry VIII in another move to finance his war with France. In the sixteenth century the guild system was in danger of breaking down and had to be supported by Acts of Parliament, without the law reducing competition or stifling enterprise. Though King Henry VIII had suppressed the guilds, Queen Elizabeth I restored their rights with a bill called the Statute of Labourers and Artificers of 1563 which put controls on prices, imposed maximum wages, restricted workers' freedom of movement and reaffirmed the seven-year apprenticeship. Though the City of London was in a powerful position and able to protect the rights of its guilds, ultimately the dominance of the guild system in London declined during the 1600s, when craftsmen who had not completed an apprenticeship opened shops instead, prompting Napoleon's famous remark a hundred years later that England was "a nation of shopkeepers."

The Workings of a Guild

After the Norman Conquests (1066 and 1071), merchants had arrived in England from France and Germany, and set up incorporated societies and guilds allowing them exclusive rights in towns and cities. There were essentially four types of guilds, the two main guilds were the merchant guild and the craftsman guild, but on a smaller scale there were also religious guilds and frith guilds. This latter guild was a hold-over from Anglo-Saxon times, and had the mandate of keeping the peace, a form of summary justice, and at the same time the frith guild was often the only form of local government, which was dispensed from Guildhalls.

It wasn't until the 14th century and the reign of King Edward III that craft guilds were able to become incorporated and thus have the same rights and protection as the more powerful merchant guilds. Guilds also answered to the Church and had to follow religious ordinances known as Canon law. Until 1534 Catholic ecclesiastic courts had considerable power in England, for example insisting that the entire population attended church every Sunday or pay a fine, and that no trading could take place on a Sunday (only repealed in 1994). Law in England was a complicated mixture of secular and Canon law, which had been taught at the Universities of Oxford and Cambridge until they were forbidden to do so by Henry VIII. In 1604, after the English Reformation, Canon law was reviewed and published in Latin and for the first time English as well. It still kept many medieval statutes but added the Thirty-nine Articles of Faith (Religion) of 1571. So essentially guilds had a three-fold governance; civil law, Canon law and their own by-laws.

Guilds were issued with documents called *Letters Patent* by either the king or town authorities, which outlined their privileges. The word "patent" means "open" in Latin meaning that the seal was pendant at the bottom of the document, so it did not have to be broken for the document to be read, indicating that it was a public document, but with the authority of the person who affixed the seal. This is the origin of the modern patent system.

The authorities in local towns formed the equivalent of a chamber of commerce and oversaw the activities of merchant and craft guilds, often sitting in on meetings; this enabled them to have a say in trade that might influence the economy of the whole town, particularly when the town was associated with a product that it had a monopoly over. The historian Austin Poole gives the example of York weavers who had received a charter from Henry II giving them the exclusive right to make dyed and striped cloth throughout most of Yorkshire.[31]

However, not all cities had guilds, those that did not were known as "free." Also, in the countryside, craftsmen did not belong to guilds rather they set up cottage industries. Some folk kept sheep, while others sheared the sheep, spun the wool, dyed it and yet others finally wove it. They would either sell their wares in a town market or to a middleman who would collect them and broker their merchandise.

There were three defining characteristics of guilds that assured their success; first, their structured education system, secondly, their well-guarded specialist skills and lastly, their welfare system. Guilds had lengthy periods of apprenticeship, which were not defined until 1563, so apprentices were often taken advantage of. They had to pay a joining fee to be accepted by a guild and then they were often overworked and under-paid for many years. If they succeeded to complete their apprenticeship they would be accepted as craftsmen, which gave them access to materials and the ability to sell their wares or services. Markets were also controlled by the guilds, so being accepted as a craftsman would give them access to these markets.

After a certain period, the craftsman would be expected to travel for a period of time, such as two years and a day, to gain further experience. They would then be known as Journeymen, from the French word for day "journée" as they would be paid daily during their travels, and would also be able to work for other masters. They were given documents that certified them as Journeymen and they would wear the guild's livery so that people would recognise that they were not vagabonds or degenerates.[5] On their return, they had to produce a qualifying piece of work, called the "masterpiece," which would illustrate their abilities as a master craftsman; this work was often retained by the guild. In this way they would become masters of their craft and, perhaps one day, master of the guild.[32] In some parts of Europe, such as Germany and France, the practice of Journeyman still exists, in Germany it is known as "der Walz" and in France the Compagnonnage has the "Tour de France."

The second characteristic of a guild was the skills and techniques that they kept secret, so as to protect their craft and ultimately their jobs.

---

[5] For an example of the livery, please see p. 24

These became what we now call trade secrets, and guilds jealously guarded the arcana of their craft.

The third unique characteristic of a guild was its welfare system. Members would pay an annual tithe which enabled the guild to support sick or elderly members, in addition they had a fund for widows and orphans of guild members, and they gave relief to those who needed to travel to find work called a "tramping allowance." Poor members of guilds were buried with honourable funerals and a mass held for them; members of the guild who failed to attend would have been fined.

Large guilds had professional beadles who were paid for ceremonial and menial functions. Chaplains were also employed, which often became a source of friction with local parish priests, as the guild chaplain would receive a fee which implied a conflict of allegiance. The devotional purpose of a guild was to celebrate the saint of its dedication, as well as funerals and obits [Requiem Mass], which enforced lay acceptance of the Catholic doctrines of purgatory and the penitential cycle. In England much of our understanding of the devotional function of a guild is based on several mystery plays, such as those performed by Corpus Christi Guild of York. Some of these religious guilds were exempt from the Act of Dissolution of 1536 and performances of their plays continued into the Elizabethan era. The guilds' major social events were feasts that had both a social and a eucharistic function.

Though one of the basic purposes of all guilds was devotional, Joshua Toulmin Smith's research also gives an insight into the daily practices of a guild. A large part of their time was spent maintaining altar lights and torches, providing for member's funerals, celebratory feasts, processions and welfare of the sick and needy. Other costs such as livery and financial support for pilgrimages were very small, as was their income from the annual levy and entrance fees. "Most of the returns included statements to the effect that the fraternity encouraged peace and brotherly love."[33]

As Ogilvie[34] shows, the dominance of guilds negatively affected the quality of products as there was no incentive to innovate or develop new skills, and they had no positive impact on the economy as their objective changed from expanding business to protecting their jobs. It has also been shown that industry actually began to flourish after the guilds started to lose their monopolies.

Powerful merchants had benefitted from the guilds' ability to organize labour and materials, and guilds created "social capital" of shared standards, reciprocal information, mutual approval processes, and collective political action. This social capital benefited guild members, even as it hurt outsiders.[35] By the 1600s the guild system had become a target of much criticism as they were seen to oppose free trade and innovation, and guilds became increasingly involved in territorial struggles to protect their "turf." The guild system did not die out completely; they maintained their ceremonies and banquets to eventually become modern day livery companies and the origin of Trade Unions.

Sacred Mysteries

The word "mystery" is derived from the Greek, meaning a revealed secret, and the guild mysteries can be divided into two, sacred and profane. The "sacred mysteries" is a term applied to the doctrines of Christianity, called the "mystery of godliness"[36] as opposed to the "mystery of iniquity."[37] The profane mysteries were the secret ceremonies performed by a select few in the honour of a deity, for example the Greek Mystery Plays of Bacchus and Ceres which had been developed from the Egyptian mysteries of Isis and Osiris. The history of these mysteries is ancient, with the Eleusinian mysteries being introduced in Athens in 1356 BC.[38] In addition to the mysteries, there were mystics who were often theologians and, in addition to the obvious meaning of the scriptures, asserted that there were other interpretations to be discovered by means of an emanation of Divine Wisdom. Mystics taught that this way the soul would be enlightened and purified, for which purpose they advocated asceticism and seclusion for contemplation. Eminent medieval mystics include Meister Eckhart (1251-1329), John Tauler of Strasbourg (1290-1361) and Jacob Boehme (1575-1624) who is known for the divine revelation he published as *Aurora* in 1612 that caused a great scandal at the time. Quakers, Hutchinsonians and Swedenborgians are considered modern mystics.

Miracle Plays, Mystery Plays and Morality Plays

The ritual of the Third Degree of Freemasonry is based on a play called the Hiramic Tragedy, or the Legend of Hiram. It is theatre in the round and is dramatic, often too much so! The question we need to ask ourselves is whether the Legend is based on a mystery play that had been acted out in Guilds for hundreds of years, or whether it was original to the Revival of 1717.

The guilds performed plays using subjects based on sacred history or accepted legends, and originally, they were intended to be performed in church, with simple stage settings and hymns. Some were performed in Latin, but most were in the vernacular. The names "Mysteries" and "Miracle Plays" were used interchangeably, but correctly the Mysteries dealt with the stories in the Gospels, and Miracle Plays were based on the lives of saints. The Miracle Plays, which were introduced by the Normans, were more popular and were performed more often.[39] For whatever reason, plays based on stories from the Old Testament were not as popular in England as they were in France or Germany. Four of the most famous Miracle Plays were from York, Wakefield, Chester and Coventry. The oldest, the York cycle of plays, dates from about 1360, followed by the Townley (the name of the owners of a fifth manuscript) and Wakefield cycles. They were called "cycles" as they were collections of smaller plays, often a set of forty, but others such as the York cycle were as many as fifty-seven plays. Some of these cycles lasted from three to even eight days and hundreds of performances were held around England. God even has a part in some of the plays, for example the Townley cycle. However, due to reaction from Protestants concerning the depiction of God, based on Jewish aniconism, the play was later discontinued.

As the performances grew in scale, with larger more complicated scenery and larger audiences, they could no longer fit into churches. Then open spaces such as the village commons had to be used, and itinerant salesmen and other performers gathered there too, so the play ended up as a pageant (from the Greek meaning "a moveable scaffold"). Sometimes the play was performed as a procession that stopped to present certain scenes, probably near a church or tavern. The transportation, accommodation of actors, food and especially beer were a large financial burden, so guilds charged their members from a penny to four-pence a year to cover costs, known as "pageant silver." In 1490 ale was twopence a gallon, so the cost to the players was not so expensive. The plays were very popular and many of the guild members wanted to act in them, so it was the responsibility of the pageant master to choose the most able performers. Sometimes the plays were subdivided by guilds to give everyone a part in the performance. In Smith's account of a Corpus Christi performance of 1415, forty-eight different guilds were involved, from Pessoners (fishmongers) and Orfevers (goldsmiths) to Fletchers (arrow-featherers) and Talliaunders (tailors).[6]

From these plays, that ranged from the pious to the lewd, came the Morality Play emphasizing subjects like the Seven Cardinal Virtues and the Seven Deadly Sins. Coinciding with a dull time in English literature, these plays dealt with abstract people rather than characters from the Bible. The morality plays sought to teach lay people what they must believe for their soul to be saved, in an attempt to bring the dramas within the sacramental teaching of the church. These morality plays also had an influence on later Elizabethan plays such as Shakespeare's *King Lear*. After the English Reformation the morality plays continued to be held, but the content was changed in line with Protestant theology.

Starting in 1382, the Catholic theologian John Wycliffe (1330-1384) published the first English translation of the Bible from Latin, resulting in an austere religious movement called Lollards who, in the early 1400s, became hostile to guilds because of their perceived idolatry, and veneration of the Trinity. The Lollard movement believed that "the Father, Holy Spirit or angels to be corporeal"[40] and they were staunchly against the Catholic dogma of transubstantiation.

The Reader will be familiar with the passion play that is still enacted in Oberammergau in Germany even to this day. The population of Oberammergau is about 5,200 and half the town is entitled to take part in the play, though the actors must have lived in the town for at least

---

[6] Following the Norman Conquest of England in 1066, Middle English incorporated many French words due in part to Norman domination and also to the prestige that came with writing in French.

twenty years to be eligible. The play is performed once every ten years to commemorate the village having been spared from the plague in 1633, while other villages nearby were decimated by disease which, according to the vow recited before every play, spared only two couples in one village.[41] The play, which depicts Jesus's life up to the crucifixion, has been performed since 1634 without break, except for one cancellation in 1770 and another in 1940, during the Second World War.

Was Operative Masonry a Guild?

The origin of Freemasonry lies in the fraternities of masons who often travelled from one construction project to the next, all over England and often overseas to help with the massive undertaking of building a cathedral. These were Operative Masons, as distinct from Freemasons after the Revival of 1717, "Speculative Freemasons." There were several guilds that comprised the building trade, but in the High Middle Ages stonemasons were not considered part of the building trade because they were not organized. Though masons of the City of London erected their first guildhall in 1463, it was only in 1677 that the Worshipful Company of Masons was incorporated under a Royal Charter, following the Great Fire of London.

Instead of a guild, Masons formed fraternities, a system of trust and the passing on of knowledge by experience rather than an apprenticeship. In the period 1100 to 1300, over sixty abbeys, cathedrals, priories and preceptories were built in England alone. Some of these buildings took decades to finish, such as All Hallows Church in Wellingborough that took twenty years to complete. In France there were major construction works, such as Chartres cathedral that took nearly thirty years to complete, starting in 1194 and finishing in 1220. However, it was often difficult to find the funds to complete such massive construction projects. In Germany, Ulm Cathedral (now a minster) took 500 years to complete. Similarly, Strasbourg Cathedral in France, was started in 1015, but after 325 years of work it was decided to leave it incomplete. The south tower is still missing.

Advances in the understanding of the physical forces involved in large buildings meant that they could be built higher and wider, especially with the aid of buttressing. Every city wanted larger churches with higher ceilings so that they could use large decorative stained-glass windows with Biblical themes to pour coloured light over the amazed congregations. It was the medieval version of wide-screen cinemas, and it meant that more people came to the Sunday masses and for the "spiritual experience," resulting in increased income for the church. It has been assumed that the boom in cathedral building in Europe 1100-1300 was paid for and directed by the Knights Templar, as it coincides with their activities, but it could also be that the Church received financing from the Templars, who had no say in the construction.

The Templars had four chateaux, twenty-three castles, ten commanderies, thirty-seven churches and three fortresses built for them between 1100 and 1314. It seems that the Templars may have also funded many cathedrals built for Benedictines and Cistercians, for example the cathedrals of Cluny, Troyes and Chartres. Consequently, there would have been a need for a vast amount of labour, including those who worked in the quarries and finished the stones. These workers would have been known collectively as masons. It is unlikely that they were educated, as the literacy rate was very low, a person had to enter a monastery if he wished to learn the three "Rs," which probably accounts for the simple "masons' marks" that are found on stones in churches such as Rosslyn Chapel.

The origin of the name of "Freemason" is still a mystery and, even as late as 1738, was being spelled "Free Mason." It has been said that in the time of the Holy Roman Emperor, King Henry III of Germany (1017-1056), the pope (probably Pope John XIX) gave a patent to Italian masons to travel around Europe building cathedrals and churches. This suggests that in Italy workers were not normally free to travel to seek employment, they needed official sanction. These masons may have been called Free Masons. These Italian masons also had a very formal and secret method of allowing other masons to join their group, who were then known as "Adopted Masons" or "Accepted Masons." This suggests that, because of labour shortages for major building projects, unskilled labourers were allowed to join their fraternity.

A second suggestion for the origin of the term is that masons in England worked with limestone, which was also called freestone, making them "Free" masons, as the stone could easily be carved for figures and decorative parts for churches and cathedrals, while other less qualified masons cut stones for foundations and walls.

A final, persuasive suggestion is that Freemason comes from "free man's son," as referred to in the earliest records of Operative Masons in Scotland, at a Lodge in Aitchison's-Haven, a small village near Edinburgh – and Rosslyn Chapel - in Scotland.[42]

There are references to meetings in Scotland of various Lodges of Operative Masons, but the information is piecemeal, and does not prove a definitive link with Freemasonry and the establishment of the Premier Grand Lodge in 1717. Sir Robert Moray, a founding member of the Royal Society and a Scottish royalist exile, was made a Freemason in a Scots regiment at Newcastle-on-Tyne in 1641, while the earliest reference to an English Mason is said to have been Elias Ashmole, who was made a Freemason at Warrington 1646. However, these Lodges were probably either Operative Lodges or Rosicrucian Lodges, because Freemasonry was not reinvented until the years 1717-1725, the Revival, with very little symbolism from Operative Masonry included.

It has been suggested that English aristocrats, particularly during the Stuart period, joined Operative Lodges to discover the secrets of Freemasonry. This would not have happened due to a strict class structure in England; no cultured person would sit with a labourer, for education or refreshment, it was so then and it is still so now. As the English philologist Frederick James Furnivall (1825-1910), one of the authors of the New English Dictionary, said sarcastically, "I should like to see the evidence of a lord's son having become a working mason, and dwelling seven years with his master." However, in 1600 there was a recorded case of the admission of an aristocrat into an Operative Lodge in Scotland. He was John Boswell, Laird of Auchinlech, and he became a member of the "Lodge of Edinburgh" (which may mean a Lodge *in* Edinburgh). He signed the register with a cross inside a circle, in imitation of a mason's mark.

The Old Charges

One of the crutches that is often used to support a medieval (or even earlier) origin for Freemasonry is the fact that many old documents have been collected that seem to indicate a glorious past. Collectively they are known as the Ancient Charges or the Old Charges, as they purport to indicate the way and manner a Freemason should behave; and these Old Charges also give a history of the Craft that even goes back to the days of King Solomon, and earlier.

In 1888, the Masonic scholar Dr. Wilhelm Begemann classified the documents into nine groups or families as he called them, as most of the documents were kept as part of a family's archives, such as the twenty-one documents in the Sloane collection amassed by the antiquarian, Sir Hans Sloane.

The oldest document dates back to 1390, known as either the *Halliwell Manuscript* or the *Regius Poem* and is now in the British Museum. Its sixty-four pages of hand-written vellum give an illustrious history of Freemasonry going as far back as Euclid's invention of geometry in ancient Hellenistic Egypt. However, as the Masonic historian Robert Gould said in 1883, "the traditional history is replete with inaccuracies, anachronisms and even absurdities." [43] The manuscript has many charges or moral requirements, including that an apprentice must serve a minimum of seven years and also contains the legend of the Four Crowned Martyrs or "Quatuor Coronati." The document is named after the member of the Royal Society who discovered it, James Halliwell, who was not a Freemason.

The first and only recorded Masonic ritual dates from 1696 and is called the Edinburgh Register House manuscript. It may give a good insight into the ritual that might have been used in an Operative Lodge, but there are some strange aspects to this document that suggest it may have been an exposé, like those of the 1720s to 1730s that proved such a thorn in the side of the newly established Premier Grand Lodge.

There are approximately sixty of these Old Charges, mainly collected by antiquarians in the 1600s. Unfortunately, they shed no light on the origins of Speculative Freemasonry as they all refer to Operative

Masonry. According to Gould, the *Regius Poem* is based on a German "Steinmetzen" stonemason's document, one of the obvious points being the reference to the Four Crowned Martyrs, who were patron saints of German Operative Masonry. The other charges all "have a common origin" which is, according to Gould, French Operative Masonry.

To quote Gould:

> ...writers, who were educated and even learned men, have introduced not so much any new legends, but rather theories founded on a legend, by which they have traced the origin and the progress of the institution in narratives without historic authenticity and sometimes contradictory to historic truth.[44]

Acts of Supremacy and Uniformity

The Act of Supremacy was another nail in the coffin of papal jurisdiction over England. This nail was directed at papal supremacy, ensuring that England would no longer be taxed by a distant hierophant, or imposed on by a German Holy Roman Emperor (the Holy Roman Empire was only dissolved in 1806).

The first Act of Supremacy was passed by Parliament in 1534 and gave King Henry VIII (and all subsequent monarchs) supremacy over the newly established Church of England, and all the rights and benefits that came with that "dignity." Thus, England had completely severed relations with Rome. On Henry's death in 1547, his granddaughter, the Catholic Queen Mary I, affectionately known as "Bloody Mary" for having 300 Protestants burned at the stake,[7] tried to claw the nail out of the obdurate English oak wood by repealing the Act in 1554. However, four years later in 1558, the Act was reinstated on Mary's death by her Protestant half-sister, Elizabeth I, finally hammering the nail home.

---

[7] The Protestants were fearful that another Catholic monarch would also persecute all Protestants in England. There is a cocktail named after Mary.

This reinstated Act included The Oath of Supremacy, making it compulsory for anyone wanting to hold public office, including priests, to swear allegiance to the monarch as the Supreme Governor of the Church of England. Failure to do so would result in a fine. Later in 1562 public disobedience of the law was made a treasonable offence, as was "sedition," meaning to "excite disaffection" against the monarch. The scope of the oath was extended to include members of Parliament and scholars at the two universities of Oxford and Cambridge. This led to all bishops losing their positions, as well as a hundred Fellows at the University of Oxford, when they refused to swear the oath.

Queen Elizabeth was tolerant and showed clemency toward Catholics as she did not want to antagonize them, many of whom held positions of power in her government. Elizabeth was twenty-five when she became queen and had to quickly establish her authority, at a time when both France and Spain were on the brink of invading England. The Spanish eventually tried unsuccessfully to invade England, with an armada of 130 ships in 1588. At this time Pope Pius V, who had already excommunicated Elizabeth, issued orders to have her killed and, as there were still many Jesuits in England, this threat was very real. However, the average Englishman was supportive of the queen and the fledgling Anglican Church, and anti-Catholic sentiment grew. Over time, Catholics who were still in power in England, not only lost those positions but their lands as well.

The second historic piece of legislation was the Act of Uniformity of 1558, which came into force the following year. It was enacted as part of a settlement by Elizabeth to unify the Anglican Church. It included the stipulation that the Anglican Book of Common Prayer be used in all churches and that every citizen had to attend church every week or be fined one shilling (the equivalent of £12 in 2015), a large amount for a poor person at that time.

After 1580, the fine for failing to attend services using the English prayer book was increased from one shilling to £20 a month. It also became a treasonable offence to convert, or attempt to convert, someone else to Catholicism, the penalty for which was to be hanged, drawn and quartered. People were arrested for attending Mass or hiding priests in priest holes, or elsewhere, though there were not many Catholics to be found, as most had converted to Anglicanism, those that refused had been burned to death. A popular song satirizing the religious situation at that time was "The Vicar of Bray," and a refrain underscores the vicar's wish to accommodate whichever sect had ascendancy:

> I will maintain,
> Unto my Dying Day, Sir.
> That whatsoever King may reign,
> I will be the Vicar of Bray, Sir!

Five Hundred Years of Change

Over a period of five hundred years, England had changed dramatically from a feudal society with knights and powerful guilds to one which rejected both the dogma of Catholicism and medieval superstition. The Tudors, from Henry VII to Elizabeth, had encouraged an era of discovery, literature, trade and adventure. Discovery: printing presses, pendulum clocks, theodolites and weaving machines; literature: William Shakespeare, Christopher Marlowe and Edmund Spenser; trade: tobacco and new trade routes; adventure: John Cabot was the first Englishman to sail to America in 1497.

In 1530, England had been a Catholic country, but then four years later Henry VIII was proclaimed Defender of the Faith, effectively joining Luther's Protestant cause by seceding from the Church of Rome. After Henry's death, his young son Edward VI continued the stipulation, but on his death Mary I, Henry's granddaughter, reverted the country to Catholicism for five years, until Elizabeth asserted herself as the Supreme Governor of the Church of England in 1558. Even within the Church of England, there was the High Church (maintaining a semblance of a Catholic liturgy) and Low Church. During her reign, Queen Elizabeth tried to reach a reconciliation with Catholics after thirty years of religious strife in England. Catholics were generally tolerated, but still there were some Catholics who wanted to exact retribution on the monarchy and on the government. This came to a head in 1605 with the Gunpowder Plot that led to the oppression of Catholics for the following 350 years.

With the death of the Virgin Queen in 1603, there was no issue to assume the throne. The monarchy then passed to James VI of Scotland, as he was the great-great-grandson of King Henry VII, as well as "heir general," (The title of king was legally constituted like property and only inheritable by children and grandchildren). James VI of Scotland became James I of England the same year. This would seem a bittersweet choice for England; sweet as it was an opportunity to join the two kingdoms into one, but bitter because though Scotland was a Presbyterian nation, many of the Scottish aristocracy were Catholic, as was James, whereas both Henry VIII and Elizabeth I had struggled to legitimize the authority of the Church of England. After the demise of the House of Tudor, the new House of Stuart faced many challenges such as threats from Jesuit plots, the problem of producing male heirs, civil war, the plague and the looming threat of the "end of the world."

Ch. 2   The House of S
Gunpowder, Treason and ɪ ɪᴏɪ

The era of the House of Stuart is one of the most interesting, and from the perspective of Freemasonry, one of the most important eras in English history as it lays the foundation for the Revival of Free-masonry. In this short outline I will focus on the themes that are important for the Revival that started in 1717.

For the first time in history, we see a king put on trial and subse-quently executed. There was trade with the far reaches of the globe and the population of England quickly doubled. The foibles of alchemy were replaced by the exactitude of science. At the same time, the kings and queens of the House of Stuart were faced with impossi-ble situations: wars, rebellions, disasters and political intrigue; and how did England end up with a German king when it had not been conquered?

History of the House of Stuart

The House of Stuart came from Scotland, and the ancestors of the Scot-tish royal family came from France with the Norman Conquest, following the Battle of Hastings in 1066, and were made Stewards of the country. The current spelling of Stuart is said to have been adopted by Mary, Queen of Scots, who was raised in France. Spelling in Eng-land was not standardized until the mid-18th century, and as late as 1538, Scotland was written as "Scotlande" and England as "Englaland." Thus, Steward became Stuart.

Mary Queen of Scots could have been queen of England, as she was the only child of King James V of Scotland and acceded to the throne on his death when she was an infant. Scotland was ruled by regents while she received an education in France. She married Francis, the Dauphin of France, and became Queen of France in 1559 on his coro-nation, but the Dauphin died the next year. She returned to Scotland aged eighteen, and six years later she married her Catholic cousin

Lord Darnley. There seems to have been hostility to the marriage, which ended tragically when Darnley was murdered, and his house destroyed in an explosion. Despite people believing that James, Earl of Bothwell, had committed the murder, he was found to have not been implicated, and after his trial he married Mary. At the time, Scotland was torn between Catholicism and Calvinist Presbyterianism and, because of her Catholic faith, there were demonstrations against the marriage led by the Protestant reformer John Knox, who preached against her. Scottish nobles imprisoned Mary briefly in a castle following an uprising, and she was forced to abdicate the throne in favour of her one-year old son, James.

One of Mary's several mistakes was that she included many Protestants in her government, which upset the powerful Catholic lairds, who openly defied her. She fled to England to seek protection from her cousin Queen Elizabeth, and it is believed that she assumed that Elizabeth would help her retake her throne.[45] However, because Mary had previously indicated her intention of becoming queen of England by rallying English Catholics against Elizabeth, she was kept under house arrest in various castles for more than eighteen years. Then in 1586 Mary was implicated in a conspiracy to assassinate Elizabeth in the Babington Plot, which was revealed by Elizabeth's spymaster, Sir Francis Walsingham. As a result, she was removed as a claimant to the English throne, and Elizabeth personally signed Mary's death warrant before having her executed for treason in 1587.

James VI of Scotland and I of England, reigned 1603 -1625

Mary's son, James VI of Scotland, did not have control of the government of Scotland until he was twelve, and the country was again managed by regents. In 1603, on the death of the last Tudor monarch, Elizabeth I , James succeeded her and as she had no children, he became King James I of England. James's claim to the throne was based on being directly related to King Henry VII, as his great-great-grandson. With James as king of both England and Scotland, this union was known as the "Union of the Crowns" but was a union of

the monarchies alone. England and Scotland continued to be sovereign states, though James wanted to establish an "imperial" throne of Great Britain with a single Parliament for both countries, but that was not to happen until the end of the Stuart dynasty.

James came to London in 1603 for his coronation and was surprised by the wealth he saw, saying he was "swapping a stony couch for a deep feather bed."[46] However, the Nine Years' War with Ireland had put the English government heavily in debt; the war had only ended a week after Elizabeth died with the surrender of the Irish army. The king's close advisor, the Earl of Salisbury, proposed to Parliament that the debts be forgiven in exchange for the king allowing certain concessions, but negotiations continued so long that in 1610, James lost patience and dismissed Parliament.

Plot inside a Plot

In 1603 a curious plot was planned by some Catholic priests and Puritans to kidnap James VI and I in an attempt at instigating religious freedom. This conspiracy was called the "Bye Plot" because after word had leaked about the intrigue, an investigation was started that discovered an even more heinous plot. When the second plot was brought to court it was referred to as the "Main Plot," with the lesser perfidy being the "Bye Plot," also known as the Surprising Treason[47] or the Treason of the Priests.[48]

At the time Catholics were subject to the Penal Laws that imposed fines on them if they did not attend Anglican church services, not attending a service was recusancy. The Bye Plot should have been put into action on St. John the Baptist's day, 24th June, but it was discovered, and the leaders rounded up and executed. Next year, 1604, King James issued an edict expelling all Catholic clergy, "Jesuits, Seminaries and other Priests," from England. [8] The plots involved two different groups of like-minded people planning independently. It is believed highly placed nobility knew of the plans, and later these co-conspirators also found themselves in prison in the Tower of London. The Main plot was more serious as it was an attempt, albeit half-hearted, to replace King James with a Protestant queen, Arbella Stuart, who was the great-great-granddaughter of King Henry VII. The leader of the conspiracy was Henry Brooke, Lord Cobham, who discussed the plot with Sir Walter Raleigh who, at the time, was the governor of Jersey.

After the discovery of the plot, Cobham and Raleigh were sent to the Tower, where Cobham soon died. Raleigh was executed fifteen years later. Raleigh had been a favourite of the previous monarch, Elizabeth I, and his execution was seen by people as being very unjust as his only guilt was a discussion with one of the perpetrators. At Raleigh's trial one of the judges stated, "The justice of England has never been so degraded and injured as by the condemnation of the honourable Sir Walter Raleigh."

Raleigh was a quintessential Tudor, a fortune hunter, politician, soldier, explorer and writer. He had been issued a royal charter authorizing him, in exchange for one-fifth of any gold or silver he might find, to explore and colonize any "remote, heathen and barbarous lands, countries and territories, not actually possessed of any Christian Prince or inhabited by Christian People."[49] He was not successful in finding gold or colonizing barbarous lands, even though he went to South America twice, but he is now known for having introduced tobacco to the West. There is a quaint story of his maid dousing him with a bucket of water on seeing smoke coming from his pipe as she thought he was on fire!

Elizabeth died in March 1603; in the summer of that year Raleigh was arrested and charged with treason for his involvement in the Main Plot. Fifteen years later, as he was about to be executed, he asked to

---

[8] There were several religious orders in England, such as the Jesuits, but their position had always been precarious. At the time, Catholics represented less than 2% of the population.

inspect the axe, saying, "This is a sharp Medicine, but it is a Physician for all diseases and miseries."[50]

The Gunpowder Plot

The Gunpowder Plot in 1605 changed the history of England. The plot not only failed, it brought about the opposite result than that the perpetrators had hoped for. The leader was a Catholic convert from Oxfordshire named Robert Catesby, who assembled a small group of like-minded people to blow up the Houses of Parliament at the State Opening when King James would be there. The plot was discovered when, on November 5th, the night before the opening, thirty-six barrels of gunpowder, enough explosive to reduce the building to rubble, were uncovered in the basement being guarded by a co-conspirator, Guy Fawkes. He did not know that the other conspirators had fled London. The conspirators were caught and hanged, drawn and quartered in public, though Fawkes cheated the executioner by jumping from the gallows and breaking his own neck.[51] This plot is still re-enacted every year in England on November 5th to the ditty:

Remember, remember the fifth of November:
　　Gunpowder, treason and plot.
I see no reason why gunpowder treason
　　Should ever be forgot.[9]

---

[9] Bonfires that burn masked effigies of Guy Fawkes have been held annually in England since 1605. This mask of an anarchist/Guy Fawkes was designed c1982 by David Lloyd.

The conspirators had intended to kidnap the young princess Elizabeth, James's Catholic daughter, from Coombe Abbey where she was living, and then start a revolution in the Midlands with the aim of installing her on the throne as a puppet queen. Elizabeth was the granddaughter of Mary, Queen of Scots, and was four years older than her brother Charles, who later became king of England.

When she was seventeen, Elizabeth married Frederick V, the Elector of Palatine, which is now a part of Germany, becoming Queen of Bohemia in 1619, but lost her title one year later after her husband King Frederick lost the Battle of White Mountain. Elizabeth was fondly remembered by the English as the "Winter Queen" or the "Snow Queen." Interestingly, one hundred years later, with the demise of the Stuart dynasty in 1714, it was Elizabeth's German grandson who was invited by Parliament to be King George I of the newly unified Great Britain, to establish the House of Hanover.

After the Gunpowder Plot, Parliament insisted on stricter controls of Catholics in England, requiring not just Catholics, but all citizens, to take the Oath of Allegiance. James took a conciliatory position as he wanted the support of powerful Catholics, saying that he would not prosecute "any that will be quiet and give but an outward obedience to the law."[52]

The Divine Right of Kings

In the Middle Ages, it was believed that the king of England received his authority directly from God, in the same way God had given authority over the Church to the pope, thus the king was not subject to the will of the people, the aristocracy, or the Church, and especially not the pope. Henry VIII received his "Verbum Dei" directly from God, who can be seen sitting at the top of the Great Chain of Being (see p46). This "Divine Right of Kings" was based on several stories in the Bible, such as Samuel anointing David as King of Israel,[53] and Peter ordering all Christians to honour the Roman Emperor even though, at that time, the emperor was a pagan.[54]

One historian wrote that Henry VIII (1491-1547) thought of God as a sort of "senior partner,"[55] so whatever he wanted was the will of God, and when things went against him, it indicated that Henry had displeased God in some way. The theory of the Divine Right of Kings became more important in the 17th century, especially under King James VI and I, and King Louis XIV of France.

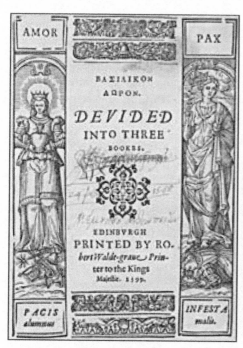

To King James, the Divine Right of Kings was an important doctrine as the Protestant Reformation had insisted that kings had absolute authority over both political matters as well as spiritual matters. James wrote a letter in the form of a book for his oldest son Henry, who died in 1612 aged eighteen, so James dedicated the book to his second son, Charles. The book is called *Basilikon Doron*, Greek for a "Royal Gift," and originally only a few copies were printed in Edinburgh in 1599, but when James became king of England it was republished in London and thousands of copies were sold. The book instructs Henry (and Charles) on how to be a good, God-fearing monarch, at the same time criticizing both Catholic papists and Puritans, which was seen to be the king's philosophy of following a "middle path." James stated in *Basilikon Doron*, "The state of monarchy is the supremest thing upon earth, for kings are not only God's lieutenants upon earth and sit upon God's throne, but even by God himself they are called gods." James's reference to "God's lieutenants" is apparently a reference to Romans 13 where Paul refers to "God's ministers." [56] This policy was also written in the preface to the Bible named after him, completed in 1611, reiterating the king's "God-given" right to rule, stating that a king "acknowledgeth himself ordained for his people, having received from the God a burden of government, whereof he must be countable." [57]

The notion that King James had been appointed by God was accepted and supported in England, it shaped how the Stuarts saw themselves as was reflected in Shakespeare's plays, Milton's poems and the political writing of John Locke.

Even today, the monarchs of the United Kingdom are some of the last to be crowned in a traditional ceremony where they are anointed with holy oil. The coronation resembles a Catholic ceremony, although it is literally "ceremonial." The monarch no longer has "absolute authority over both political and spiritual matters," but has sovereign powers, not governmental or ecclesiastical ones.

William Marshall's *Eikon Basilike* the *Royal Portrait, The Pourtrature of His Sacred Majestie in His Solitudes and Sufferings,* is a purported diary attributed to King Charles I. It was published on 9 February 1649, ten days after the King was beheaded by Parliament in the aftermath of the English Civil War.

Patriarchalism

Associated with the Divine Right of Kings was the political theory elaborated by Sir Robert Filmer in the 1620s that defended the king's right of absolute power. As he wrote in his book *Patriarcha:*

> Many, out of an imaginary fear, pretend the power of the people to be necessary for the repressing of the insolencies of tyrants, herein they propound a remedy far worse than the disease.[58]

Filmer stated that the right of fathers had been passed down genea-logically since the time of Adam, and this was reflected in the laws concerning property and inheritance. James, in his book *Basilikon Doron*, had also said that the relationship of the king to his people was "paternal" and "no misconduct on the part of a father can free his chil-dren from obedience to the fifth commandment" that of "honouring your father." [59] In time this position was regularly challenged by Parliament, particularly as the king alienated the popular opinion of citizens with a divisive religious policy, a contentious political strat-egy and an adverse foreign diplomacy.

James VI and I was not so much a man of action as a literary man, having written nine books on various subjects including kingship, witchcraft and tobacco. During his reign, he was also patron to William Shakespeare, John Donne and Ben Jonson, as well as under-writing the translation of the authorized King James Bible of 1611. Many have called him "the wisest fool in Christendom," [60] probably because of his vacillating position on religious faith, which upset Puritans. In Scotland at the time of his death in 1625, the Kirk was still divided, which became a source of future problems for his son, Charles I. Due to the volatile political situation in England in the early 17th century, many Dissenters decided to leave the country and try their luck by establishing new colonies in America, such as the hun-dred and two Pilgrim Fathers who left in 1620 in the small, thirty-three-meter ship, the Mayflower.

Witchcraft

James I saw himself as an authority on witchcraft, and even wrote a book on the subject, *Daemonologie*. It was believed that to be a witch, a person had to make a pact with the devil, and that witches always worked in covens. Since 1563, both being a witch and consulting with a witch were capital offences under the Scottish Witchcraft Act, but enforcement of the law was lax. In 1589 James visited Denmark, where a nationwide witch hunt was in progress, and this is thought to have had a strong impact on him. [61] It was reported that hundreds of witches had entered into a pact to kill the king by calling up a storm to drown him on his voyage to Denmark, because there had actually been a violent storm on his return and one ship in the fleet was lost.

Subsequently, from 1590 there were dozens of trials for witchcraft held in Scotland.

In England the situation was a little different as not all people agreed with witch hunts. In 1584 a member of Parliament, Reginald Scot, wrote *The Discoverie of Witchcraft* claiming that it was irrational and unchristian to persecute people for witchcraft. The book was a condemnation of Catholicism, showing how Catholics were responsible for whipping up the witch hunt frenzy across Europe, and sparked a debate on the subject that continued a hundred years. Though the book was quickly banned, with copies seized and burned, it was reprinted abroad and was still available in the late 1880s.

In 1604, the year after James VI of Scotland ascended the English throne as James I, he had Elizabeth's witchcraft act of 1563 broadened to include the death penalty, without benefit of clergy, to anyone who invoked evil spirits or communed with "familiars," supernatural spirits often in the form of animals.[62] However, James found that attitudes to witchcraft were different in England, so he started to distance himself from his assertion of being an expert on the subject. England was preoccupied with what was called "natural philosophy," and had no time for superstition, thus James's association with witchcraft was somewhat embarrassing.

William Harvey is an example of England's different attitude to witchcraft. He was the king's physician, famous for discovering how blood circulated through the body, and he did not believe in witchcraft. There is a story from 1632 of Harvey dressing up as a wizard to investigate a witch. He asked her if she had a familiar that helped her with her witchcraft. She produced a frog which, much to her chagrin, he promptly dissected and, finding nothing out of the ordinary with the animal, declared her innocent of the charge of witchcraft.[63] Because of his standing in society, two years later he was again asked to examine four women accused of witchcraft and likewise he had them acquitted.[64]

This is not to say that the English had abandoned their interest in spiritual matters. As late as 1768, the theologian John Wesley wrote:

> It is true that the English in general - indeed most of the men of learning in Europe - have given up all accounts of witches and

apparitions as mere old wives' fables. I am sorry for it, and I willingly take this opportunity to offer my solemn protest against this violent compliment which so many that believe in the Bible pay to those who do not believe it [witchcraft]. Such belief is in direct opposition, not only to the Bible, but to the suffrage of the wisest and best of men in all ages and nations. They well know that the giving up of witchcraft is in effect giving up the Bible. And they know on the other hand, that if but one account of the intercourse of men with separate spirits be admitted, their whole castle in the air, Deism, Atheism, Materialism, falls to the ground.[65]

By Victorian times spiritualism became a movement led by artists and intellectuals such as William Blake, Arthur Conan Doyle and Henry Sidgwick.

Charles I, reigned 1625-1649

James's son Charles acceded to the throne in 1625 and from the beginning he had difficulties working with Parliament, in particular over his right to raise taxes or armed forces without Parliament's consent, and by the end of the third year of his reign he had already dissolved three Parliaments. Charles then decided to rule without Parliament, insisting that he ruled by Divine Right. Instead of Parliament, Charles used the Court of Star Chamber as a substitute during his eleven years of Personal Rule, also known as the "Eleven Years' Tyranny."

The Star Chamber was a special council established by the Tudors to ensure that laws against the rich and powerful were fairly enforced, because lower courts would be hesitant to convict such people. The council was named after the gilt stars adorning the ceiling of the chamber. Initially, in the Tudor times, the court was well thought of because it worked impartially and quickly, but by Charles's time it was synonymous with abuse of power, particularly when investigating cases of sedition, and the court was allowed to dispatch any opposition to the king's policies. In one famous case, where the Archbishop of Canterbury, William Laud, tried to impose doctrinal uniformity on the Church of England by having an opponent branded on the face with the letters "SL" for seditious libeller, Laud himself was arrested and executed. Charles also made extensive use of the Star Chamber to prosecute Dissenters including, in absentia, the Puritans who fled to New England, which was a contributory factor in the start of the English Civil War.

Charles used the "Royal Prerogative," the special right of the monarch to confer honours and dissolve (prorogue) Parliament with impunity. Though Charles believed that he ruled by Divine Right, Protestant members of Parliament were increasingly vociferous in their opposition to him. A sign of the anti-Catholic sentiment of the times can be seen from a petition presented to the Long Parliament in December 1640. It was signed by 15,000 Londoners who called on Parliament to abolish Catholicism from all its "roots and branches," and thus was called the Roots and Branches Petition. The petition was introduced in Parliament by Oliver Cromwell in 1641, but after deliberation was defeated.

Parliament had been recalled in 1640, and although it sat for two years, becoming known as the Long Parliament, it was not able to resolve issues such as how to pay for the Bishops' Wars, where King Charles fought armies raised by bishops in Scotland. The uprising was eventually ended two years later through a settlement. The stalemate with Parliament and Protestant members' complaints against the king led King Charles to attempt to arrest five members of Parliament. He forced his way with four hundred soldiers into the House of Commons, but the five had escaped, prompting him to observe, "I see all the birds are flown."[66] The five were given refuge in the fortified City of London, which was on the Parliamentary side of the feud. That was the last time any monarch ever forcibly entered the House of Commons.

The City of London at that time, was a walled city which could easily hold off the king's forces. This, together with the financial resources available in the City, turned out to be winning factors for the Parliamentarians. The king then moved to Oxford in 1642 and established an alternative Parliament. Charles and his supporters resented Parliament's demands, while Parliamentarians continued to suspect Charles of wanting to impose unrestricted royal rule, supported by military force. In 1641 a rebellion started in Ireland with Catholics attacking Protestants, and many believed that the king sided with the Irish Catholics. Though most cities in England remained neutral in the conflict, Charles found support in rural communities and soon a civil war had started. The war pitted Parliamentarians, derisively called "Roundheads" for the round metal helmets they wore, against the Royalists, with their decorative clothes and feathered hats.

The Member of Parliament for Cambridge was Oliver Cromwell. He was an able commander, nicknamed "Old Ironsides," and soon became a leading figure in the New Model Army, which was the first full-time professional army in England. In previous eras kings had relied on part-time militias. Officers of this new army were prohibited from being elected to Parliament to avoid political factions within the army. The Royalist army was led by aristocrats who supported the king, though not all of them were Catholics. The civil war was in fact three periods of conflict, with short respites in between, and so is often referred to as "England's Three Civil Wars," or the "Wars of the Three Kingdoms," as there were battles in all three countries, England, Scotland and Ireland.

The Wars of the Three Kingdoms

The First English Civil War started in 1642, but there had been conflicts before then. The background to the conflict was that as Scotland was then Presbyterian, there were no bishops answering to the king, which he believed diminished his authority. In an attempt to control the Scottish Presbyterians, Charles introduced a new Prayer Book in 1637, partly revised by the Archbishop of Canterbury, William Laud. However, the new Prayer Book was received with fury, and a riot started at St. Giles Cathedral in Edinburgh. Scottish nobles and clergy signed a National Covenant to defend the Presbyterian Church against any intrusion from England. Then Charles tried to forcibly coerce Scotland, starting the Bishops' War of 1639.

Charles had dismissed Parliament in 1629 but continued to feud with Parliament and its Puritan leanings, which by 1642 turned into an armed conflict, the First English Civil War. The Parliamentarians sought the support of Scotland, in exchange for introducing Presbyterianism into England, and at the time nearly a third of the seats in Parliament were held by Puritans who felt that their religious creed had much in common with the Presbyterian. The conflict ended when Charles was captured by Scottish troops, supported by Oliver Cromwell, and he was imprisoned in Carisbrooke Castle on the Isle of Wight in 1646.

Though Charles had been captured, both sides in the conflict negotiated with him as it was assumed that, whatever the outcome, England still needed a king. It was believed that a Protestant monarch was the best bulwark against continental popery. So, Charles was moved between the Scots, the New Model Army and Parliament. After Charles's arrest, there was a political vacuum and, from 1646 to 1648, the gap between the Army and Parliament widened until finally the English Presbyterian party joined the Scots, signing "The Engagement" together with some remaining Royalists, to fight the New Model army which was the beginning of the Second Civil War.[67] The war lasted one year until the execution of Charles I on 30th January 1649.

The Third English Civil War started when Parliament declared England to be a republic, and Ireland and Scotland joined forces in recognizing Charles's son, Charles II as king of Great Britain, Ireland and unusually, France. [10] In 1649 Cromwell attacked Ireland, and dividing his forces, he also attacked Scotland and Charles. The remnants of the Royalist army were defeated at the Battle of Worcester in September 1651.

What had started with an argument about the Prayer Book, resulted in an intertwined series of conflicts that took place in England, Ireland and Scotland between 1639 and 1651, leaving 180,000 dead at a time when the population of England was about five million. The New Model Army occupied both Ireland and Scotland during the Interregnum. The Commonwealth government confiscated the lands of Irish

---

[10] Charles was not crowned Charles II of England until 1661, though he was proclaimed king of Scotland in 1649.

Catholics as punishment for their part in the Third Civil War and introduced harsh Penal Laws. Thousands of soldiers from the New Model Army settled in Ireland on confiscated lands which, 270 years later, resulted in the creation of Protestant Northern Ireland in 1921.

Execution or Regicide?

In 1649 King Charles I was arraigned for being "a tyrant, traitor and murderer." The trial was a noisy affair as about 4,000 people crammed

into Westminster Hall to watch the trial, so soldiers had to be called in to keep the peace. Charles had no counsel and there was no jury, just court-appointed commissioners. At his trial Charles stated that he ruled "with authority given him by God" and that no court had jurisdiction over him, so he did not enter a plea and was liable for the penalty of "peine forte et dure." The court argued that the king "was not a person but an office" and so was not above the law. Some of the king's letters had been intercepted showing that he had been trying to get help for the Royalists from Ireland and France, which was deemed treasonable. After the First Civil War, Cromwell had sued for peace, but as Charles had restarted the war by inviting the Scots to join him, it was deemed that he had "declared war on his own people."

Fifty-nine of the sixty-nine commissioners at the trial agreed and signed the king's death warrant, one of the signatories was Oliver Cromwell, though over half of the men nominated to the court had not attended the proceedings.[68] The trial was seen as an act of vengeance and was very unpopular. Cromwell thought he could make a deal with the king, for his "prodigious [extraordinary] treason," that might "vassalize us to a foreign nation."[69] The senior judge, John Bradshaw, was so fearful of reprise that he wore armour under his judicial robes and a bulletproof hat.[70] A seer, Elizabeth Poole of Abingdon, was consulted as to how the king should be punished. A short time afterwards, she claimed to have had a revelation that Charles should not be hurt.[71] The court lasted just seven days, presumably wanting to bring the proceedings to an expedited conclusion. Three days later, despite Elizabeth Poole's advice, Charles was taken to the scaffold, but was then kept waiting five hours until a death warrant could be signed by Parliament.

It is said that just before his beheading, King Charles asked for a second shirt, saying "the season is so sharp as probably may make me shake, which some observers may imagine proceeds from fear. I would have no such imputation."[72] The king's final words were, "I go from a corruptible to an incorruptible Crown, where no disturbance can be."[73] After Charles was beheaded, onlookers dipped their handkerchiefs in his blood as ghoulish mementos.[74] In February, the king was buried at Windsor Castle, rather than in Westminster Abbey, so as to avoid public disorder. Just before Charles's death, the office of king was officially abolished in an attempt to avert the automatic succession of Charles II, his son, then aged fifteen.

The horror of Charles's execution for the people was that as everything was ordained by God, it was blasphemy to change the sacred order of the Chain of Being. So Charles, who was God's lieutenant on Earth, had to be shown not only as a traitor to the people but a traitor to God as well. However, in William Marshall's *Eikon Basilike*, published a year after the execution, Charles is shown in a saint-like pose and he's holding a crown of thorns, reminiscent of Christ (cf. p54). Following the Restoration, the date of the execution, January 30th, was made a holy day that was recognized for nearly two hundred years.

Two Religious Treaties

Two important treaties had been signed just before Charles's death that weakened the position of Catholicism not just in England, but in Europe as well. During the First Civil War, the Parliamentarians thought they might lose the fight as they were concerned that Irish troops would support the Royalists. So, in 1643, the Parliamentarians made a treaty with the Scots, the "Solemn League and Covenant," in exchange for the Scots helping them fight the "papists." This treaty allowed for the Scottish form of Presbyterian church government to be adopted in England as well. However, English Presbyterians in Parliament were hostile to the execution of Charles I and the establishment of the Republic, and little was achieved by the Long Parliament resulting in Presbyterianism not being enforced in England (except in a small area of Lancashire), and England reverted to episcopalianism in 1661. Secondly, though the Solemn League and Covenant was signed in 1643 by both Scotland and England, the Covenant left many loopholes in the law because of its ambiguous wording, which were later used to advantage by English Dissenters. The problem remained that the king was at that time under arrest, but in theory, still head of state. This made the Covenant's legality a moot point, but the Westminster Assembly of Divines, a council of theologians who sat in Parliament, ratified the agreement in 1649 making it law. This was one of their last formal documents, as the assembly ceased to function after Cromwell's dissolution of the Rump Parliament in 1653.

The second important settlement was the Treaty of Westphalia in 1648, which was signed by 109 European delegations, including the Holy Roman Emperor, Ferdinand III. This was to bring an end to the Thirty Years' War which had pitted Protestants against Catholics, and it effectively ended the pope's power base in Europe. Pope Innocent X issued a papal bull declaring the treaty "null, void, invalid, iniquitous, unjust, damnable, reprobate, inane, empty of meaning and effect for all times!" His comments, however, were ignored by Catholics and Protestants alike.

Fifth Monarchy

A group of zealous Protestants in the Rump Parliament formed a gathering in 1648 calling themselves the Fifth Monarchists and were active mainly during the Interregnum. Their name is based on a story in the Book of Daniel that tells of a prophecy that the king of Babylon, Nebuchadnezzar, had seen in a dream, showing that the four ancient monarchies of Babylon, Persia, Macedonia and Rome would precede a fifth monarchy, the kingdom of Christ, which would stand forever.[75] The Monarchists believed that King Charles I was in league with the antichrist, the pope, and only by removing the king would the "Second Coming of Christ" occur. Another spur to their side was the fact that the year 1666 was close at hand and this, they claimed, indicated the end of human rule on earth, as given in the Book of Revelation. The year would also herald the beginning of the Fifth Monarchy, as quoted in a Fifth Monarchy manifesto *A Door of Hope* printed in 1660, which may have been influenced William Blake when he wrote the anthem *Jerusalem*:

> We therefore freely, of a ready minde, and with a most chearful heart ... give up our lives and estates unto our Lord King Jesus, and to his people, to become soldiers in the Lambs Army... neither will we ever... sheath our swords again, until Mount Zion become the joy of the whole earth ... until Rome be in ashes, and Babylon become a hissing and a curse.[76]

The Commonwealth of England 1649–1653

In 1648 the Long Parliament was purged of all members with Royalist sympathies, this then became known as the Rump Parliament, and it handled legislative functions leaving the new Council of State to handle executive functions. Policy was mainly dominated by the wishes of senior officers in the New Model Army known as Grandees. These Grandees were landed gentry who served in the army to oppose the Levellers (see below).

The Interregnum followed the execution of Charles I in 1649, an eleven-year period of republican rule in the three kingdoms of England, Ireland and Scotland. During this period, government affairs were carried out first by the Commonwealth (1649-1653) and then by the Protectorate of Oliver Cromwell (1653-1660) until the Restoration of Charles II in 1660.

Parliament initially established the Commonwealth of England, which was de facto military rule in the name of parliament. However, it was a time of economic depression in England, and the Rump Parliament was ineffective as it could not decide on what type of government to introduce. Many members of parliament saw the government as illegal, based on regicide, while others believed the alternative would have been a military dictatorship. Elizabeth I's Act of Uniformity of 1558, to unify the Anglican Church, was repealed in September 1650 and independent churches were tolerated.

In 1653, the Rump Parliament was also dissolved and replaced with one with 140 nominated representatives, headed by Oliver Cromwell, which became known as the Parliament of Saints. The representatives believed that they were ordained by God to rule the country, later calling the assembly Barebone's Parliament, after a member with the colourful name of "Praise-God Barebone," a fundamentalist who believed that Jewish Mosaic Law should replace the British Constitution.[77] It seemed that radical changes were going to be introduced, the least of which was that there would be a constitutional government in England and Ireland, with London as the centre of political power.

The Protectorate of Oliver Cromwell 1653–1658

In 1653 Oliver Cromwell, with the support of leaders in the New Model Army, declared England a Protectorate with himself as Lord Protector, a de facto king, leaving the Fifth Monarchists feeling betrayed. Protestants took this opportunity to call for a greater purity of worship and piety among the population, becoming known as Puritans.

Many people now believe that the Puritans were soulless, religious fanatics. For example, the Rump Parliament outlawed

Christmas celebrations, as had the Protestant Kirk in Scotland ten years earlier, as it believed the holiday should be a solemn one. However, the people thought otherwise, and a ballad called *The World Turned Upside Down* was written to protest the solemnity. Though it wasn't all doom and gloom, and the first truly English opera *The Siege of Rhodes* was written during the Interregnum.

The Fifth Monarchists also wanted to turn England into a more "godly" nation, expecting "King Jesus" soon to be enthroned. Among their number were women who acted as prophets for the movement. One, Mary Cary, called for Jews, who been expelled from England since 1290, to be allowed to return, believing that if they were allowed to enter England and convert to Anglicanism that this would precipitate the Second Coming of Christ. The Fifth Monarchists did not believe that the Rump Parliament would fulfil this request and plotted twice in 1657 and 1659 to overthrow the government, but the plots were discovered. Though the Fifth Monarchy men were religious, they were also determined to fight for their beliefs. Whether Cromwell had sympathy for the Fifth Monarchist cause is difficult to say, as one of their plots was aimed at him, but Jews were at last allowed to live in London for the first time in 360 years, without converting to Christianity, and in 1657 they built London's first synagogue.

After military campaigns in Ireland and Scotland, Cromwell died of what is now assumed to have been malaria and was buried in Westminster Abbey. Three years later, after the restoration of the monarchy with the crowning of King Charles II, Cromwell's body was exhumed, and to exact revenge on the brutal leader for the "murder" of Charles's father, was subjected to a posthumous execution, with his head on display on a pole in Westminster for twenty-five years.[78]

Richard Cromwell

Following Cromwell's death, command passed to his son, Richard "Tumbledown Dick" Cromwell, the second of only two commoners to have ever been head of state in England. His government lasted only nine months until 1659 when he resigned and was pensioned off. He was allowed to remain in the Palace of Whitehall, where his father had lived as that was, and still is, the centre of English government.

Richard "was never formally deposed or arrested, but allowed to fade away."[79]

In 1660 the Long Parliament was briefly reinstated and Charles, son of Charles I, who had fled to France when he was fifteen, was invited to return on his thirtieth birthday to become Charles II, with many calling him "The Fifth Monarch."[80]

Levellers

Many forms of Protestantism started in England following the repeal of the Act of Uniformity in 1650, and one of the most important was the Levellers. The Levellers called for equality before the law, suffrage, religious tolerance and "popular sovereignty" and thus were popular with the New Model Army. However, some of their beliefs were before their time and they were often imprisoned for those beliefs. One of their leaders was Richard Overton, who had been active writing pamphlets during the Civil War and the Interregnum. Among the pamphlets he penned was an important one, written anonymously, concerning immortality and his denial of it, based on a verse in the Bible, "man hath no pre-eminence above a beast: for all is vanity. All go unto one place; all are of the dust, and all turn to dust again."[81] Overton claimed that until a person's soul is resurrected there is no salvation or condemnation.

This pamphlet caused an uproar in a time of religious tension and Parliament ordered the Stationer's Company to find out who the author was. The Worshipful Company of Stationers had been incorporated during the reign of Mary I, and it had the legal power to arrest authors of books that were offensive to public morals and bring them before an ecclesiastic court for trial. Cromwell had pushed a bill through Parliament to end royal censorship of books in 1641, but censorship was not completely abolished until nearly 50 years later. Overton's tract had been published in Amsterdam, and though he signed it only with his initials, he was discovered and in 1646 was imprisoned in Newgate Prison. However, with the support of the New Model Army, he was released a year later.

On the back of the publicity of Overton's pamphlet, a small sect called "Soul Sleepers" was established, though the sect did not survive long.

Overton's support of Christian mortalism (see chapter *Religious Turmoil*) was taken up by other restorationist sects, such as the Jehovah's Witnesses two hundred years later.

John Milton 1608–1674

Milton worked as a civil servant for the Commonwealth at the Council of State under Oliver Cromwell, but is better known as the poet who in 1667 wrote *Paradise Lost*.

Milton's father, being a man of means, allowed his son John an independent income, though he also taught the children of wealthy people to supplement his income. Milton wrote tracts defending the right of the people to hold their rulers to account, sanctioning regicide, and thus favouring him with Cromwell. Milton's pamphlet *Areopagitica*, named after a similar speech by the Greek orator Isocrates, attacked pre-printing censorship that stifled freedom of speech, which he saw as a uniquely Christian freedom. Milton had studied at the University of Cambridge and wrote in Latin, Greek, Hebrew, French, Italian and Spanish, and had a solid understanding of each of those countries' cultures. After the fall of Richard Cromwell, Milton proposed a free republic or "free commonwealth" to be brought about by 1660, hoping to revive the "Good Old Cause."[82] The reason the soldiers of the New Model Army had been motivated to fight on behalf of Parliament in the first place, was because many were independents who wanted local congregational control of church matters, which they called "The Good Old Cause." Regrettably, Milton's opinion was in opposition to that of the public, which was then calling out for the return of the monarchy.

By 1654 Milton had become totally blind and had helpers write manuscripts for him. Then by 1660, with the Restoration of King Charles II, his situation had become precarious. He had not been a successful writer, his books sold in small numbers, and he had been living off his father's inheritance, supplemented by some teaching. After the Restoration, Milton had to go into hiding, as a warrant for his arrest had been issued and his books had been burned. Two years later he received a pardon, but by then he was living in an impoverished state. However, in 1667, on publishing the epic poem *Paradise Lost*, his fortunes improved. Scholars say that the poem reflects his feeling of personal disappointment at the failure of the Commonwealth, and has encoded references to the "Good Old Cause," while proclaiming the optimism of human potential.[83] He also espoused heterodox religious opinions such as mortalism, and Arianism that rejected the Trinity, believing that the Son was subordinate to the Father; a belief that was steadily gaining momentum in the late 17th century.

Just before his death, Milton wrote his last major work, *Of True Religion*, which argued for religious toleration for everyone but Catholics. The book became part of the debate on the Exclusion Bill, or how to stop James, the Duke of York, the heir to the throne after Charles II, from becoming king, as James, like his brother, was also Catholic.

Charles II, reigned 1660-1685

1660 starts the period known as the Restoration, when Charles II was restored to the thrones of England, Scotland and Ireland. The term is used rather loosely to describe the king's restoration as well as the period of his reign and, by some historians, the period up to and including the Glorious Revolution in 1688. Interestingly, after his restoration, all legal documents were backdated to 1649 as though the Interregnum had never happened.[84]

Charles II's epithet, the "Merrie Monarch," was due to his proclivity for mistresses and a certain hedonism at court. His wife bore him no children, but it is estimated that he had twelve children with thirteen mistresses, one of the most famous being Nell Gwyn, actress and one-time theatre orange-seller. The first act that Charles passed through Parliament was the Indemnity and Oblivion Act of 1660, where he pardoned all those accused of treason against the crown, with the exception of those involved in the trial and execution of his father, Charles I. Fifty-nine judges had signed the king's death warrant and thirty-one were still alive. Of these, twelve were sentenced to death at Tyburn or Charing Cross. The Leader of the Fifth Monarchist Army,

Thomas Harrison, was the first person found guilty of regicide, and was hanged, drawn and quartered because he was considered to still represent a threat to Charles's government. The potential for the Fifth Monarchists to overthrow the king was proved the next year with "Venner's Rising."

The new Parliament, known as the Cavalier Parliament, soon set to work to solidify the authority of the Anglican Church. Over the period 1661 to 1665, Parliament, which was now dominated by Anglicans, introduced a series of laws called the Clarendon Code, named after Edward Hyde, 1st Earl of Clarendon, Charles's chief minister. The impetus for these laws was a failed rebellion by the Fifth Monarchy Men in January 1661 in what became known as "Venner's Rising."

Thomas Venner was a wine-cooper who, with fifty like-minded men, attempted to take London in the name of "King Jesus" because they feared the dreaded date 1666 and Armageddon were getting nearer. The uprising lasted only four days before most of the men were either killed in the conflict or were later hanged, drawn and quartered for treason. After this the Fifth Monarchy dissipated and other radical groups, which at the time included the Quakers, also decided that it was useless to fight and became pacifists.

The four laws that became the Clarendon Code were introduced to limit not only Catholics but also Dissenters who were thought to be social revolutionaries. The first law limited official posts in the government to Anglicans, the second reinforced the authority of Elizabeth I's Prayer Book and formed the basis of the 1662 Act of Uniformity, resulting in 1,910 ministers and university dons having to leave their positions, in what became known as the Great Ejection of 1662. The third law prohibited meetings of Dissenters and the last, the "Five Mile Act," disallowed Dissenters from preaching or teaching within five miles of any town or city. These acts resulted in a period of persecution of Dissenters, but despite the Code, the movements flourished in England near the end of the 17th century.

Puritans had abolished many aspects of the Anglican Church during the Interregnum, but with the Clarendon Code the Church was restored as the national Church of England. People took to the streets to celebrate, danced around Maypoles and taunted Presbyterians, with the hangman publicly burning copies of the Solemn League and Covenant.

Rats

Plague was a severe problem that hurt England's economy. A linear view of history suggests that the plague suddenly happened in 1665, but it had been affecting London for many years before that. Bubonic plague is a flea-borne bacterial disease that causes necrosis and pneumonia, with an 80-90% death rate. The fleas travelled quickly on rats, their hosts, because as there was no proper sewage system in London in the 1600s, the streets were littered with filth. The poor lived in houses that were close together, and as the winter of 1665 was warm, rats spread the disease quickly. Even as late as 1852, Charles Dickens, in his book *Bleak House*, recounts how the poor were paid by the rich to sweep horse droppings and other refuse from the road so that they could cross from one side to the other.

The first large scale plague was around 500-550 AD when up to a quarter of the world's population died; the second large outbreak was from 1330 to 1347, starting in Mongolia and spreading along the Silk Road to Italy and parts of Europe, killing up to one third of the world's population. The plague was known as the "Black Death," probably because of the blackening of the skin due to necrosis. The first major outbreak during the Stuart era started in London around 1603 with 38,000 deaths that year. From 1604 to 1612 there were between 5,000 and 11,000 deaths from the plague every year in London. The deaths abated for ten years, but the numbers suddenly spiked in 1625 to 63,000. Then every five years there would be an outbreak with between 10,000 to 20,000 deaths per year. Presumably Charles I was too busy when he ascended the throne in 1625, particularly with his problems with Parliament, to pay attention to the increase in deaths in London at that time. Secondly, he lived in the City of Westminster, about five miles from the old City of London, and did not witness the problem first-hand. The population of London was about 300,000 in 1665, and, by the end of the year, 65,000 people, one person in five, had died.

Our knowledge of the epidemic comes from the journalist, Samuel Pepys, who wrote a detailed account in 1665 of the government's inability to do anything useful to halt the disease. Pepys wrote:

> This day, much against my will, I did in Drury Lane see two or three houses marked with a red cross upon the doors, and 'Lord Have Mercy upon Us' writ there – which was a sad sight to me, being the first of the kind...that I ever saw.[85]

Death figures were recorded in weekly Mortality Bills from the 130 parishes in and around the City of London, but some religious groups such as Jews and Quakers had their own graveyards, so the recorded numbers may be understated. Also, because of the large numbers of dead, the coroners could not keep up with recording them and carcasses were summarily burned. Wagons were pulled through the streets by people in fantastic costumes and masks to protect from the disease, ringing bells while calling out "bring out your dead!" Pepys wrote on 4th September 1665:

> I have stayed in the city till above 7,400 died in one week, and of them about 6,000 of the plague, and little noise heard day or night but tolling of bells.

Bodies were also left in the street and collectors, "plague doctors," (left)[11] had to be paid to take them away at night. In an attempt to control the spread of the disease, the government stopped people from entering or leaving the City of London, however, rich people could buy passes to get away to their country houses. Charles II, with his family and court, escaped to Salisbury on June 29th 1665, during the height of the plague, while members of Parliament moved to Oxford.[86] The rapidity of the infestation must have caught everyone by surprise; in June there had been only forty deaths a week, that rose in July to a thousand deaths a week and a peak of 6,800 in September, falling to 500 deaths a week in November. By January 1666, the number of deaths had fallen back to around fifty a week.

---

[11] The long raven beaks on the plague doctors' masks were filled with lavender and other flowers to counteract the miasma, the "bad air."

Physicians of that time generally did not understand the aetiology of disease, for example they believed that the stars "influenced" a person's health, so fever became known as "influenza." Likewise, with the plague, people believed that the disease was transmitted by miasma, "bad air:"

> Ring-a-ring of roses,
> A pocketful of posies,
> A-ti-shoo, a-ti-shoo,
> We all fall down.

In this ditty, the ring of roses refers to the red blotches on the skin from having been bitten by a plague-carrying flea. The posies of flowers were to protect from the "bad air," and sneezing was thought to be a symptom of the plague. Of course, every-man-jack had a home-made remedy that they were eager to sell, and most of the cures, such as tobacco smoked in clay pipes, which even children smoked, were based on this irrational idea of bad air. The College of Physicians suggested that burning brimstone would purify the bad air that they also believed caused the plague.[87] Shop-keepers would put change in a bowl of vinegar as patrons did not want to accept potentially infected coins, and charlatans sold all manner of lucky charms and a cure called "plague water" made from powdered "unicorn" horns.

However not all physicians were blinded by superstition; a German Jesuit in Rome, Athanasius Kircher, looked at the blood of plague victims through the newly invented microscope and seeing "small worms," he suggested these were the responsible pathogens. Though his conclusion was probably correct he would not have been able to see bacteria with a 17th century microscope. However, he did make sensible recommendations to contain the disease such as wearing masks, quarantine, and burning victims' clothes.

Samuel Pepys was one of the first to record that the number of deaths was being under-reported, as the clerks were overwhelmed by the number of the dead. He gave as an example the week of August 31st 1665, where 6,100 deaths were recorded. Pepys believed the number was closer to 10,000. By October of that year, Pepys noticed that the worst was over, the number of deaths had declined dramatically, and people were venturing out of their houses, though shops remained closed.

The English Father of Medicine: Thomas Sydenham 1624–1689

Thomas Sydenham was one of the first physicians to base his treatment on close examination of the patient, rather than taking advice from medieval books. Until then, the Doctrine of Signatures was the major form of therapy in England, based on a theory by the Greek physician Galen who stated that a herb shaped like a human organ should be used in treating that organ. This idea was also promoted by the English botanist William Coles, who said that God had so designed the plants in order that man could identify their use.

In 1666 Sydenham wrote a book on curing fevers, followed two years later with an update on the plague. He added more information to the third edition in 1676, and this text, *Observationes Medicae*, became the standard textbook on medicine for two centuries. He was an advocate of using laudanum (a tincture of opium) saying, "Of all the remedies it has pleased almighty God to give man to relieve his suffering, none is so universal and so efficacious as opium."[88]

Medicine was still very primitive at the time, and doctors used blood-letting (phlebotomy) to cure disease, though King James I's physician and the discoverer of blood circulation, William Harvey, wrote disparagingly of the practice in 1628.[89] However, even two hundred years later in 1838, Dr Henry Clutterbuck, a lecturer at the Royal College of Physicians, wrote "blood-letting is a remedy which, when judiciously employed, it is hardly possible to estimate too highly," and as late as the 1880s the Canadian physician and one of the four founding professors of Johns Hopkins Hospital, William Osler, spoke in favour of blood-letting.[90] Often it was the job of the barber to perform blood-letting, as is seen in the red and white stripes that coil around a pole outside their establishments, the red for blood and the white for bandages.

Sydenham rejected the superstition that most physicians employed. In one famous case where he was called to see a patient that had already had a copious amount of blood let and who looked very poorly, Sydenham prescribed him "roast chicken and a pint of canary (a fortified wine)." Sydenham was also one of the first to use "Peruvian Bark" (quinine) for the treatment of Malaria. After his death, his importance as a medical pioneer was recognized, with people calling him the English Hippocrates. His legacy was in teaching that observation was a powerful diagnostic tool; "I have [often] consulted my patients' safety and my own reputation most effectually by doing nothing at all."

Out of the Frying Pan into the Fire

As if things could not get worse after the plague, on Sunday 2nd September 1666 a fire broke out at the king's baker in Pudding Lane in the south of the old city of London, and fanned by intense winds, quickly spread. Efforts to slow the progress of the fire were chaotic, with firebreaks made by pulling down houses, and eventually gunpowder, as suggested by Pepys, was used to clear the houses. By the following Thursday it was brought under control. The last flames were extinguished at Pye Corner in Smithfield. Pepys recounted the horror:

> I saw a fire as one entire arch of fire above a mile long: it made me weep to see it. The churches, houses are all on fire and flaming at once, and a horrid noise the flames made and the cracking of the houses.

St. Paul's Cathedral early 16th century

In all about 13,000 buildings were destroyed, including St. Paul's Cathedral, the Royal Exchange, eighty-seven churches and forty-four livery halls, covering an area of about sixty percent of the City. The fire was so intense, with the heat reaching 1,250°C, that the lead on the roof on St. Paul's melted and flowed in the street like water. About 80,000 to 90,000 people were displaced, and many sought refuge from the heat in boats on the river Thames.

The old City of London is not the same as the present Metropolitan London but was a small area which is now the financial centre, the "Square Mile." There were many small side roads and passages, with houses standing shoulder to shoulder. During the fire, thieves, pretending to help people to safety, used these passages to escape after taking people's possessions and leaving them for dead. Surprisingly, very few people were recorded as having died in the fire, between six and eight people. However, there were also lynchings of Dutchmen living in London, as well as people using the fire as an opportunity to attack Catholics. Infanticide was common, as was leaving the old to fend for themselves, and such was the heat that many bodies were incinerated to nothing, so, the number of dead may have been much higher. At the time of the fire, England was winning a war against the Netherlands, and so the start of the Great Fire was originally attributed to the Dutch.

This time the royal family stood their ground, with King Charles helping the firefighting and ordering navy rations to be released from stores in the East End for the homeless. Charles put his younger brother James in charge of firefighting operations, as the Lord Mayor was nowhere to be found. James distinguished himself, as a spectator commentated, "The Duke of York hath won the hearts of the people with his continual and indefatigable pains day and night in helping to quench the Fire."[91]

After the fire, the king organized evacuations to the countryside for those that had been displaced, and work started on rebuilding the city. The loss had been tremendous, estimated at £10 million (£1.5bn at current values)[92] which was an enormous sum as the National Income at that time was only £40 million; but on the other hand, the fire had burned away slums, open sewers and the remnants of the plague. In 1667 the first London Building Act was passed dictating that future buildings in London had to be made from stone not wood, with only doors, floors and window frames allowed in wood. The same year, the Worshipful Company of Masons was incorporated to help organize labour and materials. As so many people had died during the Great Plague, there was a labour shortage and wages had risen considerably.

By introducing a tax on coal, money was found to rebuild St. Paul's Cathedral; churches were rebuilt, a new underground sewage system was engineered, and within a decade much of the City of London was rebuilt in stone. The new St. Paul's Cathedral was not completed until December 1711. Despite several proposals, such as one by John Evelyn (below), of a system of avenues like in Paris, the layout of streets hardly changed at all.

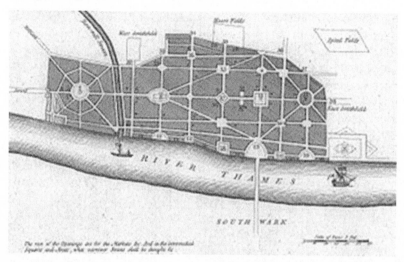

The strange story of Robert Hubert illustrates the level of hysteria at this time among the people. He was a French watchmaker working in London and was apparently slightly unhinged as he admitted to starting the fire and was hanged for the offence. He said incorrectly that the fire was set five miles away in Westminster, and even stranger, it was proved later that he wasn't in England at the time of the fire!

The astrologer, William Lilly, wrote a tract in 1651, fifteen years before the fire, entitled *Monarchy or No Monarchy* in which he prophesied the future of England. The series of woodcuts showed London on fire, plagues of rats, death, starvation and England's navy engaged in war. As historian Rebecca Rideal wrote, "Unsurprisingly, Lilly was called in for questioning following the fire of 1666."[93] Another interesting prophesy was by Old Mother Shipton, whose real name was Ursula Southiel, said to have been so ugly that she had to live in a cave to avoid people's scorn. She predicted the fire of London in 1641, and also prophesied that when Christ started the Armageddon, the Lion (Britain) would be defeated by the Eagle (America) and "Eagles shall be preferred by the people." People of this era were both very religious and superstitious, so after the tragedies of the Great Plague and the Great Fire, many people were convinced that Armageddon was close at hand.

The rebuilt London was different from the old city. Rich aristocrats preferred to live in Westminster to be near the king, who lived in Whitehall Palace, until that was destroyed by fire in 1698, when he moved to St. James's Palace. The mercantile centre was still the City, which was connected by a rural lane called Piccadilly to the new West End, with its fashionable houses and the City of Westminster.[94] Christopher Wren was appointed to rebuild many significant churches, as well as the gutted St. Paul's, with the assistance of the city surveyor, Robert Hooke. This was also a difficult time for the Royal Society, as both men were members and, instead of surveying the destruction in the name of the Society, Wren and Hooke undertook the work in their own names, leading to criticism from some quarters. However, Hooke is said to have done exemplary work in trying to identify property lines where there were no structures left to guide him.

Anti-Catholic Sentiments

The Great Fire of London had destroyed most of what had been the mediaeval City of London. So, in 1677, to commemorate the Great Fire, Wren and Hooke designed a tall column the same height (62m) as the distance from where the fire had started, the baker's shop in Pudding Lane. In the spirit of the Royal Society, they made the column to double as a scientific instrument. The column is hollow with stairs inside and an observatory deck at the top. It was designed to hold a zenith telescope, and there was a laboratory underneath it. The golden urn of flames at the top hinges open to allow a view of the night sky.[95]

Following the "Popish Plot" (see below) the City added an inscription to the Monument in 1681 written in Latin, "Sed Furor Papisticus Qui Tamdiu Patravit Nondum Restingvitur," meaning "the popish frenzy, which wrought such horrors, is not yet quenched," thus wrongly blaming the Catholics for the fire. It was still believed that if a person were a Catholic, he or she could not be a good citizen. The plaque was not removed for one hundred and fifty years until 1831, showing how deeply ingrained were feelings against Catholics at that time. The column, "The Monument to the Great Fire of London," now better known as just The Monument, still stands near London Bridge. The fire is said to have ended at Pye Corner, in Smithfield, where there is now a small golden statue to commemorate the event.

War with the Netherlands

Charles II had inherited a war with the Netherlands from the Commonwealth for control of trade routes, which were then dominated by the Dutch, as England fought to expand its commercial strength. In 1631 Charles I had covertly colluded with Spain to weaken Dutch sea power, which was then at its zenith, holding secret negotiations with the Spanish for assistance. Then in 1652 Oliver Cromwell started a three-year war with the Netherlands, this was followed by Charles II starting the Second Anglo-Dutch War in 1665, which ended three years later in stalemate as Charles had been financially crippled by the plague, the Great Fire, and extravagance at court. Charles was determined to gain dominion of the seas to help private companies, such the Levant Company (est. 1592) and the East India Company (est. 1600), corner the world market in products such as silk and spices. The conflict began well for the English with the capture of New Amsterdam, which was renamed New York after Charles's younger brother James, the Duke of York. Eventually, a treaty was signed giving the Dutch valuable sugar plantations in Suriname off the coast of South America and allowing England to keep New York.

The Third Anglo-Dutch War started in 1672. There was political instability in The Hague at the time, where a leading republican politician, Jan de Witt, opposed the royal House of Orange-Nassau. For his pains, he and his brother were lynched by a mob, and their livers roasted and eaten. Two years previously, Charles had signed the secret Treaty of Dover with his cousin King Louis XIV of France for his help in the war, in exchange for Charles secretly converting to Catholicism "at an unspecified future date." [96] However, the Third Anglo-Dutch War went against England and Parliament forced the king to sue for peace. The troubles with the Netherlands continued into the late 18th century, the last war being concluded in 1784.

England Bankrupt

An issue that continually dogged Charles II was a lack of money; his court spent extravagantly, even though the country was in financial difficulties, and in 1672 England was officially bankrupt. Known as the "The Great Stop of the Exchequer," the country could no longer repay its debts, so Charles ordered that no principal on loans was to be repaid and only "six pounds per cent" interest. [97] The king appealed to banks for a loan but was refused, the resulting crisis lasted a year and also bankrupted several London banks. One, a goldsmith who had turned banker, Sir Robert Vyner, sued the Exchequer for compensation in a civil case, "The Goldsmith Bankers Case," that dragged out more than twenty years without resolution. [98] The result of this dilemma was the foundation of the Bank of England, which received its charter in 1694, with the charter members' names kept secret, as were all dealings between the Bank and the government. [99]

More Resistance

Charles II attempted to extend religious freedoms to Protestant non-conformists and Catholics by introducing the Royal Declaration of Indulgence in 1672. However, it had little backing in the Cavalier Parliament and the next year the king was forced to repeal it.

In 1678 Charles II was informed of a "popish plot" against his person, and he had one of his ministers, the Earl of Danby, investigate the charges. The protagonist was Titus Oates, a sometime priest and navy chaplain, afterwards called "Titus the Liar." He had invented conspiracies that included more than eighty famous and aristocratic Catholics, as well as the forty Kemble Martyrs, saying that they had threatened to assassinate the king, but on investigation it was all found to have been fabricated. Though Oates recanted many of the spurious charges, he still denounced the king and his brother, the Duke of York, as being Catholics. Based on Oates's false charges at least twenty-two people were executed, including the Catholic Archbishop of Armagh. It was enough to start a wave of anti-Catholic hysteria throughout the land. Charles showed mercy on Oates as he feared the public backlash, but when the Duke of York became king, he had Oates retried, pilloried and imprisoned for three years.

The Popish Plot is of significance as it helped precipitate the Exclusion Bill Crisis, which bifurcated both the country and Parliament. John Milton may also have had a hand in moving public sympathy against Catholicism with his book *Of True Religion*, written in 1673, a polemic against popery. James, the Duke of York, had been given the honorary appointment of Lord High Admiral at the age of three, and after Charles II ascended the throne, James was reaffirmed in the position. He commanded the Royal Navy during both the First and Second Anglo-Dutch Wars. However, the continued anti-Catholic sentiment and fear of Catholics' influence at court led Parliament to introduce a new act in 1673, the Test Act, (or correctly "An act for preventing dangers which may happen from popish recusants"). Like the Clarendon Code, the Test Act expanded the ban on Catholics in government to include all civil and military officials, requiring each person to make a declaration against three Catholic doctrines; the invocation of saints, transubstantiation and the sacrament of the Mass. James refused to take this oath, so he had to relinquish his post as Lord High Admiral, and in doing so confirmed that he was Catholic. Originally the act did not include peers,[12] but five years later in 1679 the act was enlarged, becoming the Exclusion Bill, to include all members of Parliament, including peers, partly in response to the Popish Plot. However, five nobles, the Five Popish Lords, were able to delay the passage of the act and, by adding a clause that excluded the Duke of York, the future King James II, substantially weakened the act.

Parliament also was divided, with those against the Exclusion Bill called Abhorrers, later becoming the Tory party, and those in favour,

---

[12] Any of the five classes of the aristocracy: duke, marquis, earl, viscount and baron. Cf. Do Masons Ever Visit Boston?

the Country party, later called Whigs. The bill was introduced into the House of Commons in 1679 by the Earl of Shaftesbury, with the aim of stopping James from being nominated successor to King Charles II, but the king, using his Royal Prerogative, dissolved Parliament.

The Abhorrers expressed abhorrence at the fact that some of the members of Parliament were trying to force Charles II to reconvene Parliament, and sentiment both inside and outside the House was strong against Catholics with both sides campaigning vehemently. The Country Party (Whigs) tried to fan the flames of fear by rekindling the fabricated Popish Plot of a year earlier, and paraded effigies of the pope and cardinals through London before putting them on a bonfire. The Abhorrers (the Tory party) likewise distributed propaganda reminding the people of Oliver Cromwell's tyranny and Puritan excesses. Dr Samuel Johnson, the literary critic and lexicographer, as well as a zealous Tory, joked that "the first Whig was the Devil."[100] The English lawyer and biographer Roger North wrote, "the frolic went all over England" with speakers from both camps giving speeches throughout England. By 1681 public interest had largely died down again, and the Exclusion Bill was defeated in the House of Lords.

Still, there was life left in the cause. In 1683 a plot was discovered to kill Charles and James when they were together. Many members of the aristocracy thought that Charles's relationship with his Catholic cousin King Louis XIV was too close, and though Charles and James were publicly Anglicans, James's refusal to take the oath as required by the Test Act, convinced many that though their skin was Anglican their hearts were Catholic. After the Exclusion Bill had been defeated and the Whig party was in disarray, a group of Whig assassins concealed themselves in a fortified mansion in Hertfordshire, near Newmarket, where the king and duke would often spend a day at the races, hoping to surprise them and take their lives on the return journey. The mansion was called Rye House, and subsequently this has been called the Rye House Plot.

Unfortunately for the plotters, there had been a large fire in Newmarket in March of 1683, destroying half the town, and the races were cancelled forcing the king and duke to return early, thus avoiding the attack. However, word of the perfidy eventually leaked out and in

June the conspirators were rounded up; twelve were executed, ten imprisoned and ten exiled. Sixteen of the conspirators were aristocrats. One of the conspirators, the Earl of Essex, committed suicide by cutting his own throat while imprisoned in the Tower of London.

Historians have suggested that Charles may have fabricated the plot in order to rid himself of his obstreperous political opponents. Whatever the case, it was obvious that some politicians, with support from the aristocracy, were planning a rebellion against the Stuart monarchy, so Charles took advantage of the Rye House Plot to enforce stringent and repressive measures against those who did not support him. The Plot forewarned of further attempts to overthrow the monarchy, which were to come in James II's reign.

In 1685 King Charles II died from a stroke, called apoplexy in those days, and to fulfil his promise to his cousin, he reverted to Catholicism on his deathbed.[101] Charles's reign brought many changes to London, with new buildings designed by Inigo Jones, such as the piazza at Covent Garden. Wealthy landowners built city residences to be near the royal court, and several new streets bearing the names of Stuart royalty were created around St. James's Palace.

James II, reigned 1685-1688

As Charles II had no children that could legitimately succeed him, his brother James ascended the throne in 1685 as King James VII of Scotland and James II of England and Ireland. Surprisingly, considering the political manoeuvring to disqualify him, he was met with public rejoicing.

Before the restoration of Charles II, his brother James had caused controversy by announcing his engagement to Anne Hyde, daughter of Edward Hyde, 1st Earl of Clarendon. People at court did not take this seriously as James was a well-known philanderer, but in 1660 James secretly married Anne, and his affection for her made him popular with the public.[102] While James and Anne were in France during the Commonwealth, she converted to Catholicism. This was kept secret and even on their return to England James and Anne continued attending Anglican services.[103] In 1671 Anne died of breast cancer, and two years later, the forty-five-year-old James married a fifteen-year-old Italian princess, Mary of Moderna. The Duke of York was twenty-five years older than his bride, scarred by smallpox and afflicted with a stutter.[104] It is said that Mary disliked James so much that she burst into tears every time he entered the room, though later she grew to warm to him. However, the people of England thought this new queen was a "popish spy."

Three months after James ascended the throne, one of Charles's many illegitimate children, the Protestant James Crofts, the 1st Duke of Monmouth, who at the age of thirteen had been given a dukedom and made a Knight of the Garter, was implicated in the Rye House Affair, but had escaped to the Netherlands in self-imposed exile. Monmouth then conspired with Archibald Campbell, 9th Earl of Argyll, to seize the throne of England. Argyll was also in the Netherlands avoiding a charge of treason for his part in the Rye House Affair. In May of 1685, Monmouth and Argyll pawned their valuables to raise a small army in Holland and hire some Dutch warships. Then Argyll headed for Scotland, and Monmouth the south-west of England, hoping to raise armies to capture the Crown. Surprisingly, the Dutch prince, William of Orange, did not interfere with their plans, even though he was married to King James's sister, Mary. This may have been because James was aware of the plot and local militias were waiting for Monmouth when he arrived.

Argyll's three ships landed in the Orkney Islands hoping to engage the king's army in Scotland, while Monmouth's army marched on London, but Argyll was unable to drum up enough Protestant supporters and disagreements within the leadership, as well as opposition from the Marquess of Atholl, led to the forces dispersing. Argyll and his supporters were captured, and he was executed by guillotine in Edinburgh in June 1685. Monmouth arrived in Dorset on June 11, proclaiming himself king. He was also unable to raise much support and was defeated by James's larger and better equipped army. A month after landing in England, Monmouth was executed at the Tower of London.

Following this debacle, James II decided he had to consolidate his power to protect himself from further insurgency. The first step was to enlarge the regular army, but after the experience of the New Model Army, this move alarmed many people, particularly as the soldiers, when not fighting, tended to cause trouble. James also skirted the Test Act allowing Catholic officers to command troops without taking the required oath, as well as giving Catholics positions in his cabinet. Parliament objected, and James responded by dissolving it in November 1685.

The Glorious Revolution

In 1688, James II enforced the Royal Declaration of Indulgence that his brother Charles had issued in an attempt to extend religious freedom to Catholics. This required Anglican priests to read the Declaration in church, despite resistance from seven Anglican archbishops. Three months later in June, a son and potential heir was born to James and his wife Mary and was quickly baptized a Catholic. Many people believed that the child, James Stuart, the future "Old Pretender" was a spurious changeling, that had been smuggled inside a bed-warming pan into the queen's bedchamber.[105] England suddenly awoke to the possibility of the continuation of the Catholic dynasty, as James's only other possible successors were his daughters Anne and Mary who, at Charles II's insistence, had been brought up as Protestants.[106]

Seven Protestants consisting of six noblemen, both Whigs and Tories, and one bishop, afterwards called the "Immortal Seven," had secretly invited the Protestant Prince William of Orange[13] to bring an army to England and claim the throne. Now the birth of a potential Catholic heir strengthened their resolve. The reason for their choice of William was that ten years earlier in 1677, King Charles had approved of his brother James, who was at that time the Duke of York, allowing his daughter Mary to marry the Calvinist Protestant Prince William, though James himself had been reluctant to consent to the marriage. It was now clear that Prince William was planning to invade England.

James felt that he had a sufficiently large army to repel Prince William's smaller army, so he refused assistance from King Louis.

---

[13] Huis van Oranje-Nassau is the name of the Royal House of the Netherlands

Also, he felt that bringing Catholic French troops on to English soil would only exacerbate the situation. James was very short of money at the time, and unable to pay soldiers and sailors. This was aggravated by a run on the banks, so he issued a proclamation against defaming the government with "*False and Seditious News and Reports.*"[107] What he did not count on when William arrived, carried on a "Protestant Wind," on the 83rd anniversary of the Gunpowder Plot in November 1688, was that many of his Protestant officers would defect to William's side. More infuriating was the fact that his own daughter, the Protestant Princess Anne, wrote to William approving his action and met with him when he arrived in England. On hearing this James exclaimed, "God help me! Even my children have forsaken me."[108]

James gave up on the idea of fighting William and tried to escape. It was claimed that he first threw the Great Seal of the Realm into the River Thames, and then got as far as Kent, before being captured by William's troops.

King James is attacked by a mob, who mistook him for a Jesuit priest as he made his escape at the Isle of Sheppey in Kent, December 1688. [109]

To avoid him becoming a martyr, William let James travel on to France, where James's cousin Louis XIV greeted him and found him suitable lodgings in a palace. James made an attempt to regain the throne of the three kingdoms, but he was defeated at the Battle of the Boyne in 1690, a fight between the Protestant Dutch king of England, William of Orange, and a Catholic ex-king of England leading a coalition of French, Jacobite and Irish forces, fought in Ireland. After the rout, James II hurriedly returned in ignominy to France.

A year later, there was another battle at Aughrim where a total of 7,000 soldiers died, and seeing their desperate situation, the Irish coalition forces signed a military and civil settlement with William, the Treaty of Limerick the same year, 1691. Following this, Protestants in Ireland showed their allegiance to William by calling themselves "Orangemen." 14,000 Irish took this opportunity to leave the country in what is now called "The Flight of the Wild Geese." James died in 1701, aged seventy-seven; surprisingly, of all the Stuarts, his reign was the shortest, but his life was the longest.

The coup d'état, called the Glorious Revolution, has also been called the "First Modern Revolution" by Prof. Steven Pincus. Alternatively, it is also incorrectly known as the "Bloodless Revolution," because in the few skirmishes between the armies fewer than one hundred people died on both sides - not exactly "bloodless." The peaceful transition of power meant that for the first time in a very long time, Parliament had a monarchy with which it could work to rebuild the country.

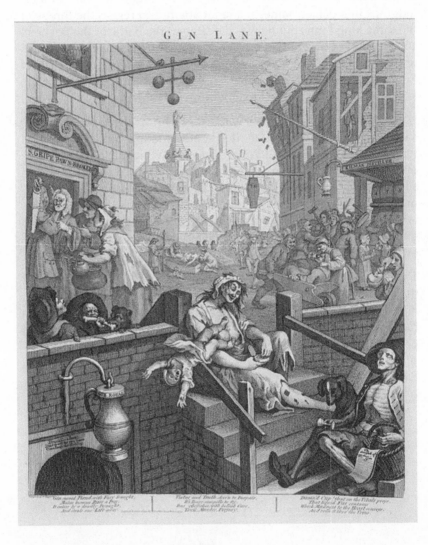

Gin Lane by William Hogarth, 1751

Ch. 3   The End of the House of Stuart and the End of the World

After the failure of the Commonwealth, which had been usurped by Puritan excesses, the country hoped that the Dutch Prince of Orange, William III, would support the Church of England that Queen Elizabeth had fought for one hundred years earlier. However, there also remained many threats to the monarchy, both religious and supernatural.

William III, reigned 1688-1702 & Mary II, 1688-1694

James II had two children with his first wife Anne Hyde, Mary and Anne. After Anne Hyde's death, James married Mary of Modena, and they had a boy, James Stuart. However, it is now believed that the child was stillborn, and the potential heir to the throne was "supposititious."[110] The Immortal Seven, six nobles and a bishop, had formally invited William to "invade" England in June of 1688, however William had been planning the coup since the year before and had been seeking assurances from Parliament that he would be welcome and not meet with resistance. Coincidentally, James Stuart was born the same day that William received the letter from the Immortals. At the time of the Glorious Revolution in September of 1688, Princess Mary was twenty-six and Princess Anne was three years younger.

In 1689 the indefatigable James II landed in Ireland in a last-ditch attempt to regain the throne of England. A battle ensued the following year at Drogheda in the east of the country near the sea. It was fought on both sides of the river Boyne, becoming known as the Battle of the Boyne, and resulted in James's defeat, so he had to flee to France again. His loss of support to take the triple thrones led to the continued ascendency of Protestantism in Ireland, and the Battle of the Boyne is still today celebrated by the Protestant Orange Order. After James died in 1701, his son James Stuart was attainted for treason the next year, and forfeited his titles.

After James II's flight, Parliament asked Princess Mary to accept the throne, and she agreed on the condition that her husband, William of Orange, could be co-regent. This was acceptable to Parliament as he was a Protestant, and they were crowned King William III and Queen Mary II. To Parliament, the fact that a foreigner was now king of England was less of a concern than his religion, and being royalty was fortuitous. This is interesting as in modern times Queen Elizabeth II married Philip, Prince of Greece and Denmark in 1947, and although technically he became a naturalized British subject before marrying Elizabeth, he did not become king or co-regent, but rather consort.

William took his new responsibilities very seriously, fighting to defend England from the Dutch, which from a modern perspective is surprising given that England and the Netherlands had been at war for twenty-two years up to fifteen years before William was asked to "invade" by the Immortal Seven. Another way to look at this situation is that William was born in 1650 and, from the age of two until he was 24 years old, England was his enemy. Then at thirty-nine he was asked to become king of England, a position which he discharged honourably.

By 1688, in England religious problems had abated, but there were still religious disputes in Europe, and the same year William led English and Dutch troops to battle with the king of France, Louis XIV, starting the Nine Years' War. The war ended in 1698 with the Treaty of Ryswick. Louis had to recognise William III as the legitimate king of England, and that Louis would no longer give assistance to the deposed James II or his followers, the Jacobites. After James II died, Louis infuriated William by recognising the claim of the Old

Pretender, James's son, to the English throne as James VIII and III. Following France's lead, Scotland, Spain, the Papal States and Modena also renounced William III, Mary II, and later Queen Anne, as legitimate sovereigns.

Subsequently, in 1702 England became embroiled in the War of Spanish Succession. Charles II, king of Spain, had suddenly died in 1700 and ceded parts of Spain to Louis XIV, who instead decided that he wanted the whole Spanish peninsula, which upset not only the Spanish and the Austrian Habsburg Holy Roman Emperor, but also other monarchs in Europe. The war continued until 1713 and the very complicated and lengthy negotiations that eventually resulted in the Peace of Utrecht, which prevented the unification of the French and Spanish thrones under one monarch.

Pretenders

There were attempts by Jacobites to assassinate King William in 1695 and 1696, followed by a planned invasion of Scotland in 1708 by French troops.[111] The plots were foiled. The outcome was that the Whig party strengthened its position in respect to the Tories in the House of Commons, claiming that William's escape was due to God's intervention and divine providence, reiterating the Stuart kings' claim to govern by the Divine Right of Kings. Because of the Jacobites's dastardly actions, London citizens denigrated them, calling them "Sawneys," after stories about a clansman called Sawney Bean, who had reverted to cannibalism, started to circulate. These rumours were fanned by an amateur historian, Nathaniel Crouch, writing under the pseudonym of Richard Burton, who published such stories in the 1680s, portraying Jacobites as cannibals.

William's reign in Britain was the beginning of the move from the "personal rule" of the Stuarts to rule by Parliament. Queen Mary II died of smallpox in 1694, and William, who was devoted to his wife, was recorded as saying, "from being the happiest [I am] now going to be the miserablest creature on earth."[112] After lying in state, Mary was buried at Westminster Abbey, and it was the first time that both Houses of Parliament attended a royal funeral service. King William died eight years later in 1702 due to complications from a fall from his horse which had stumbled on a mole's burrow, and he was buried next to his wife in the Abbey. Jacobites afterwards took delight in toasting the mole, "the little gentleman in the black velvet waistcoat."

New Laws

A year after the Glorious Revolution, William and Mary brought in new laws to end several centuries of tension and conflict between the monarchy and Parliament, and to ensure that a Catholic could never again rule England. In 1689 Parliament passed the "Bill of Rights" that denounced James II for abusing his power by suspending the Test Act, prosecuting Seven Bishops for having petitioned the crown, and establishing a standing army. More importantly for Britain, the bill also declared that no longer would a Catholic be allowed to ascend the throne, nor could any British monarch ever marry a Catholic.

The act established that the succession to the throne was to be determined by Parliament and not by any "divine right." It also set out the foundations of a constitutional monarchy, establishing several important rights, such as: freedom from interference with the law by the monarch, freedom from taxation by royal prerogative, freedom to petition the monarch, and the freedom to elect members of Parliament without interference from the sovereign. The Bill of Rights was amended in 2013 to allow the first-born child to ascend to the throne, regardless of gender.

The Act of Toleration of 1689 gave freedom of worship to denominations other than Anglicans, so long as they rejected the dogma of transubstantiation and swore an oath of allegiance to the Crown. This act purposely excluded Catholics, non-trinitarians and atheists.

Lastly, other bills were later passed to assure Parliamentary agreement to this new situation; the most important of these were the Act of Settlement of 1701 and the Acts of Union of 1707, passed in the reign of Queen Anne. The Act of Settlement was brought about by the fact that William and Mary had no issue, so the act mandated the succession to the throne on the German Princess Sophia of Hanover, and to her heirs, though her famous mother, Elizabeth of Bohemia, was Scottish and Catholic, because Sophia was a Protestant and a granddaughter of James I of England.

The Right to Bear Arms

Until the time of Cromwell, English armies were made up of conscripts as there was no standing army. Weapons would then be issued to those men, but often after the battle they were not all collected by the authorities, so some weapons remained in civilian hands.

Knights had used broad swords, sabres and cutlasses but with the demise of knights, the use of these swords also fell into disuse.[113] The right to wear a sword then became the prerogative of the nobility, who preferred the lighter, thrusting, dress sword known as a rapier.[14]

In the Bill of Rights of 1689 were included injunctions concerning an Englishman's right to wear a sword, and the fact that this clause was included suggests that the right to bear weapons was very much part of English life:

> Disarming Protestants, &c.
>
> > By causing severall good Subjects being Protestants to be disarmed at the same time when Papists were both Armed and Imployed contrary to Law.
>
> Subjects' Arms.
>
> > That the Subjects which are Protestants may have Arms for their Defence suitable to their Conditions and as allowed by Law.[114]

William III included this clause to rein in potential Catholic opposition to his authority. Though it is doubtful that aristocratic Catholics, such as the Duke of Norfolk, would have paid much attention to this provision. This injunction emphasized that Catholics were not allowed to have arms, but also that contrarily Protestants were allowed arms to protect themselves from Catholics - but of course the weapon had to be "suitable to their conditions," in other words, not excessive.

---

[14] From the Spanish "espada ropera" meaning dress sword

In a famous print of Amadeus Mozart attending a Lodge in Vienna, painted by the Austrian artist Ignaz Unterberger in 1789, it can be seen that all the Brethren were wearing swords. We also see from the Palser Plate of 1812[15] that gentlemen were still wearing swords in England as well, over one hundred and twenty years after the Bill of Rights.

The Gin Craze

William III was looking for a way to improve people's living standards, when he enacted laws in 1689 and 1697, aimed at making ale more expensive and banning French brandy imports and instead encouraging the production of gin. In 1690 the government ended the Worshipful Guild of Distillers' monopoly which then enabled anyone to make gin, however the legislation did not take into account how to control the production.

The objective was threefold, first, to expand the market for English grain, wheat, rye and barley. There had always been a surplus of barley as it was not such a useful crop, mainly being used for animal fodder or to ferment beer, and north of the border as porridge or gruel; however, barley is the main ingredient in gin. Ale in those days would have been made from any of maize, oats or poor-quality barley.[115] Wheat farmers either rotated their crops with barley or left their fields fallow to avoid taxing soil nutrition, but with the demand for gin they had an incentive to grow more barley. Much poor-quality land was then made available for its production, and landowners growing barley not only became very rich they also quickly became a powerful lobby in Parliament.

---

[15] See *Freemasonry: Spiritual Alchemy*

Secondly, as England was at war with France, gin helped the Protestant cause by providing the troops in the Thirty Years' War with the "Dutch courage" to triumph over the Catholic opposition. Also, it was seen as patriotic to drink gin as it was an English drink, compared to foreign drinks such as wine or even tea. William stopped the import of French wine and brandy,[16] substituting them with the cheaper gin, which in turn encouraged brandy smuggling and piracy along the south coast of England.

Lastly, juniper, the flavouring for gin, was produced in the Netherlands, so importing it helped William's home country as well. The name "gin" derives from the Dutch word "jenever" for juniper berry, the only fruit to come from a conifer tree, which was grown in the Netherlands. In England gin went by the epithet "Queen Jennifer;" later Jennifer was abbreviated to "jen" and then "gin."

Unlike beer and ale, which were mainly men's drinks and sold in ale houses, or wines that were sold with food in taverns, gin was sold in gin shops or "dram shops" ostensibly as a medicine. It was purported to be a cure for many things from high blood pressure to rheumatism, as well as being an aphrodisiac: "Tis the juniper berry that makes the heart merry!"

Gin was more attractive than beer for women as it was served in small glasses, so it became to be seen as a woman's drink, and it was often made by women in their kitchens for extra income. As making gin was not regulated, small distilleries sprung up everywhere, and by 1730 there were 1,500 distillers in London. Nearly all the gin in England was made and consumed in London, but much of it was of suspect quality and often watered down.

England in the late-1600s was a hard-drinking culture, people drank beer, ale or wine all day long as the water was unfit to drink but, until the advent of gin, spirits were not so popular. Children would drink low-alcohol beer, even for breakfast, called small beer. Gin was a drink that spanned social classes, poorer people nicknaming it "mother's ruin" or "the devil" and in better society, "the drink that shall not be

---

[16] "Brandy" is from the Dutch for "burnt wine," "verbrande wijn." The correct word for the French variety is cognac or "eau-de-vie."

named." Princess Anne of Denmark, later to be Queen Anne, was said to be fond of gin. The rich drank whatever they wanted and often hid bottles of gin besides bottles of contraband cognac in their cabinets.

By the 1720s the situation had turned into an epidemic of extreme drunkenness, with magistrates complaining about gin as "the principal cause of all the vice and debauchery committed among the inferior sort of people."[116] This drunkenness provoked moral outrage from not only Dissenters, but writers and artists as well. The popular writer Henry Fielding wrote a pamphlet complaining about the increase in crime,[117] and William Hogarth made the now famous print called "Gin Lane" (see detail on p.88) that depicts a sorry scene with a man fighting a dog for a bone, a dying man in a soldier's coat, a suicide hanging from a rafter, a carpenter pawning his saw and a woman trying to sell her child's clothes so she could buy a drink. A notice on the gin house reads:

> Drunk for a penny
> Dead drunk for twopence
> Clean straw for nothing[118]

The poem at the bottom of the etching reads:

> Gin, cursed Fiend, with Fury fraught,
> Makes human Race a Prey.
> It enters by a deadly Draught
> And steals our Life away.
>
> Virtue and Truth, driv'n to Despair
> Its Rage compells to fly,
> But cherishes with hellish Care
> Theft, Murder, Perjury.
>
> Damned Cup! that on the Vitals preys
> That liquid Fire contains,
> Which Madness to the heart conveys,
> And rolls it thro' the Veins.

The natural philosopher and clergyman Stephen Hales, who had a scientific bent, inventing all sorts of medical devices and elected to the Royal Society in 1718, lobbied Parliament about gin, writing a famous pamphlet against gin and other distilled spirits, *A Friendly Admonition to the Drinker of Brandy and other Distilled Spirituous Liquors*. Hales did not oppose drinking alcohol per se, but he felt strongly that gin was "the bane of the nation."[119]

Around 1720, the "Society for the Reformation of Manners" was established, with politicians, lawyers, tradesmen, constables and even informers, working together to reduce crime and prostitution, as well as the idleness that had affected work productivity. The Dissenters drew up economic arguments to ban gin and petitioned Parliament, but the Prime Minister, Robert Walpole, resisted enforcing legislation or introducing tougher laws as he did not want to antagonize landowners, who by then had a strong lobby in Parliament. The Society brought 1,363 prosecutions in 1726-7 and continued until the mid-1750s.[120]

Gin's success was due to its low price and the fact that it could be made without a licence; however, once the door was opened it was difficult to close it again, and the first legislation restricting the sale of gin was forty-six years after William had first introduced it into England in 1689, and it then took a further twenty years to bring the gin craze under control.

> No more can I seat me to Study
> Than a Fish can swim without Fin,
> My Brains are confus'd and quite muddy
> By losing my Comforter Gin.[121]

Censorship

The printing press had been developed in Germany in the 1450s and by 1600 there were already hundreds of presses in London alone. Originally the appetite from devout readers was for Bibles and Prayer Books, but academic readers called for books on Greek and Roman classics as well as books from the Renaissance. Later, books such as the 14th century explorations of Marco Polo and even translations of Chinese classics such as Confucius (translated in 1687) became available. Newspapers started to be circulated from about 1620.

England's strong support of Protestantism led to the government allowing not just the freedom of religious belief, but eventually also more freedom to express one's opinion. In 1637 the Star Chamber banned all new books because of complaints from Spain and Austria that newspapers in England had been writing lies about the Thirty Years' War, but this just resulted in the same stories being printed in Amsterdam and then smuggled back into England. Pope Paul IV had set up the *Index Librorum Prohibitorum* the first *Index of Prohibited Books* in 1559 with, five years later, the king of France introducing laws so that all new books to be published had to have his approval first - pre-publication censorship. This stipulation was soon copied by monarchs across Europe who saw it as a way to suppress opposition to their rule, particularly in time of war. This dual system of secular and ecclesiastical censorship was also used in the colonies of America.

Due to the Star Chamber's abuse of Dissenters, in 1641 the Long Parliament abolished the court and instead instituted the Habeas Corpus Act, one of the most important and historic pieces of legislation to protect an individual's rights. Following this, in 1643 Parliament introduced the Ordinance for the Regulating of Printing, also known as the Licensing Order, requiring authors to have a license approved by the government before they could publish; this act had to be reapproved every two years. John Milton wrote a pamphlet, *Areopagitica*, which forcefully challenged this system of pre-publication censorship, without first getting permission, thereby breaking the law; the pamphlet became a testament for freedom of speech. The Licensing Order was followed in 1662 by the Licensing of the Press Act, making it illegal to set up a printing press without the authority of the Stationer's Company, and giving the Company the authority to raid people's homes in the search for illegal printing presses, which was mercilessly enforced for two years until the Great Plague. Following the Great Fire of London in 1666, the censorship laws were less frequently enforced which led to a growth in pamphleteering by religious and political groups.

By 1692, because of the works of "freethinkers" such as John Locke, who campaigned against the law, and others also who espoused the principles of freedom of speech and religion, the censorship laws were allowed to expire, and in their place the Copyright Act (Statute of

Anne) was introduced in 1710. However, the Church of England still wielded the Blasphemy Act against atheists and Unitarians, among others, and this ecclesiastical law was not abandoned in Great Britain until 2008.

Freethinkers

The term "freethinker" was attached retrospectively to those people who emerged in the late 1600s to oppose the dogma of the Church, and especially a literal translation of the Bible. They believed that by understanding the workings of Nature one could understand the world. One of the earliest freethinkers was William Molyneux (1656-1698), the Irish natural philosopher who was famous for inventing, among other things, a sundial accurate to within fifteen seconds! He corresponded with the physician and philosopher John Locke, and later with the author of the popular book *Discourse of Freethinking* that promoted Deism, Anthony Collins (1676-1729). Freethinkers insisted that truth should be based on logic and reason, rather than tradition, authority or revelation.

John Locke, 1632–1704

Locke was one of the most influential philosophers of the English Enlightenment, and a follower of the Baconian tradition. Some of his ideas are said to have influenced the American Declaration of Independence, and he is accredited with defining the modern concept of consciousness. Locke was an empiricist, believing that all knowledge should be based on sensory experience. At Oxford he worked with Robert Boyle and Robert Hooke, and later, after being invited to join the Royal Society, he met with Isaac Newton and England's first Poet Laureate, John Dryden.

Locke had to live in the Netherlands for five years as he had been accused of involvement in the Rye House Plot, though this was unsubstantiated, and he only returned after the Glorious Revolution in 1688. With his revolutionary ideas about human rights and government, he became an intellectual hero for the Whig party. Locke's strong advocacy of religious tolerance, as expounded in his *Letter Concerning Toleration* written after the religious wars in Europe had ended with the Peace of Westphalia, provided the philosophical structure for the 1689 Act of Toleration. He was also a Stuart era environmentalist, as he promoted the idea that things that were not being used or were perishable were an offence against nature,[122] but conversely durable goods are acceptable as they do not decay or spoil.

Following the Restoration, all the faults of the earlier Stuarts were reinstated: the cult of a divine monarchy, where the king was father of country, Patriarchalism, the Divine Right of Kings and the King's Touch. These were attacked by Locke, who criticized the absolute power of the king, insisting that men are born free, that they have inalienable rights and if the government or ruler fails then the people have a right to resist. For the first time the argument moved away from Biblical proof of kingship to proof based on reason. Locke also attacked Charles II in print, as he believed him to be a popish king.

John Toland, 1670 – 1722

Toland was an Irish philosopher who wrote extensively about the philosophy of politics and religion, and one of the first to be called a freethinker.[17] His first book *Christianity not Mysterious*, written in 1696 after the expiry of the censorship law, caused a scandal as he challenged inherited and "uninvestigated authority," stating that the Bible did not contain miracles as they could be explained by natural principles. In England the courts sought to arrest him for blasphemy, so he escaped to his homeland Ireland, where he faced being burned at the stake, so he hurriedly returned to England denouncing the Irish authorities as "popish inquisitors," and the Irish had to settle for burning his books instead of the author himself. He was able to avoid prosecution, but not poverty, and died in 1722 aged fifty-one, surrounded by his books.[123]

---

[17] Attributed to Bishop George Berkley

Anne, reigned 1702-1714

James II's youngest daughter Anne succeeded to the throne when William III died in 1702. She had married Prince George of Denmark and Norway twenty years earlier, in an attempt to form an Anglo-Danish alliance to restrict Dutch maritime power, which naturally upset her brother-in-law William. England now had more influence in Europe than in the past due in part to England's victories abroad. John Churchill, 1st Duke of Marlborough, had made a name for himself as one of Europe's great generals, having won several important victories during the War of Spanish Succession (1701-1714), for example the Battle of Blenheim, after which he named his palace in Oxfordshire.

Now, after one hundred years, Anne was able to unify the kingdoms of England, Scotland and Ireland by the Acts of Union, a feat her ancestor King James I had not been able to do, even with the help of his Lord Chancellor, Sir Francis Bacon, both openly and sub rosa. England and Scotland had been ruled by a union of monarchies for nearly one hundred years, in the Union of the Crowns, but the countries had separate legislatures, and the Scots were not keen on seeing the end of their independence; however, pressure by England and financial pressure at home led to Scotland capitulating and signing the Acts of Union. The act was in fact two acts that were ratified by each Parliament, Scotland in 1706 and then England in 1707, resulting in Britain becoming "United into One Kingdom by the Name of Great Britain."[18] The vote had not been unanimous as the House was split 69 Noes to 106 Ayes. Historian Simon Schama wrote, "What began as a hostile merger, would end in a full partnership in the most powerful going concern in the world ... it was one of the most astonishing transformations in European history."[124]

---

[18] Article I of the Treaty of Union

A new House of Commons of Great Britain was established with Scotland sending forty-five members to join the English members, and sixteen Scottish peers joined the House of Lords. The flag for the United Kingdom of Great Britain was redesigned. In 1606 James I had introduced a flag that incorporated England's cross of St. George with Scotland's cross of St. Andrew, but the Scots protested that England's cross lay on top of Scotland's one, and the flag does not seem to have been used extensively. Then in 1707 a new design was presented to Queen Anne where Ireland's cross of St. Patrick was added to give the current Union Flag, affectionately called the Union Jack, now with the English cross of St. George on top of both the Scottish and Irish crosses.
[19]

Despite the political progress, the Test Act was still enforced, and non-Anglicans could not sit in Parliament, this included all non-Conformists, Unitarians, Jews and Catholics. The act remained in force until the nineteenth century. Though Catholics and Dissenters were not hunted down after the new laws were passed, they still had no right to assemble or pray. Both Anne and her sister, the former Queen Mary II, had been raised as Protestants, and Anne favoured the Tory party, which shared her Anglican beliefs. During the War of Spanish Succession, the Whigs had grown in power due to the Whig Junto, also known as "the Five Tyrannising Lords," a group of five powerbrokers who had worked to manipulate the office of Ministers of the Crown. One of the Junto was Thomas "Honest Tom" Wharton, later Marquess of Wharton, the father of Philip, 1st Duke of Wharton, who later became the fifth Grand Master of Freemasons in 1722. Anne was continually frustrated with the members of the Junto until 1710 when she expelled them from government, together with Lord Treasurer Sidney Godolphin. Her friend Sarah, Duchess of Marlborough, had also championed the Junto and had abused her friendship with the

---

[19] 1) England, Scotland and Wales: Celtic Britons 1st century AD; called Britannia by the Romans, later abbreviated to Britain 2) Kingdom of England and Wales 1535: Henry VIII colonized the Kingdom of Ireland in 1542; 3) Great Britain: England, Scotland, and Wales, 1707; 4) United Kingdom: United Kingdom of Great Britain and Ireland 1800; 5) now The United Kingdom of Great Britain and Northern Ireland, 1922 to date.

Queen, so Anne also dismissed Sarah from court, leading to the end of the career of the heroic general, the Duke of Marlborough.

Though Anne's marriage had been an arranged one, she was fond of her husband, Prince George, and was left desolate by his death in 1708. Anne had a weak constitution, and though she gave birth to seventeen babies in sixteen years, only one had survived infancy, Prince William, who had lived to just eleven. For six years she mourned her husband's death, and the culmination of the fact that she had no heir, as well as political intrigues in court, matters of state and the thought that after her death the throne would go to her German cousin, Sophia, Electress of Hanover, probably depressed Anne, as she put on a lot of weight. When she died in 1714, she was so heavy that people joked that she had been buried in a square coffin. Her doctor wrote to Jonathan Swift, "I believe sleep was never more welcome to a weary traveller than death was to her."[125] With Queen Anne's death a curtain was drawn over the tumultuous dynasty of the House of Stuart.

A Thorn in Her Side

Even though James II was defeated at the Battle of the Boyne in 1690 and died eleven years later in 1701, the Jacobite cause was not dead. His son, James Stuart, the Old Pretender, attempted to invade England in 1708. He had raised a small fleet of ships and attempted to land in Scotland, however the harsh weather impeded him, and Admiral Sir George Byng prevented the ships from landing, so James abandoned the expedition.

Problem Palaces

When William and Mary came to London in 1688 to assume the throne, one of the first projects they embarked on was rebuilding the old Tudor palace of Hampton Court. The palace, which is about eighteen miles from Westminster by river, had been used by King Henry VIII. William and Mary hired Christopher Wren to design extensions to the building, so that it might rival Versailles, or the Binnenhof Castle at the Hague, where William had been born. However, after the death of Mary in 1694, William lost interest in the project. Ironically, it was at Hampton Court in 1702, that William's horse stumbled on a molehill, leading to his death.

After the Duke of Marlborough ("he never fought a battle he did not win")[126] had defeated the French at the battle of Blenheim in 1704, during the War of the Spanish Succession, Queen Anne underwrote the cost of building the duke an enormous stately house in Oxfordshire, called Blenheim Palace, as a gift "from a grateful nation." It quickly became evident that the duke's grandiose plans meant that the palace was bigger (200 rooms) and more splendid than any royal palace. Secondly, expenditures got out of hand and the budget for the building was quickly overspent.

In 1710 Jonathan Swift wrote an article in the *Examiner*, attacking the Whigs, and accusing the Marlboroughs of embezzling funds that had been set aside to build Blenheim.[127] In Parliament, questions were asked about the large amounts of money being used, and riots started in London protesting Whig extravagance. Following this, the duke's wife Sarah fell out of favour with the queen, and in 1712 funding for the building was stopped. By then, the building was already four times over budget and money was owed to many workers. The Duke of Marlborough died in 1722 and the palace was eventually completed around 1735 by the duke's widow, Sarah, being the only palace in England not owned by the monarchy. The Crown now owns the freehold and charges the tenants one French flag a year, on the anniversary of the Battle of Blenheim, August 13th.

Longitude

Accurate navigation had been a challenge for centuries. Daniel Defoe called navigation one of the two daughters of trade, the other being manufacturing.[128] Though mariners were able to ascertain their latitudinal position, that is the degree north or south of the equator, using astrolabes, sextants and a directional compass, they were not able to accurately calculate longitude.

In 1707 there had been a serious shipwreck near the Scilly Isles where, during the War of the Spanish Succession, Admiral Sir Cloudesley Shovell commanded a fleet of twenty-one warships that became caught up in a storm, and four of the ships, including the flagship Shovell was on, were broken up on the rocks. As accurate records were not kept, it is not known exactly how many people lost their lives, but it is estimated at between 1,400 and 2,000,[129] making it one of the worst maritime disasters in British history.

Legend has it that Shovell was warned by a native of the islands, who was familiar with the rocky coastline and was on watch in the crow's nest that day, about the danger but Shovell chose to ignore it. After the shipwreck, Shovell was washed up on shore, barely alive, along with hundreds of corpses, and a local woman killed him to steal the emerald ring he was wearing.

Travelling by sea was more reliable than going by land, so the various seaports were better connected to each other, than ports were with inland cities.[130] Dr. Samuel Johnson is quoted as saying "being in a ship is being in a jail, with the chance of being drowned." Another time he added, "a man in a jail has more room, better food, and commonly better company!"[131] There were no maritime clocks or almanacs and even maps were very sought after – when pirates attacked a ship, often the first things they looked for, besides bounty, were chronometers and maps.[132] So until the introduction of a marine chronometer, an hourglass was used to estimate longitude.

One idea put forward was to make a map of magnetic declination, because a compass gives slightly different readings according to its position, though at the time the difference between true north and magnetic north was not understood. In 1700, Edmund Halley had sailed the seven seas in the ship Paramore, often captaining the ship himself, to take magnetic readings around the globe.[133] On his return in 1701 he made a map of the isogenic lines, which showed where the magnetic declination had the same constant value. Later it was realized that such a map would not be useful in estimating longitude because Earth's magnetic poles were found to "wander." Halley succeeded Flamsteed as Astronomer Royal in 1720.

Queen Anne's government established the Board of Longitude for "the safety of merchant ships and to improve trade," after the mathematician and theologian William Whiston had been instrumental in the passing of the Longitude Act of 1714. The act offered a prize for the best idea to calculate longitude accurately. Whiston also attempted to win the prize, worth about one million pounds in today's currency, which motivated many people to try their hand. The prize was paid out in instalments, with the first going to John Harrison in 1737 for his clock, and later Thomas Earnshaw receiving a part for a clock that utilized a unique spring escapement which was used on H.M.S. Beagle, one hundred years after the establishment of the award.

William Coward

Though his name is now lost in the pages of history, the physician William Coward caused an uproar in England because of a book he wrote in 1702 under the pseudonym "Estibius Psychalethes," with the unwieldly title of *Second Thoughts concerning Human Soul, demonstrating the notion of human soul as believed to be a spiritual, immortal substance united to a human body to be a plain heathenish invention ... the ground of many absurd and superstitious opinions, abominable to the reformed churches and derogatory in general to true Christianity.* In the book, Coward stated that the soul did not exist, calling it "a heathenish invention." It is now thought that he was influenced by John Locke's writings, but it started other writers to write on the mortality of the soul, which was to become a major controversy in the coming years.

Though it might seem strange to us now that Parliament would involve itself in such matters, but because of the uncertain situation of the law concerning censorship at the time, Coward's book was debated on in Parliament and found to be blasphemous. Luckily for Coward, the only penalty was to have his books burned by the hangman which, paradoxically, just increased the popularity of the book. We will meet Coward again later in this narrative.

Pamphleteering

Tracts had been written defending or attacking contemporary issues from the time of the Civil War. They were printed cheaply, widely distributed and many people, including Milton, found them a useful vehicle to broadcast their opinions. Such people became known as pamphleteers.

At the end of the Stuart era, there was a Whig movement against the Stuart kings' assertion of the "Divine Right of Kings" published in a tract titled *Vox Populi, Vox Dei*, Latin for "voice of the people, voice of God." Later, Jacobites used the same title in tracts against the Whigs. Historian Netta Goldsmith writes:

> Until the 1750s men were flogged and imprisoned if convicted of spreading propaganda in support of the Stuart cause, while in 1719, a young printer John Matthews, who published one of the Jacobite pamphlets, *Vox Populi, Vox Dei*, was hanged. In these circumstances Jacobites learned to write obliquely or in a code which escaped the notice of all but the initiates. [134]

The code was so successful that even now, few people realize that the English national anthem originally called for "God save the Stuart king," or that the carol "O Come All Ye Faithful!" originated as a Jacobite rallying cry."[135]

The Legacy of the House of Stuart

By the end of Queen Anne's reign, Britain had become a force to be reckoned with. From three divided countries, fighting over religious beliefs, as well as fighting on the continent to stop the expansionist ambitions of King Louis XIV, Britain was now a successful rural economy, with agricultural output twice that of any other country, exporting large amounts of grain.[136]

People's lives were improving, and more people were able to buy manufactured items such as silk and fine fabrics from around the world. The East India Company had received a Royal Charter from

Elizabeth I in 1600, making it the second oldest joint-stock trading company, initially formed to trade in the East Indies, it eventually turned to trading with the Indian subcontinent and Qing dynasty China. At one time the company accounted for half the world's trade in commodities such as cotton, silk, tea, opium, saltpeter and indigo dye; it also brought sugar and tobacco to England from the Americas.

The East India Company was often involved in skirmishes with Dutch, Portuguese and Spanish ships as they tried to secure ports in China and India. In Japan in 1613 Tokugawa Ieyasu gave trading privileges to the company, and through the good offices of William Adams, was able to open a trading house in Hirado in Kyushu, Japan. However, unable to purchase raw silk to sell to China, the company closed the trading post ten years later.

In 1720 the population of England was about 5.2 million people and London had grown significantly as well, to about 700,000.[137,20] Though the plague, smallpox and other diseases had kept the growth in check, many people left the countryside for London in search of fame and fortune. There were also migrants who came predominantly from Germany and Holland. In 1685 the Revocation of the Edict of Nantes by Louis XIV reversed a law from a hundred years earlier that allowed Calvinist Protestants, known as Huguenots, to live in Catholic France; following the revocation a large number of Huguenots fled to England, many helping to establish the silk industry in London.

At the time of the Great Fire, the wealthy lived in the west part of London, called the city of Westminster, and everyone else lived in the east, the City of London However, following the Great Fire, people who had lost their homes in the City were resettled in the surrounding countryside. Queen Anne had approved an act allowing for fifty new churches to be built to cater for these people. William III, who was then living in Whitehall Palace, could not endure the smoky air of London as it gave him asthma. Following a fire at the palace in 1691, he converted a large hunting lodge in a village called Kensington into Kensington Palace, and the court followed.

---

[20] The population of London included not only the two cities of Westminster and London, but also the docklands south of the River Thames.

The restrictive Puritanism of the Interregnum had been replaced by the dissolute abandon of the gin craze. Literacy had risen to about 45% but people still kept time by the ringing of church bells. Gambling and duels were common, as was prostitution, giving Dissenters ammunition to rail against the decline of family values and the rise in promiscuity. With the general increase in living standards and the growth in the population came a rise in crime by both individuals and also street gangs. In response to this, more offenses, even shoplifting, became capital crimes, though many offenders were just shipped off to the Americas. The penalty for returning from penal transportation was also hanging.

Most people, including scholars, believed that God intervened in their lives somehow, which explained the disasters that befell them, even though the new science showed that the world did not function completely by God's magic. Letting the Licencing Act expire in the 1690s allowed people to express their opinions more freely in print, and Dissenters took advantage of this opportunity to write pamphlets supporting their cause. The term Dissenter had originally been used in relation to Scottish Presbyterians, but it became to mean any of twenty different groups of Protestant Dissenters, as had been defined by the Act of Toleration of 1689.

The End of the World: Catastrophes

One of the defining characteristics of the Stuart dynasty is the start of the scientific revolution, and the move away from superstition to trusting reason. People were challenged by events that seemed to be God-sent, that fell into two categories; the first was tribulation, such as the Great Fire, comets and mega-storms, and the second category, the Second Coming of Christ. Naturally people believed the two were connected.

Dozens of people published predictions showing that the end of the world was nigh. Christopher Columbus had calculated the world would end in 1658, 7,000 years after Creation, which happened, he believed, in 5,343 BC. The Fifth Monarchists used the forecasts of their prophets to show that the coming of the antichrist and the final apocalypse would happen between 1655 and 1657, but as nothing happened, they then promoted the inauspicious date as 1666, based on "666" given in the Book of Revelation. As misfortune would have it, the Great Fire of London did happen in 1666, but the antichrist did not appear. A dozen other prognosticators, including Cardinal Nicholas of Cusa, similarly published their dire forecasts.

Everyone had a theory: Martin Luther had predicted that the end of the world would happen before 1600; the famous diviner, Michel Nostradamus, predicted in 1530 that the world would end in 1800, though Isaac Newton was more conservative, proposing that the world would not end until much later, the year 2060, based largely on deciphering Biblical codes. The Scottish mathematician, Sir John Napier, also analysing the Book of Revelation, calculated the end of the world would happen in 1786.[21] However, few took such drastic actions as Johann Zimmermann, the German theologian and astronomer, who was a follower of the mystic, Jakob Boehme. Zimmermann developed a following in the city of Hamburg, creating elaborate theories predicting the end of the world. He assembled followers to go to America with him to start a new spiritual community there, having already negotiated for land from William Penn, the governor of Pennsylvania. From watching the night sky, he calculated the end would come in 1693, so the band of settlers set out the same year for America. Unfortunately, Zimmermann died on the voyage, and it is not known if the others ever completed the journey.

One of the driving forces behind these warnings was the list of "Fifteen Signs before Doomsday" that everyone knew as the list was printed in the Book of Common Prayer, and had been part of the Chester Mystery Plays since the early 1400s.[138] Shakespeare had even borrowed from the list to include in his play, *Hamlet*. The events were supposed to have originated in the apocryphal book of the Apocalypse of Thomas, and were expected to happen in the two weeks before the end of the world:

> Day 1, Earth's waters rise above the mountains
> Day 2, the waters sink so low they cannot be seen anymore
> Day 3, the waters return to their original position

---

[21] Napier invented logarithmic tables for just this purpose.

Day 4, all sea animals gather on the surface and bellow
    unintelligibly
Day 5, the waters burn from east to west
Day 6, plants and trees fill with dew and blood
Day 7, all buildings are destroyed
Day 8, the stones fight each other
Day 9, great earthquakes occur
Day 10, all mountains and valleys are levelled to a plain
Day 11, men come out from hiding but can no longer
    understand each other
Day 12, the stars and constellations fall out of the sky
Day 13, the bones of the dead come out of their graves
Day 14, all men die, the earth burns
Day 15, Judgment Day [139]

According to some theologians at the time, a few of these events could be accounted for by: the Great Storm (Day 1 - see below) that flooded most of the West Country in 1703, the Great Fire of London (Day 7), celestial objects seen in the sky (Day 12) and the plagues (Day 14).

Comets

The first telescopes were made in the Netherlands by Hans Lippershey in 1603, but they were not so powerful with only a 3x magnification. Many people studied the problem of improving them, and among them was Isaac Newton, who in 1668 invented a reflecting mirror telescope which helped obviate chromatic errors in the lenses. In 1672 he presented an improved version of his telescope to the Royal Society with a purported 38x magnification. Mathematics also played a major role in early astronomy. The astronomers Jeremiah Horrocks and William Crabtree first calculated in 1639 the complicated path Venus takes through the sky, a transit that happens about once every 105~120 years. Horrocks and his friend were lucky to observe the predicted event from their homes the same year.

Charles II understood the importance of having a strong maritime trade based on accurate navigation, so in 1675 he not only established the Royal Observatory in Greenwich, but also appointed the first Astronomer Royal, John Flamsteed. The king charged him:

forthwith to apply himself with the most exact care and diligence to the rectifying the tables of the motions of the heavens, and the places of the fixed stars, so as to find out the so-much desired longitude of places, for the perfecting the art of navigation.[140]

A second unspecified task was to seek out any comets that might destroy the capital, as the city had many times been thrown into panic by the threat of unforeseen disasters raining down from the heavens. In March 1652 there had been a solar eclipse, which the Scottish historian Thomas Carlyle dismissed as:

Much noised of by Lilly, Booker, and the buzzard Astrologer tribe ... mass panic had been stirred up and after it passed with little incident there was a fierce backlash against such prognosticators and their arts. [It occurred] Munday last, which according to their calculation should have produced an Egyptian darkness, and the greatest that hath been seen in this latter age.[141]

The eclipse passed without event, and as it happened on a Monday that day became popularly known as Mirk Monday.

William Whiston and the Deluge

In 1680 a "Great Comet" was seen in the skies in daytime, which again panicked the nation and Europe. Newton quotes Johann Zimmermann as having seen it, and again in 1682 another very bright comet lit up the skies. Pamphlets were printed all over Europe forecasting the imminent end of civilization, or at least major catastrophes.

It was commonly thought that comets forewarned of disasters such as droughts, pestilence, floods and the defeat of armies, to quote Cicero: "From the remotest remembrance of antiquity it is known that comets have always presaged disasters."[142] The fact that the comet of 1680 was followed so soon by another large comet, caused people to expect the worst.

In 1696 William Whiston published a *New Theory of the Earth* in which he claimed that comets appeared in cycles, and that the one in 1682 was the same one that had been observed many times before in history, including 44 BC, the year of Caesar's assassination. He even calculated that the same comet had been responsible for the Flood depicted in the Bible, which he claimed happened in 2346 BC. When Newton became president of the Royal Society in 1703, Whiston was chosen to take the position vacated by Newton as professor of mathematics at Trinity College, Cambridge.

Then came a storm of Biblical proportions that struck the south coast of England in December 1703 and lasted three days. It was said that more than 2,000 chimney stacks were blown down in London alone, and twice that number of oak trees were blown over. Ships were sunk in their hundreds, many were blown out to sea, and over 1,000 sailors were drowned on the treacherous sandbanks in the English Channel. The flooding was particularly severe in the West Country, where hundreds of people and thousands of cattle were drowned. One ship was even found fifteen miles inland[143] and it took months for the extensive flood waters to recede. In total, probably as many as 15,000 people lost their lives.

While Queen Anne sought refuge in the basement of St. James's Palace, the Church quickly declared that the storm was "God's vengeance for the sins of the nation." Others, such as the writer Daniel Defoe, were more pragmatic blaming the storm on divine punishment for England's poor performance in the War of Spanish Succession against the Catholics.

Astrologers in Opposition

In the time of the Tudors, astronomy and related occult arts were well regarded, and Queen Elizabeth herself employed an occultist, John Dee, to be her advisor. Dee worked with Sir Edward Kelley, a spirit medium, who claimed the ability to summon up spirits and angels, as well as purportedly knowing the secret of alchemically transmuting base metal into gold.

During the English Civil Wars, astrologers were used by both sides to find the opportune time to get an advantage in the war. On the Parliamentary side were William Lilly and John Booker. Lilly had published many books and almanacs on astrology as well as one called *Christian Astrology*. As it was the first such book written in English instead of Latin, it sold very well, making him wealthy. Booker was a celebrated astrologer who, in 1631, had accurately predicted the deaths of Frederick V Elector of Palatine and King Gustav II of Sweden. In 1640 Booker was made a censor at the Company of Stationers.

The Battle of Naseby in 1645 was a decisive turning-point in the Civil War. Lilly wrote a pamphlet, *The Starry Messenger; or an interpretation of that strange apparition of three suns seene in London, 19. Novemb. 1644. being the birth day of King Charles,* predicting that Cromwell would win, and his pamphlets were printed and distributed among the Royalist forces. It is said that so much credence was given to Lilly's predictions that the Royalists became demoralized and lost the battle. Cromwell later said that "a favourable prediction from Lilly was said to be worth more than half a dozen regiments."[144] Both Lilly and Booker were summoned to be at the siege of Colchester in 1648, to encourage the Parliamentarian troops.

The Royalist's astrologer was George Wharton, a cavalier who had befriended the antiquarian Elias Ashmole. In 1647 Both Wharton and Ashmole attended the first meeting of the Society of Astrologers, of which Lilly and Booker were also members. Wharton was imprisoned in 1649, at the end of the Interregnum, perhaps on charges of treason, but was released due to the intervention of Lilly and Ashmole. Afterwards he published yearly almanacs and was later remembered for a falling out with Booker over the licensing of books on astrology.

After the Restoration of Charles II, Lilly became unpopular with the aristocracy, but because of the success of his books he was wealthy enough to buy a small estate in Surrey, where he ended his days practicing medicine, having educated "a nation in crisis in the language of the stars."[145]

The Knighting of a Pirate

In 1692 there was an earthquake on the other side of the world that had repercussions in England. On June 7th Port Royal in Jamaica was hit by an earthquake, followed by a tsunami, which destroyed the port, as well as 2,000 buildings, and killed upwards of 5,000 people. In the space of two minutes, nine-tenths of the city was under water, probably due to liquefaction.[146] Port Royal had become wealthy from pirates operating in the Caribbean Sea, the city was a "place of debauchery" and so people believed that the earthquake was an Act of God to destroy the wicked city. The moral message of this calamity was given in sermons across England and America.

One pirate in particular is of interest, Henry Morgan, who had made his base in Port Royal.[22] Originally from Wales, Morgan died four years before the earthquake. Morgan had been given a licence in 1667, known as a "letter of marque," to attack and seize Spanish vessels. However, England and Spain had signed the Treaties of Madrid in 1667 and 1670, ending the six-year Anglo-Spanish War. So, to appease the Spanish following his successful marauding career, Morgan was arrested by the English authorities. However, when he arrived in London, he was feted as a hero. For his services to the Crown, he was knighted in 1674 by Charles II, and on his return to Jamaica he became its Lieutenant Governor.

The Second Coming of Christ

The five decades of calamities, from the Great Plague, the Fire of London, the Great Storm, to enormous comets lighting up the sky, even in daylight, all pointed towards an extraordinary event, the like of which had never been seen before, one that had been predicted in the list included in everyone's Prayer Book.

---

[22] Morgan's house "Firefly" was once owned by Noel Coward.

The educated would have called this event the Parousia, Greek for an "official visit," but others knew it as the Second Coming. In the 1600s people were very pious for two reasons, first, it was the law that every citizen had to attend church every week, but more than that, they saw religion as a way to understand the world they lived in.

Following the execution and ascension of Christ, the Gospels suggested that he would come to Earth again. This is also part of the Nicene Creed, promulgated in 325AD, "He will come again in glory to judge the living and the dead," and though the average parishioner would not have known the Nicene Creed, it is certain that priests would have taught the Second Coming as an article of faith.

The Second Coming weighed heavily upon the conscience of the nation, so much so that after the Great Fire had destroyed St. Paul's Cathedral, King Charles II expressly ordered that the cathedral be rebuilt in order to receive the King Jesus, whose arrival he thought was imminent. Even before the completion of the cathedral, many people claimed various dates for the awaited visit, such as the Fifth Monarchists who now claimed the New Millennium would start in 1673, whereas another Fifth Monarchist, Henry Archer, basing his calculations on the Book of Daniel, forecasted 1700 to be the date. Jacob Zimmermann had predicted 1694, as had the German theologist Johann Alsted.

The events of the three-year reign of James II starting in 1685, which ended with the Glorious Revolution and James escaping to France, probably distracted people's attention from the Second Coming of Christ. Meanwhile, the new king, William III, was more concerned with stopping the second coming of James II.

The House of Hanover

The Act of Settlement had been ratified a year before Queen Anne took the throne, with the act making provision for the contingency that should the royal line of succession be extinguished, the crown would be inherited by the Protestant Sophia, Electress of Hanover. Although more than fifty Catholics had closer blood ties to Anne than Sophia, her legitimacy was based on the fact that she was the daughter of Elizabeth of Bohemia, James I's only daughter, and thus was his granddaughter, as well as the fact that Sophia was Protestant - the Bill of Rights of 1689 had stipulated that no Catholic could ever be a British monarch. Sophia died in June of 1714, two months before Anne died, so the crown was inherited by George, Sophia's son, the Elector of Hanover, starting the British House of Hanover.

George I, reigned 1714 – 1727

Though in Hanover, George was an absolute monarch, conversely in Britain he had to work with Parliament. From the start the situation in Parliament was difficult, and the year after he assumed the throne the Whigs took control of the House. Many of the Tories sympathized with the Jacobite cause, and this turned into a rebellion. The leader of this uprising was Lord Mar, a Scottish Jacobite lord, who was at the time the British Secretary of State. He was relieved of his post by George I and, embittered, he joined the Jacobite cause. Mar was nicknamed "Bobbing John," as he tended to change allegiance from Tory to Whig or Jacobite to Hanoverian, and back again, very easily.

"The Fifteen," as the insurgency was later called, was a dismal failure. James Stuart, the Old Pretender, had hoped for the support of his Catholic half-brother the Duke of Berwick, who was in France serving Louis XIV as a marshal in the army, but was refused. Lord Mar raised the unconstitutional standard of "James VIII and III" in Braemar outside Aberdeen in 1715, but the government had caught wind of the rebellion and offered any tenant their landlord's property if the tenant refused to support the Jacobites, so support was low. When James arrived in Scotland from France by sea, he did not have enough money, arms or supporters. He had mistakenly thought that the Duke of Marlborough would bring an army to his support, regretfully James decided he had come too far to retreat, saying, "I think it is now more than ever, now or never."[147] The Duke of Marlborough returned to England and oversaw the battle against the Jacobites from an office in

London. He later became sick and was confined to his half-built palace, where he died in 1722.

Indemnity

Within months the uprising had collapsed, and James Stuart escaped back to France, taking Lord Mar with him. Many insurgents were executed, and Lord Mar was tried in absentia for treason. King George was generally lenient with the rebels; money he took from forfeited estates he used to build schools in Scotland and to pay down the National Debt.[148] Two years later the Indemnity Act of 1717 pardoned all those who had taken part in the attempted rebellion, with the exception of the whole of the Gregor Clan, including Rob Roy MacGregor, who were deemed bandits.[149] The persecution of the MacGregors ended nearly sixty years later, in 1774, when the stipulation was repealed.

To commemorate the Indemnity Act, also called the Act of Grace and Free Pardon, a silver medal was issued by the Royal Mint. On the obverse is the head of George I in relief, the reverse has the winged figure of Clemency standing behind a short pillar. In her left hand she holds an olive branch, in her right a caduceus that touches the head of a fleeing snake, representing the thwarted Rebellion.[23]

As many Tories were implicated in The Fifteen, George distrusted them, which in turn helped the Whigs. Though it has often been said that George did not like living in Britain, preferring Hanover, and that he did not speak English, this is partly due to the prejudices of historians. He was reticent to the point of shyness, and awkward in public, preferring a simple game of cards to court receptions, as his mother said, he "was more sensitive than he cared to show." [150] Besides German, he spoke Dutch, French and Latin, and documents show that in later life George also understood English. He proved to be a reformist monarch, who encouraged the Enlightenment and allowed writers to publish without fear of censorship.

---

[23] See Broken Column Lecture in *Alchemy by Degrees* in *Freemasonry: Initiation by Light*

The Forty-Five

As can be seen, the Jacobite cause was deeply embedded among the Scottish clans. Scotland had been an independent nation, that went back as far as the House of Alpin from 848 AD, but was coerced to join the Union in 1707. Even after the death of King George I and the succession of his son, George II, the flames of the Jacobite cause were still being fanned, this time by the Old Pretender's son, Charles Stuart, retrospectively called "Bonnie Prince Charlie." In 1745 he raised enough money to buy just two ships and sailed to Scotland in an attempt to raise an army in order to seize the throne of Great Britain. The insurgency was quickly snuffed out, with Charles Stuart being defeated at the Battle of Culloden Moor in 1746, in a battle that lasted only fifteen minutes, and with it the Jacobites became politically irrelevant. Following this, "Highland Clearances" were enforced in a mismanaged attempt to reorganize Scotland's failing economy, eventually leading to large-scale emigration to America and Canada. Songs and books depict Charles Stuart as a "romantic figure of heroic failure," and thus his legend lives on.[151]

Further Penal Laws

The Disarming Act of 1716 sought to remove any resistance remaining in the Scottish Highlands, where the clans supported the Jacobites. The act stated that it was to "secure peace in the highlands" but its objective was to outlaw the ownership of any "broad sword or target, poignard, whinger, or durk, side pistol, gun, or other warlike weapon." After the uprising of "The Forty-Five," this act was followed in 1746 by the Dress Act, which sought to further suppress any disaffected or rebellious clans, by making it illegal for anyone in Scotland to wear "Highland Dress," especially tartans and kilts. There was an exception for tartans worn by military regiments such as the Black Watch regiment, which became known as the "Government Tartan." The law was repealed in 1782

Capitulation

Following the death of James Stuart in 1766, Pope Clement XIII no longer acknowledged the Jacobite cause. He had supported James as the future "James VIII and III" of Great Britain, instead the pope now accepted George I as the legitimate ruler. This had been a major point of contention and basis for the Penal Laws against Catholics in the first place. In England in 1771, 1778 and 1793 Catholic Relief Acts were passed, giving more emancipation to Catholics. It was a slow process and discrimination against both Scottish and Irish Catholics took a long time to heal. The Stuarts had schemed to introduce religious toleration for Catholics, and because they had a strong belief that their sacred right to rule was guaranteed by the Divine Right of Kings, this became a cause célèbre for disenfranchised highlanders. Unbelievably, Charles Stuart was a conspirator in yet another plan to invade Britain in 1759 during the Seven Years' War; this time the French proposed to either send him ahead of an invading French fleet or to Ireland to raise an army. The French later changed their mind, considering Charles Stuart to be more of a liability than an asset. The fleet never left port.

Charles Stuart, the Young Pretender, died in Rome in 1788, aged 67. He is buried in the crypt of St. Peter's Basilica in the Vatican, next to his father and brother.

Summary

The end of the House of Stuart and the beginning of the House of Hanover forms the foundation for the Revival of Freemasonry in Britain. The limitations of the printed word mean that I have to write the story sequentially, but in fact many of these events were happening at the same time.

The history of the Stuarts is like an octopus, as the legs go out in all directions but are part of the one, the intellectual revolution and the religious one, scientific developments, the death of alchemy and the growth of trade. The history of the Stuarts also has to include the machinations used to either suppress or promote Catholicism in Britain, which to the British meant giving obeisance to the pope.

King Charles I had tried to preserve his throne by asking for Spanish assistance, and it cost him his head, the first time an English king had been executed. King Louis XIV had hoped to unite France with Spain, and eventually Great Britain, as one great Catholic empire, but that was thwarted by the Dutch king of England, William III. Among the public, there was also the fear of retribution, that the punishment inflicted on Catholics by Henry VIII would be returned on Protestants manyfold should Catholics take power in Britain.

The Civil Wars were a series of confrontations between the king and Parliament, which sought to wrest power from the king, and the situation was made worse by religious acrimony. Initially, England's landowners formed the power base in Parliament which became Anglican and Tory, some of whom were sympathetic to the Jacobite cause, and only with Queen Anne, and then later with George I, did the Whigs find a voice.

People at the end of the Stuart era thought that they had entered the Tribulation with so many catastrophes: a barren Queen, the threat of a Catholic invasion, the Great Plague, the Great Fire, the Great Storm, the Jacobite uprisings, and comets that might at any time destroy much of the country. The kings and queens of the House of Stuart were faced with enormous challenges not just from wars and rebellions but also these horrendous disasters, leading people to believe that it was all punishment from God.

James II was the last monarch to govern by divine right, he had been able to appoint ministers at wish and rule by decree. James had received money directly from the Treasury, as well as all taxes on imports, to maintain his household and standard of living, but Parliament withdrew these powers.

William III's Bill of Rights of 1689 and Queen Anne's Acts of Union of 1707 steered the country out of danger and set the course for Great Britain for the next two hundred years. Traditionally Anne has been portrayed as running a petticoat government, that is to say, under the influence of her favourites at court and lacking political astuteness or even interest, but modern historians believe that this portrait is based on male prejudice.

Despite being a woman in a male dominated world, and even with her health problems, "theologically fit to rule, but biologically cursed,"[152] Anne steered the ship of state with resolve. The stability of her reign led to greater prosperity for citizens and a general strengthening of the economy. Arts and literature flourished under her reign, made possible by laws she enacted to abolish censorship, and these in turn gave a voice to subjugated Dissenters, about whom we will learn more in the next chapter.

A Tory politician remarked about a flattering statue of Anne that had been erected in front of St. Paul's Cathedral just before her death, depicting her with her back to the cathedral. The politician's comment just about sums up the sentiment of the age, "it was fitting she was depicted with her rump to the church, gazing longingly into a wineshop!"[153]

The Defenestration of Prague 1618. Two Catholic lords are thrown out of windows by Protestant lords, in an act that is often seen as precipitating the Thirty Years' War (1618-1648) between Protestants and Catholics.

In the Middle Ages, defenestration was a common form of lynching. In this case, the two men fell 70ft. from the third-floor window but survived the fall.[154]

Ch. 4   Religious Turmoil

During the hundred years before James VI of Scotland ascended the throne of England as King James I, the movement to remove Catholicism from England had already started. Then, following the Protestant Reformation of 1517, Arian and other non-Trinitarian sects started to proliferate, both in Europe and in England.

The Doctrine of the Trinity states that though God is the one God, God can also be expressed as "three coeternal consubstantial persons," the Father, the Son and the Holy Spirit.[155] This doctrine was, and is, unique to Christianity. However, even Church fathers found it difficult to reconcile it as it raised profound theological questions, such as whether the three were of equal status or whether they always acted in unison.

The Catholic theologian John Wycliffe translated the Vulgate (meaning "commonly used") Latin New Testament into Middle English in 1382, and the remainder of the Bible was translated by associates and completed in 1395. Each edition was laboriously transcribed by hand by monastic scribes, so only about 250 of his Bibles were ever made. It then became possible for people other than the clergy to read the Bible, and one of the results of this was that Wycliffe's followers, known as Lollards, started to preach the Bible throughout England.

In 1525, just before King Henry VIII's break with Rome, William Tyndale was also translating the Bible, but from Hebrew and Greek directly into the vernacular English of the times. His Bible was composed of the New Testament and part of the Old Testament, and the invention of the printing press in 1438 helped it to become widely distributed. Tyndale fell out with the king as he disagreed with him divorcing Catherine of Aragon, asserting his Protestantism saying, "the pope's dogma is bloody," and it cost him his life.[156,157]

The Catholic Church in England was outwardly concerned about the veracity of the translation of Tyndale's Bible, but secretly worried more about the erosion of its power should just anyone be able to read the Bible. However, that concern was unnecessary as King Henry VIII passed the Act of Supremacy in 1534, closed Catholic monasteries, confiscated their land and made himself head of the Anglican Church and Defender of the Faith.

The Latin mass was replaced by a mass in English, and a Book of Common Prayer was published for the first time. Queen Mary I, Henry VIII's daughter, tried to reverse the English Reformation by repealing the Act of Supremacy. She took revenge by murdering 300 Protestants, resulting in her nickname "Bloody Mary," and hundreds more, known as the "Marian Exiles," had to escape to the Netherlands. Mary died in 1558 and was followed by the staunch Protestant, Queen Elizabeth, who restored the Act of Supremacy.

On Elizabeth's death, James VI and I inherited the problems of the Kirk, or national Scottish Church, that had started to adopt the Calvinist Presbyterian doctrine introduced by John Knox. It was run by ministers and elders, doing away with the Catholic system of bishops and dioceses. However, James saw the Catholic bishops as allies and so came in conflict with the Kirk as he tried to support the bishops in Scotland, threatening the Kirk saying it would get no protection from the king, "no bishop, no king."[158]

Finally, James I assembled a group of theologians who revised the Bible, correcting errors and making the language easier for the common man to understand. The King James Bible was admired for its "majesty of style," even a Catholic theologian commented that "It lives on the ear, like music that can never be forgotten, like the sound of church bells, which the convert hardly knows how he can forego."[159]

When James I arrived in England, he found that there were more Catholics there than there were in Scotland, and that they were suffering under the Penal Laws. However, it was the Catholics, not the Protestants, who tried to kill the Catholic monarch with three assassination attempts, hoping to replace him with Arbella Stuart. The outcome was harsher laws being introduced, such as the Oath of Allegiance and the Test Act, resulting in a wave of anti-Catholic sentiment. James I tried to marry his son Charles to the Spanish Infanta Maria Anna, the daughter of King Philip III. Negotiations started when Charles was fourteen and continued for ten years, eventually Charles married another Catholic, Henrietta Maria of France instead. The result made Parliament uneasy, as they feared a continuance of the Catholic monarchy.

The Interregnum (1649-1660) was a turning point in religious freedom in England. Europe had suffered with the Thirty Years War (1618-1648) that had left nearly 20% of the population of Germany dead. Then Civil War started in England over the type of government the country should have; this war pitted Puritans against Royalists, many of whom were Catholics. It is estimated that over half a million people died in three countries over the three civil wars. Violence on such a scale prompted people to seek out metaphysical truths that superseded religion that were, as Galileo said, "Written in the book of Nature" or as Lord Herbert of Cherbury, the "Father" of Deism said, "engraved on the human mind by God."[160]

Stuart England had championed Anglican Protestantism (the Church of England) while at the same time trying to reintroduce rights for Catholics. Later, Interregnum Puritan values were found to be too severe for English tastes and the country sought new religious freedom while maintaining the national religion. Dozens of dissenting religions or sects, called Dissenters, were established which in turn challenged long-held beliefs about immortality, the Divine Right of Kings and even a ritual called the "King's Touch." In the latter part of the Stuart dynasty, the Book of Common Prayer was updated, but not without much controversy.

Dissenters were mainly centred in cities, while Anglicanism was stronger in the countryside and in the two universities. From these beginnings a small movement led by two brothers at the University of Oxford later became a world-wide religion, Methodism. Things were made difficult for Dissenters by the Toleration Act of 1689, after which they had to have licences to preach. Dissenters were often discriminated against in courts, and were not allowed to perform marriage or funeral ceremonies, which was the preserve of Anglican clergy.

Though religious toleration for Dissenters was introduced during the Commonwealth, the Church still had the power to punish those that denied the theology of the Trinity or the authority of the Bible, using the Blasphemy Act of 1697. In that year a student in Scotland was the last person executed in Britain for blasphemy.

Protestants continued to fear that Catholics, who were often living in remote regions in England, might collude with other Catholics in either France or Spain in an attempt to overthrow the Protestant government, which resulted in the continuing persecution of Catholics. Finally, during the latter part of the reign of Queen Anne, the Tories tried to enforce the position of the Church of England as they believed that dissension would get out of hand, and spread dramatically, which would have threatened national security, but an escalation did not happen.

The Interregnum and Religious Freedom

Cromwell had successfully brought about a Puritan movement that forced out the remnants of Catholicism in England, and at the same time restructured the Church of England. The uncertain future of Anglicanism was a fiercely debated topic. Meanwhile, Cromwell lost the support he had achieved during the Civil Wars, and many went as far as to call for the abolishment of the aristocracy. This, together with the higher taxes that he had imposed to maintain a standing army because of constant threats of rebellions in Ireland or Scotland, led to public outrage.

A tract was published called *Killing No Murder*, where the author advocated the assassination of Oliver Cromwell; someone attempted to carry out the plan but was caught and executed. The author was also arrested and put in the Tower of London, where he became deranged and died within the year. The plot so distressed Cromwell, that from that day on, he never slept in the same lodgings for more than two nights in a row.

High Church

Puritans had demanded that the Church of England reform its liturgy, which they thought was too similar to Catholicism. The Church's reliance on the leadership of bishops and other aspects, such as the use of incense and ostentatious church bell change-ringing, "smells and bells," came to be called High Church, and later High Churchmen endorsed the 1662 Prayer Book as a bond between the Church of England and the State. In contrast, the Latitudinarian Low Church, commonly called the Broad Church, asserted that human reason when combined with the Holy Spirit was sufficient to guide the believer. They wished to make the Church as inclusive as possible and accepting of other Christian viewpoints.

Three Sets of Articles

Five years after Henry VIII introduced the Act of Supremacy, the Catholic Church in England issued the Six Articles in 1539 to redefine its doctrine and solidify its position. The articles, called by the people "the bloody whip with six strings," reaffirmed the need for confession, celibacy of priests and more importantly, the belief in transubstantiation - that the bread and wine of the mass were transformed into the body and blood of Christ. This was difficult on two levels; first, it sounded to the people like witchcraft, and secondly, half the population was illiterate and did not understand the concept. Penalties were severe for denying any of the six articles, with death reserved for the denial of transubstantiation.

In 1552, Archbishop Thomas Cranmer issued an expanded Forty-two Articles of the Anglican faith. The Articles were not so much a statement of doctrine as a mission statement that invalidated the position of Catholics and Dissenters, such as Anabaptists. However, Queen Mary did not allow the Articles to become law. After the succession of Queen Elizabeth, the number of articles was reduced to thirty-nine in 1563, including the contentious Article XXIX, which asserted that "the wicked do not eat the Body of Christ,"[161] meaning that sinners do not need to take the sacrament (the Eucharist) to atone for their sins. In retaliation, the pope excommunicated Elizabeth in 1570. The following year the Articles were made law and printed inside every Book of Common Prayer.

Over the next sixty years, the Thirty-nine Articles were revised many times, but in 1628 the literal interpretation of the Articles was made law by Charles I, with serious penalties for priests and dons who interpreted them differently. This was followed by the Clarendon Code and Great Ejection of 1662. Lastly, the Test Act of 1672 stated that anyone who wanted to hold a civil office had to profess a belief in the Articles, which was maintained until its repeal in 1824. The Test underlined the Anglican doctrine by requiring people to make a declaration against the invocation of saints, transubstantiation and the sacrament of the Eucharist, recognizing only two sacraments, baptism and Holy Communion.

Since the Act of Establishment enacted by William III in 1701, the Church of England has been England's official religion, and the monarch its supreme governor and the "Defender of the Faith." Today the monarch, with the consent of Parliament, can appoint bishops and, in exchange for this right, twenty-six bishops, "The Lords Spiritual," have ex officio seats in the House of Lords.[162]

Surprisingly, witchcraft was not seen to be a concern. The number of witch trials had declined by the end of the 1600s, and reinforcing the existing Witchcraft Act that James I had enacted in 1604 was not seen as necessary. The last execution for witchcraft in Great Britain was in 1727 when the Scottish woman Janet Horne was burned alive, though the name of the unfortunate soul is probably different as in north Scotland "Jenny Horne" (devil's horn) was a common term for witches. It was not until 1735 that George II introduced a new, more lenient, Witchcraft Act.

The Abrahamic Faiths

Protestantism

Protestants now recognize the concept of an invisible church, in contrast to the Roman Catholic view of the "visible one true Church founded by Jesus Christ."[163] Starting in the 16th and 17th centuries, many new Protestant denominations were fighting for recognition.

Lollards: 1382

Following his translation of the Bible in 1382, Wycliffe became more convinced that transubstantiation was a fallacy and in saying so, brought the wrath of the Catholic Church down on his head. As he had once been Master of Balliol College at the University of Oxford, the university protected him as they believed in safeguarding the academic freedom of the dons. Though Wycliffe had to defend himself against the Church authorities until his death in 1384, aged sixty-four. In 1415 he was posthumously declared a heretic and excommunicated.

Followers of Wycliffe's teachings, the proto-Protestant Lollards, probably got the epithet from the Old Dutch word for mumble, "lollen," as his followers were wont to say prayers under their breath. The Lollards pushed for reforms in Catholicism, and eventually they were also seen as heretics. Though they were constantly persecuted through the 15th century, it was during the reign of Mary I and the reintroduction of the Heresy Acts that Lollardy was finally suppressed.

Arianism: 1517

Arianism is a theological dispute that had been persecuted since the time of the First Council of Nicaea in 325 AD where, not only was the doctrine of Catholicism decided, but also Arianism was declared to be a heresy. Arianism had been in Europe since medieval times, but it was the Protestant Reformation of 1517 that encouraged followers to start to proselytize in England.

Arianism is named for the teachings of Arius in third century Egypt. What put him in opposition to the Church was his anti-Trinitarian message, that Christ was the son of God and therefore subordinate to his father, which was heretical. The Catholic Church believed then, and still believes, that God, the Son and the Holy Ghost are "consubstantial," the original Greek word being "homoousion," meaning to be "of one substance."

For various reasons, the label "Arian" was also associated with the Socinians and later Unitarians. Isaac Newton also supported an anti-Trinitarian theology, based on his research of the Bible which he started in around 1672. However, he kept his Arian beliefs concealed.

Anabaptists: 1534

Anabaptists from the Netherlands and Flanders started congregations in England soon after the start of the English Reformation, but were quickly persecuted. The word Anabaptist means to baptise again, as believers insisted that a profession of faith as an adult was necessary to join the congregation, rather than the traditional infant baptism, where a child is accepted into the Church as long as one of the parents is a member of the faith. The term Anabaptist is misleading as many smaller Protestant sects were labelled with that blanket term, even the Protestant reformer William Tyndale was once accused of being an Anabaptist.

In the reign of James I, though Anabaptists still continued to distribute literature and preached openly, many were executed for heresy. Then in 1590 they were expelled from England, joining up with like-minded believers in Europe. Anabaptists' relationship with the Baptist denomination was difficult after the Baptists issued an anathema against the denomination in 1624, which pertains today, and it is believed that many Anabaptists were absorbed by Baptist churches over time.

Puritans: 1559

During the reign of the Catholic queen, Mary I, hundreds of Protestants, the Marian Exiles, fled to the Netherlands for safety, only to return after her death. These Protestants were more extreme than most, and were often described in similar terms to the Cathars in France, as separatists who sought to "purify" the Church of England, becoming known as "Puritans," but the term Puritan was moot as it was more a collection of Protestant sects. By the time James I arrived in England, there were already hundreds of Puritan clergymen there, and they presented him with a petition asking for the abolition of outward badges of "popish errours" including the wearing of wedding rings.[164] James ignored their requests and instead began to persecute them.

During the eleven years of the Interregnum, Puritans were allied with Cromwell's military regime. The Long Parliament had overturned the episcopacy of the Anglican Church, replaced the Book of Common Prayer, and for a time Presbyterians temporarily led the Church of England. The Commonwealth advocated more religious freedom and so the Rump Parliament revoked Elizabeth's Act of Uniformity requiring every citizen to go to church once a week. Many of the newer Protestant sects took advantage of their new-found freedoms to expand their congregations and to worship more openly, for example the Ranters, Fifth Monarchists and Quakers.

Calvinism: 1640

John Calvin was a French Protestant theologian living in Switzerland. The Catholic Church, calling his teachings heretical, named them Calvinism, from whence the sect got its name. John Knox had been chaplain to the king of Scotland when Mary I was crowned, thereby restoring Catholicism to the country. Knox then had to leave Scotland and moved to Switzerland where he met Calvin. Knox was so impressed by Calvin that after the death of Mary, he returned to Scotland to promote Calvin's teachings and led the Scottish Protestant Reformation.

The Solemn League and Covenant had been signed in 1643 by both England and Scotland, helping protect the young Protestant Kirk. However, by 1651, following the defeat of the Royalist and Scottish army at the Battle of Worcester, the importance of the Solemn League and Covenant was in question and Presbyterians lost support on both sides of the border. By 1707, with the signing of the Acts of Union, Scotland was then able to safeguard the rights of the Presbyterian Church.

The Presbyterian Church introduced governance by elders, called in Greek "presbyteros," instead of bishops. With echoes of Freemasonry, Calvinist Presbyterians introduced the term "Architect of the Universe,"[165] and in a commentary on Psalm 19, Calvin referred to God as the "Great Architect." Calvin was perhaps basing his terminology on the writings of Saint Thomas Aquinas, who said in his book *Summa Theologica*, written in 1274, that God was the creator of everything in the same way that an architect is the creator of designed buildings.

Socinians 1680

In the decade from 1680 to 1690, the Socinian Controversy was a theological argument about the relationship between Christ and God, based on the Gospels, and the concept of the pre-existence of Christ, where he is identified with the divine hypostasis called the Logos or the Word,[166] an argument that raged in churches across England. It was started by tracts written by non-Trinitarian Protestants called Socinians, named after a similar group in Poland, the Polish Brethren, who were labelled as Arians or Socinians. In England the foremost proponent of the non-Trinitarian cause was a Unitarian, John Biddle, who had been imprisoned by Charles I on several occasions for denying the Trinity. Others before him had met a worse fate, execution. With the establishment of the Commonwealth, Biddle thought he would be free to express a non-Trinitarian doctrine, however Cromwell needed to be politically shrewd with the Church of England and so in 1652 had Biddle exiled to the Scilly Isles.[167]

The reason that Cromwell had acted strictly with Biddle is based on the fact that the Act of Toleration, though it gave religious toleration to Protestants, contained a clause excluding anti-Trinitarian beliefs. The Socinian Controversy confirmed that tolerance would not be extended to include anti-Trinitarianism, and this was also enforced by the Blasphemy Act of 1697. Isaac Newton had taken a close interest in the controversy and collected many books from the Polish Socinian School, the Racovian Academy.[168]

Judaism in England

Jewish settlements had started with the invasion of William the Conqueror in 1066,[169] though there are records of earlier visitations. William established the English feudal system with lords designated to manage estates that belonged to the king. Serfs working on the estates were accountable to the lords, but merchants were exempt, as were Jews, who were deemed direct subjects of the king. Jews were dependent on the king giving them a charter that worked like a modern visa, granting them a right of stay in England, but Jews had no rights as citizens. Their function as moneylenders was vital to the king at that time, because the Church proscribed charging interest on money loaned, as did Judaism and Islam, but Mosaic Law did not forbid Jews lending money with interest to non-Jews. As a result, Jews in England became very wealthy, and the king could tax them heavily, without needing the approval of Parliament.[170]

In 1215 Pope Innocent III had ruled that Jews:

> in every Christian province and at all times shall be marked off
> in the eyes of the public from other peoples through the

character of their dress. Particularly, since it may be read in the writings of Moses[171] that this very law has been enjoined upon them.[172]

So, in 1218 Henry III instituted the Edict of the Badge, requiring Jews to wear a badge resembling the two tablets of the commandments on their coats to identify themselves.

The Expulsion

When the next king, Edward I, returned from the Ninth Crusade, he found that many citizens had mortgaged their lands to Jews, and some had become destitute. He himself had become deeply in debt to Jewish moneylenders who had funded the Second Barons' War and the Welsh Wars. So, in 1275 and again in 1290 Edward had all the Jews in England expelled, though at the time it is estimated that there were no more than 2,000 living in England. All debts payable to Jews reverted to the king, and it is said that the eviction was handled expeditiously and without violence.[173]

In the period of the Interregnum, a small group of Spanish Sephardic Jews approached Cromwell concerning his policy of religious freedom, asking for the right to live in England. They had entered England after the Reconquista and were accepted as Spanish citizens. The word Sephardim is Hebrew for "Spanish Jew," one of the three Jewish ethnic communities that wore a distinctive dress with turbans. In 1656 Cromwell gave them permission to remain and allowed them to build a synagogue and a burial ground. Though their lives were safer, there was still widespread discrimination based on stories passed down from the Middle Ages, such as the Wandering Jew.

The Wandering Jew

The Bible relates the story of a Jew who insulted Christ as he carried the cross on the way to being executed, because of this, the Jew was condemned to roam the world despondently until the Second Coming of Christ. He was personified as a Christ-hater and people associated the legend with extortionate moneylenders and criminals like Dickens's Fagin the pickpocket. In the Middle Ages, Jews had also been executed on false accusations of "Blood Libel," kidnapping

Christian children for their blood. All of this combined to exacerbate the public's perception of Jews, and discrimination was rampant.

Catholics

One of the paradoxes of the balance of religion in England at the time of the Stuarts was that it was the Catholics who tried to assassinate the Catholic King James I, as they believed he had betrayed them. James inwardly understood their grievances and was working with Parliament to ease the Penal Laws. However, in order to increase security in England following the Gunpowder Plot, James also had to take measures such as the Oath of Allegiance to suppress Catholics. He believed that English Catholics took their orders from the pope and not their monarch, an "imperium in imperio," so the oath was to confirm that the pope had no authority over the king, making it possible to identify any potentially disloyal subjects. To work around this restriction, Catholics professed to being Protestants though secretly praying, and sometimes hiding, in spaces hidden between walls in large houses - priest holes. At the same time, James, even though he was Catholic, had been supportive of the Anglican Church, even commissioning the new authoritative English Bible.

James's successor, Charles I, attempted to ease persecution of Catholics, which was another factor that probably led to his execution. The Long Parliament in 1643 restructured the Church of England and gave freedoms to Dissenters, which turned out to be a headache for following governments. Following the Restoration, Charles II enacted further Penal Laws such as the Clarendon Code and later the Test Act, necessitating an oath of a belief in the Thirty-nine Articles of faith. The fact that his brother, James II, failed the Test Act led to the exclusion crisis and ultimately the Glorious Revolution of 1688. The one insightful act that changed the course of history, despite having Catholic monarchs ruling over Protestants, was that Charles II insisted that his brother James's children be brought up as Protestants. This simple act may have saved England much bloodshed during the Glorious Revolution.

Future policy concerning religion in Great Britain was determined for the next 150 years by the Toleration Act of 1689. This allowed non-conformists, including Dissenters, to have their own places of worship, at the same time censorship was relaxed, and the Church of England was reinforced as the national religion.

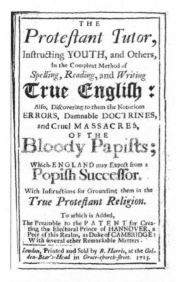

Anti-Catholicism

The three plots against the life of James I by Catholics were still in the memories of people when in 1662 Charles II married the Catholic princess, Catherine of Portugal, and formed an alliance with France against the Protestant Netherlands. At the time France was the leading Catholic power in Europe, and people were naturally suspicious of the king's intentions. Then in 1666 the Great Fire of London enflamed the populace's animosity towards Catholics. Although at the time the fire was attributed to Dutch immigrants, later it was blamed on a "popish frenzy," and led to rioting and many lynchings. Some obviously wanted to take the situation further, for example the fabricated "Popish Plot" invented by Titus Oates that resulted in the execution and banishment of dozens of leading Catholic citizens and nobles between 1678 and 1681.

The Act of Settlement of 1701 enacted by the Dutch Protestant King William III, ensured that no Catholic could either be a future monarch of England, nor marry one, on pain of exclusion from succession and, until recently, this was the situation in England.[24] However, the rights of Catholics were restored with the abolishment of Penal Laws by the Roman Catholic Relief Act of 1829. In the 1880s Ireland was said to be "distracted, disloyal and impoverished."[174] The problem still may not have been resolved; as late as 1972, there was an inter-denominational riot in Derry in Northern Ireland, known as Bloody Sunday, leading to the growth of the Catholic resistance organizations, Sinn Féin and the IRA, established in 1905 and 1916 respectively.[175]

---

[24] This act was replaced by the Succession to the Crown Act 2013, allowing the first born, male or female, precedence, and ending the disqualification of Catholicism.

Islam

Pope Pius V had excommunicated Elizabeth in 1570, calling for her to be stripped of the crown, and the next pope, Gregory XIII, financed a failed assassination attempt, the Throckmorton Plot. Spanish ships were stopping English merchants from trading not just in the Spanish Netherlands, but also across Europe, while at the same time Elizabeth also sought new markets for merchants. So, Elizabeth I established diplomatic relations with the Ottoman Empire in 1580, hoping to secure its support in case of an attack by Spain on England. The Ottoman Empire's economy was many times the size of that of England, so to be competitive, Elizabeth had encouraged the formation of joint-stock companies: the Turkey Company to trade with the Ottomans, the Muscovy Company to trade with Persia, and later the East India Company that eventually helped to colonize India. However, the Ottomans never came to the aid of Elizabeth in her various naval fights with Spain. In the reign of James I, England lost over 460 ships from skirmishes with the famous Barbary pirates, who then sold the crews into slavery, what became known as "White Gold."[176] There is even evidence that Muslim ships also raided parts of England in search of slaves.[177]

Though thousands of Englishmen travelled the globe for trade, very few Muslims ever settled in England, but by around 1700 there were a few living in London. In contrast, there had been hundreds of Indian seamen employed on British ships, such as the Lascar sailors from Bengal working with the East India Company. The problem of employment issues became so great that in 1660 the government had to introduce the Navigation Act to ensure that at least a quarter of the crew on an English ship was English.

At the time there was a strong interest in studying Islamic sciences and philosophy. The fifteenth century Bodleian Library at the University of Oxford had already built up an extensive collection of Arabic manuscripts on a wide variety of subjects, from astronomy and mathematics to medicine and horticulture. Chairs of Arabic Studies were established at both the Universities of Cambridge (1632) and Oxford (1636).

Dissenters

The year after the outbreak of the First English Civil War in 1642, Parliamentarians signed the Solemn League and Covenant with Scotland, in exchange for Scotland's help should Irish (or French) forces land in England in support of the Royalists. The Covenant required the Presbyterian parish government system to be adopted in English churches. On top of this, many changes were made to Anglican Church liturgy to rid itself of any traces of Catholicism. In 1661, following the Restoration, the Solemn League and   Covenant was repealed when Parliament passed the Sedition Act, and people took to the streets to celebrate.

Following the introduction of the Clarendon Code and then the Great Ejection of 1662, many Dissenters had to preach in private homes in "conventicles," which became the beginnings of the Baptists and other congregations. Further legislation was introduced to restrict these types of meetings, then the Five Mile Act was passed, and this led to many ministers such as the Baptist minister and author, John Bunyan, being imprisoned.

Finally, the Act of Toleration of 1689 allowed certain freedoms to Dissenters such as Congregationalists, Baptists, Presbyterians, and Quakers, giving them the ability to coexist with the Church of England; but Catholics were still excluded by the Act. Despite this 'toleration' most of the upper classes spoke out against the more fanatical sects as it was thought that they might threaten social order and property rights.

The division between Presbyterians and other Dissenters became more apparent towards the end of the 1690s, with Lutheran Pietism based on frugality becoming the basis of Evangelical Protestantism, especially in America in the Puritan settlements in New England, which became the basis for American Protestantism.

Over twenty different Protestant sects sprung up once Cromwell passed the Act of Toleration. Many of which were centred on a charismatic preacher, such as the Barrowists, though some movements had no leadership, like the Sabbatarians. They can be roughly divided into two groups, home-grown Dissenters and Protestant groups that expanded into England from Europe.

Catalogue of the severall Sects and Opinions in England and other Nations With a briefe Rehearsall of their false and dangerous Tenents.

...a numberless crew of locusts have sprung out of the bottomless pit, assuming to themselves the names of Arians, Arminians, Socinians, Antinomians, Anabaptists, Familists, Antiscripturists, Antisabbatarians, Antitrinitarians, Libertines, Erastians, Levellers, Mortalists, Millenaries, Enthusiasts, Separatists, Semiseparatists, Quakers, and many more of the same brood. No country from the foundation of the world hath brought forth and brought up, so many monstrous births as it [England] hath done.

The Catalogue of the several Sects and Opinions - Thomas Hall, minister, 1660

Home-Grown Dissension

Baptists

The origin of the Baptists in England is not clear; it is known that there was a sect in Amsterdam in the time of James I, and that by the 1620s there were five clandestine churches in London, the first of which was founded in 1612. In the Netherlands at the time there were several sects such as the Anabaptists and Mennonites that had similar views, believing in a similar dogma of adult baptism, Arminianism and separation of church and state. However, after a schism in 1624 the Baptists issued an anathema against the Anabaptists, and following the Act of Toleration of 1689, the Baptist denomination went from strength to strength.

Brownists

In the 1550s a group of English dissenters called the Brownists formed around their leader Robert Browne. They were early separatists from the Church of England who, in 1620, boarded the Mayflower for a new life in America. As a majority of those on the Mayflower were Brownists, the Pilgrims were, until the 19th century, called the "Brownist Emigration." The term "Brownist" was also used in a derogatory way by Shakespeare in *Twelfth Night*, however, their importance is that they were the antecedents of the larger movement of Seekers. In 1640, 2,000 Brownists stormed the old St. Paul's Cathedral in a demonstration, not an insignificant number at a time when the population of London was about half a million souls.[178]

Seekers

The Seekers were a religious society, rather than a sect, that emerged around the 1620s, inspired by three brothers, Walter, Thomas, and Bartholomew Legate who taught that Catholic churches were corrupt and that the faithful should wait for God's revelation. In 1612 James I met with Bartholomew Legate who told the king that he had not prayed for seven years. The king was so horrified that he had Legate burned at the stake.[179] The Baptist leader Thomas Helwys had interceded asking the king to forgive Legate, but for his pains he was also thrown into prison, where he died four years later. The Seekers did not have services, rather they sat in silence waiting for God to inspire them.

Quakers

The Quakers grew out of the meetings of the Seekers, and still today practice their faith in the same way, sitting quietly waiting for inspiration. They were first organized by George Fox, who in 1652, had a vision of Christ on Pendle Hill in Lancashire. He believed that it was possible to have a direct, spiritual experience without the need of priests, and such was his charisma that he preached to thousands at a time. Fox was imprisoned many times for protesting people's rights; once when called before a judge, Fox had said that all people should "tremble before the Lord,"[180] consequently the judge called him and his followers "Quakers." Though the epithet was used in derision, it stuck in people's minds, however, Quakers describe themselves as "Children of the Light," calling each other "Friends."

Ranters

The Ranters were a movement that grew quickly in the time of the Commonwealth, made up largely of common people, and though there were no leaders or organization, the movement grew organically and was widespread throughout England. Ranters were seen as a threat to society as Parliamentarians worried about the mob element of the movement. It was also alleged that the Ranters was a free-sex movement, though there is no evidence for the accusation. Ranters believed that as God was in all living things, they were the "chosen people" and did not owe obedience to anyone. This principle is known as "antinomianism," that obedience to the law is based on an internal spiritual urge rather than any external compulsion.[181] Ranters also believed that they would be saved by Divine Grace and so they rejected the concept of immortality. One of their spokesmen was John Robbins, who claimed his wife was the Virgin Mary and his son was Christ, and that he was on a mission to convert Jews to Christianity.[182] George Fox is quoted as stating that at the time of the Restoration most of the Ranters joined the Quakers.

Grindletonians

The Grindletonians were another small Puritan sect with antinomian beliefs, that started in the Lancashire town of Grindleton in the north of England, early in the reign of King James I, lasting until the death of its founder in 1680. The movement started near where the Quaker leader, George Fox, had also started his ministry. Grindletonians stressed an "inner light" of mystical enlightenment, allowing anyone so inspired to preach.

Muggletonians

The Muggletonians was a small, unique sect that grew out of the Ranters, and though always a small congregation, it survived until the 20th century. It was started by a Protestant tailor, Lodowicke Muggleton, who, with his partner, declared in 1651 that they were the last two prophets who had been prophesied in the Book of Revelation. They were well known for putting curses on people who mocked them, which disturbed many well-known people as the malediction often had an effect on them.

Philadelphians

The Philadelphians was a group formed in the 1650s around the Anglican priest and mystic John Pordage who, like so many people at the time, was also studying astrology and alchemy. He was influenced by another Christian mystic, the Lutheran Jacob Boehme. Pordage was rector at a church which was the benefice of Elias Ashmole, who valued Pordage's knowledge of astrology highly. In 1668, a seer known for her visions, Jane Leade, joined Pordage's group, which upon Pordage's death became the Philadelphian Society, a name taken from the Book of Revelation.

The members continued to attend their Anglican churches while maintaining their spiritualist beliefs that the Holy Spirit existed in each person's soul, and by seeking truth through the wisdom of God (Sophia) anyone could become enlightened. After the death of Leade in 1704 the number of followers declined. The numerous books and pamphlets published by the Philadelphian Society, particularly those by Jane Leade, were to influence other groups such as the Behmenists, as well as Christian mystics and esoteric Christians.

Levellers

The Levellers were a political movement of militant Protestants who demanded extended suffrage and religious toleration. They found dedicated support in London and in the New Model Army. Levellers met in taverns and inns, and were known for wearing sprigs of rosemary in their hats for recognition. In 1648 nearly one-third of the inhabitants of London, including many women, were said to have been Levellers. That year they signed a petition to Parliament, bemoaning the king's power over the austere body, and calling for many changes to be made in how Parliament worked.

However, the Grandees in the Army, with the support of the Rump Parliament, marginalized the Levellers and other Dissenters, so that by 1650 they no longer had influence with the new government. That did not stop some over-enthusiastic Levellers, such as the mutinous Miles Sindercombe, from blowing up Whitehall Palace in 1657 in an attempt to assassinate Cromwell.[183]

Diggers

The Diggers, who have been called "Protestant agrarian communists,"[184] were a movement that started during the Civil War, so named because they attempted to farm on common land. The original concept came from a passage about common ownership in the Bible.[185]

The movement rallied against the fact that, following the Inclosure Acts [sic] from 1604 on, the common man had the right to produce his own food taken from him. Enclosure took small landholdings to create one large farm, and former common land could no longer be used communally, creating a working class that then had to work for the landowners. The Diggers were constantly harassed by landowners, imprisoned and tried. Small communes were established mainly in the north of England, but within twenty years the movement had dissipated.

Enthusiasts

Originally the term "enthusiast" had been applied to mystics and prophets who believed they were divinely inspired, though the use was later extended as a general term for Protestants, particularly those that were revelling in their newly won religious freedom after the Commonwealth came into existence. However, following the Glorious Revolution, "enthusiast" became a derogatory word used to describe the excesses and fanaticism of the Puritans, and it was also used to mock Presbyterians after the repeal of the Solemn League and Covenant.

In 1662 the Royal Society introduced byelaws that stipulated the discussion of politics or religion was banned, and anyone discussing these subjects would be expelled for being an "enthusiast." Critics of the Royal Society, such as Meric Casaubon[186] and Henry Stubbe, asserted that the materialism of new science was as detrimental to society as were religious fanatics, with Casaubon calling enthusiasm just "a degree and species of epilepsy."[187] The Royal Society often charged followers of Francis Bacon's ideals as being scientific enthusiasts because they rejected traditional learning in favour of new science.

Imported Dissension

The establishment of the Commonwealth, and the passing of a law in 1649 that abolished kingship, as well as the introduction of the Act of Toleration in 1689, led many European sects to see England as fertile ground for proselytization.

Familists

The Familist sect is the English name given to the "Familia Caritatis," Latin for "Family of Love," that had developed based on the teachings of the Dutch mystic Hendric Niclaes. He had been visiting England from the 1550s and converted a Dutchman who was working in London as a carpenter, Christopher Vitell.[188] Vitell translated and published Niclaes's works, quickly bringing condemnation from the Government, and a censure in 1580 from the Archbishop of Canterbury.

The Familists' view was that Nature, not God, ruled Earth, that heaven and hell were both present on Earth at the same time, and that Satan's influence was mental and never physical. Reginald Scot, a member of Parliament and author of a book on witchcraft, was a Familist. It is said that the Familists continued to prosper until the 1650s when they were also absorbed by the Quaker movement.

Behmenists

Jakob Boehme (Böhme) was a German cobbler who became a famous mystic claiming he had had a divine revelation,[189] and through his numerous books developed a following in Europe and in England in the 1640s. Boehme believed that mankind was in a state of sin, but with God's grace man could restore his state of divine grace. His cosmology consisted of three levels, that of hell or "Dark Fire," the harsh human experience of "Fire Light" and the third, of paradise, being "Light Fire." The Behmenists were a short-lived group and many members eventually joined the Quakers. Boehme's ideas had a lasting influence on German philosophers such as Fredrich Schelling, who was a Behmenist, Georg Hegel and Arthur Schopenhauer. *Aurora*, which Boehme started to write in 1612, but did not finish, was seen as heretical in Germany, causing a scandal across the country. A theologian, Gregorius Richter, condemned it, writing:

> There are as many blasphemies in this shoemaker's book as there are lies; it smells of shoemaker's pitch and filthy blackening. May this insufferable stench be far from us. The Arian poison was not so deadly as this shoemaker's poison.[190]

Camisards

A few members of the Camisards arrived in London in 1706, they were followers of the Huguenot leader Jean Cavalier, who led French Protestant peasants in uprisings against the persecution of Protestants in South France following the Revocation of the Edict of Nantes in 1685. Camisard is the name of the traditional smock worn by French peasants at the time. Cavalier came to England in a regiment of refugees which had taken part in the Spanish expedition with Sir Cloudesley Shovell in 1705. Cavalier was made a general and later Lieutenant-Governor of Jersey. The Camisards in London were a millenarian sect (see below) led by pastors called prophets, notably Élie Marion, whose visions supported the followers. Another English Camisard prophet was Thomas Emes, a doctor of dubious education, called a quacksalver in Dutch, who treated the poor and had joined the Camisards hoping to become famous. The books published by the Camisards are said to have influenced the spiritual outlook of the Swiss philosopher, Jean-Jacques Rousseau, as well as Ann Lee, founder of the millenarian restorationist Christian Shaker movement.

Controversies

Around 1700, memories of the Great Plague and the Great Fire of London continued to fuel ideas of millenarianism, the Second Coming of Christ, and "the End of the World" which were still important topics of conversation from tavern to coffee shop.

We can understand the religious fervour of the age by the large number of churches in the City of London. At the time of the Great Fire, there were eighty-seven churches serving the spiritual needs of the people living in the square mile of the City of London. After the fire, in 1751, we can see from *A General View of the City of London*[25] that at least fourteen of the churches had already been rebuilt. There were many religious controversies at the time, including the Chinese Rites controversy; some of the most important controversies that have a bearing on Freemasonry follow.

Millennialism

There are two similar words in theology that have different meanings; millenarianism, which is also written as millenarism, and millennialism.

Millenarianism refers to a belief in a major transformation of society, often brought about by a dramatic event. Whereas, millennialism is a Christian term based on the prophecy in the Book of Revelation, that Christ will come to Earth a second time, and his kingdom will last a thousand years, which in those times implied "forever." Both words are based on the Latin for thousand "mille," though scholars at the time preferred to use the Greek word for thousand "chilia," resulting in chiliasm sometimes being substituted for millennialism.

In England the strongest proponents of millennialism were the Fifth Monarchists, who were most active during the Interregnum, believing that "King Jesus" was to arrive before 1666 and establish a fifth monarchy. The rout of Venner's Rising, the failed rebellion by the Fifth Monarchists, sealed their fate and those that were not executed

---

[25] See the cover of *Freemasonry: Spiritual Alchemy*

dispersed and may have joined other millennialist groups such as the Diggers or the Quakers.

Many Christian intellectuals at that time were also millennialists such as Thomas Hobbes, John Comenius, Samuel Hartlib, John Milton, Robert Boyle, Isaac Newton and the Platonist philosopher Henry More.[191]

Unitarianism

The Unitarian position was, and still is, that God is one entity, and so Christ is son of God but not God; this was in opposition to the Trinitarian belief that was enforced by the Act of Toleration. Though Unitarianism came to England in the early 1700s from Poland and Lithuania where it had a strong following, it was not established as a formal denomination in England until 1774. Prior to that it was more of a concept that was part of the theological argument of the time. Being an anti-Trinitarian doctrine, followers of Unitarianism were severely persecuted.

One of those followers was Arthur Bury, rector of the University of Oxford, and the author of the *Naked Gospel* published in 1690. This book was ordered to be burned and Bury was charged with Socinianism, the concept of the pre-existence of Christ, thus losing his university post.[192] Over the following ten years more than twenty books were published either attacking or defending the opinions in the *Naked Gospel*, including books by luminaries such as John Locke and the Deist author, Matthew Tindal. Twelve years later Bury published his last book *The rational Deist satisfy'd by a just account of the Gospel* which did not stir up as much passion as the *Naked Gospel*; he died ten years later, in 1712.

Atheism

It has been said that the Reformation had attacked the authority of the Catholic Church and, in a similar manner, freethinkers and others attacked the authority of the Protestant movement.[193] The concepts of Atheism and Deism started to get noticed in France, Germany and the Netherlands through the works of philosophers such as Baruch Spinoza who wrote his *Short Treatise on God, Man, and His Well-Being* in 1661, though published posthumously. In his lifetime he was labelled an atheist because he used the word God in a different, more impersonal way, than was used in the traditional Judeo-Christian monotheism. As the American philosopher Frank Thilly said, "Spinoza expressly denies personality and consciousness to God; He has neither intelligence, feeling, nor will; He does not act according to purpose, but everything follows necessarily from His nature, according to law."[194]

The German religious critic, Matthias Knutzen, the Polish philosopher and former Jesuit, Kazimierz Lyszczynski, and the French priest, Jean Meslier, all followed openly atheistic positions. In England however, John Locke wrote that the government should not tolerate atheism, as a denial of God's existence would result in social chaos.[195] Voltaire, who was also a critic of atheism, emphasized that the fear of God was an important factor in maintaining social order and is famous for having said, "If God did not exist, it would be necessary to invent Him!"

The argument over atheism continued well into the 1770s, with the philosopher Edmund Burke denouncing atheism and Baron d'Holbach in France promoting it. As it is chronologically outside the timeframe of the beginnings of Speculative Freemasonry, it is necessary to leave the conversation here, except to say that atheism was vigorously opposed in Britain. Atheism was summed up by the Deist philosopher and friend of John Locke, Anthony Collins, who wrote, "Ignorance is the foundation of atheism, and freethinking the cure of it" [196]

Deism

The word Deism comes from the Latin word for God, "Deus." There is a similar word for God in Greek, "Theos," that forms the English word Theism. Again, there is a slight difference in their usage; both Deists and Theists believe in one Almighty God, but the Theist believes that God remains active and interested in the world of His creation, whereas the Deist believes God has left control to the beings He created.[197] Deists rejected the notion that God, whom they referred to as Divine Providence and the Supreme Being, would reveal His plans for creation, and taught that revelation as a source of guidance was spurious. To Deists what was important was observation of Nature and the powers of reason. During the 1600s, the two terms,

Deist and Theist, were used interchangeably, and though the term Deist first appeared in the 1621 book *The Anatomy of Melancholy*,[198] interest in Deism grew quickly in England between 1690 and 1740. The term Theism is first attributed to the theologian Ralph Cudworth from his 1671 book, *The True Intellectual System of the Universe: the first part, wherein all the reason and philosophy of atheism is confuted and its impossibility demonstrated* where the term Theism was used as the opposite of atheism.

During the Enlightenment, Deism became a subject of much discussion among the intelligentsia. In Europe, the Enlightenment is considered as having started in the 1700s, but in England it is recognized as having started with the publication of Sir Francis Bacon's book, *New Atlantis*, in 1627. By the time of the Interregnum all ideas were being challenged, not just Trinitarianism and other Christian concepts, but also the accuracy of the Bible, miracles and the existence of the supernatural. This was brought about by advances in science, such as astronomy, where the theories of Copernicus and Kepler could be verified, challenging the Catholic Church's outdated opinions. An example of Biblical accuracy that Newton challenged was to be found in the First Epistle of John, "For there are three that bear record in heaven, the Father, the Word, and the Holy Ghost: and these three are one."[199] Newton, who was a scholar of Greek, knew that the description "and these three are one" was not to be found in the original Greek Bible but had been added during the writing of the authorized King James Bible to justify the doctrine of the Trinity.

Scientists such as Newton were discovering laws of Nature that were not only supported by repeated testing, but also showed that these laws, not God, controlled nature. The widely held belief was that God had put everything into motion, but then was no longer concerned with day to day operations, so the universe was thought of as a vast machine that worked without divine intervention. Also, the study of science, in particular geometry and astrology, was equated with seeking and worshiping God, as the universe was constructed on those harmonic principles.

> The Church's view of the universe as a fixed unchanging system existing through divinely produced order was replaced by a clockwork-like, mechanistic universe.[200]

The Bible was also viewed differently, it was no longer the infallible word of God, but rather the writings of a different culture that was Jewish rather than Christian. The West was now trading with dozens of countries outside the Mediterranean, unlike the Tudors, which brought new cultures and religious diversity to England, especially in London. Jesuits had brought the teachings of Confucius from China and translated them into Latin, which had a strong influence on Enlightenment philosophers, who considered integrating this unique system of morality into Christianity.[201, 202]

Within Deism there were several factions and the more radical Deists rejected Christianity outright, calling it mere superstition, to which Christian apologists accused the Deists of being atheists. Professor of philosophy, James Force explains:

> Defining the essence of English deism is a formidable task. Like priestcraft, atheism, and freethinking, deism was one of the dirty words of the age. Deists were stigmatized – often as atheists – by their Christian opponents, as the 17th century minister William Stephens said, 'DEISM is a denial of all reveal'd Religion.'[203]

The "Father of Deism" is considered to be Lord Herbert of Cherbury, who defined Deism in his book *De Veritate* written in 1624. Later, Matthew Tindal's book *Christianity as Old as Creation* written in 1730 was quickly adopted as the Deist bible. Other notable Deists included John Toland (1670–1722), Thomas Woolston (1669–1731), William Wollastson (1659–1724), Charles Blount (1654–1693), Thomas Chubb (1679–1747), the Jacobite Henry St John 1st Viscount Bolingbroke (1678–1751), Anthony Collins (1676–1729) and Peter Annet (1693–1769). These last four were also known for either doubting or even denying the immortality of the soul.[204]

The Assembly of the Divines

As mentioned in the section on the Long parliament and Oliver Cromwell, the Assembly of Divines was a council of 140 theologians established by the Long Parliament just before the beginning of the First Civil War, that met for the first time in 1643. Its objective was to bring the Anglican Church into closer conformity with the Presbyterian Church of Scotland. However, disagreements over

church government meant that little was achieved, though a *Directory for Public Worship* was written in 1644 to replace the Book of Common Prayer, and was adopted by Parliament the next year. Some of the Assembly's recommendations were even taken up by Scottish Presbyterians. The divines were particularly concerned with antinomians, people who believed that civil law was not relevant for Christians, a position the divines believed was even more threatening than Catholicism.

Predestination

Initially, the Assembly was committed to the reformed Calvinistic doctrine of predestination, the concept that God had chosen certain people to be saved and enjoy eternal life, rather than eternal punishment. There was another position, that Christ had died with the purpose only to save those who were eternally chosen to be saved, a doctrine called "particular redemption." A third view was that of "hypothetical universalism," where Christ's death, as well as saving those who had been chosen, offered salvation to all people on condition that they believe in him. These three concepts of predestination were argued over by the Divines, and eventually a position close in wording to hypothetical universalism was adopted.

Purgatory

The idea of praying for the dead may have started in early Judaism, as it was part of the grieving process. Originally, Catholic purgatory was not a place but a temporary condition, though later it was thought of as an annex to hell, however, the laity were taught that if they could complete penance in their lifetime, they would escape purgatory, so it also was thought of as an entrance to Heaven. Pope Gregory the Great wrote in around 590 AD, "And yet is it more clear than day that the souls of them that be perfect, do, straight after death, possess the joys

of heaven," but he then added that sinners suffered in a "purgatory fire" after death, and this image has persisted. The fire was said to burn away all evil the individual had attracted to himself and leave only a pure soul, the truth. The soul was then able to stand in the presence of God, known as the Beatification. The idea of the soul being purified by fire was an anathema to the Eastern Orthodox Church and was one of the factors contributing to the schism of 1054.

A doctrine of purgatory came to dominate medieval eschatology. The Catholic Church had changed its stance on immortality at the Council of Florence in 1439 introducing the doctrine of purgatory, dictating that the souls of the dead were conscious and "capable of pain or joy even prior to the resurrection of their bodies," which was again endorsed at the Fifth Council of the Lateran 1512–1517. At this council it was decreed that "souls stay in purgatory temporarily to be purified for entering heaven," based on a disputed verse in Corinthians (below), which incensed the Protestant reformer Martin Luther.

In the Bible there is little to support a concept of purgatory, except in Matthew, "whosoever speaketh a word against the Son of man, it shall be forgiven him: but whosoever speaketh against the Holy Ghost, it shall not be forgiven him, neither in this world, neither in the world to come."[205] Paul states;

> Every man's work shall be made manifest: for the day shall declare it, because it shall be revealed by fire; and the fire shall try every man's work of what sort it is. If any man's work abide which he hath built thereupon, he shall receive a reward. If any man's work shall be burned, he shall suffer loss: but he himself shall be saved; yet so as by fire.[206]

Starting in the 11th century, to help those in purgatory, the family of the deceased could buy indulgences from the Church (from, for example, the Pardoner in Chaucer's *Canterbury Tales*) or pay to have Masses said for them, and this would shorten their suffering. The idea that redemption could be bought was also abhorrent to Luther. A jingle written by a Dominican priest illustrates this concept well:

> As soon as a coin in the coffers rings,
> the soul from purgatory springs. [207]

There were other ways of helping a soul out of purgatory besides praying and alms, such as confession and pilgrimages. Knights going on crusades would often buy indulgences or pay for masses to be said for them in advance for forgiveness of their future sins. The Church claimed that the money received from selling indulgences was used for building new churches, but even by the time of Chaucer (1343-1400) people knew the system was corrupt, and was just a money-making enterprise for Catholics. The nascent Church of England took an ambivalent position concerning purgatory when it issued the original Ten Articles of Faith of the Church of England in 1536, which were expanded in 1571 to the Thirty-nine articles. It was stated that the laity could pray for the dead, though "the place where [departed souls] be, the name thereof, and kind of pains there" were "uncertain by scripture."

Immortality

The English theologian and chemist, Joseph Priestly, said that the division of body and soul was "originally a doctrine of Oriental philosophy," that had spread into the West. The early Church fathers added to that concept Greek Platonism, resulting in a combined concept of a Last Judgement with that of an immortal soul.

One of the theological arguments that concerned people during the Restoration and after was whether humans possessed an immortal soul that could be destroyed. The difficulty was that the Bible provides little guidance about immortality, for example in the Old Testament Ezekiel states:

> Behold, all souls are Mine;
> The soul of the father
> As well as the soul of the son is Mine;
> The soul who sins shall die. [208]

In the New Testament Christ taught:

> And do not fear those who kill the body but cannot kill the
> soul. But rather fear Him who is able to destroy both soul and
> body in hell (Gehenna). [209]

In I Corinthians Paul introduces the concept of the "sleeping dead" saying that humans do not have immortality, but they have to "put on immortality" so that "Death is swallowed up in Victory."[210]

To explain this problem, early interpreters of the Bible taught that God, rather than the text of the Bible itself, was absolute. Also, changes were made to the Bible by each new denomination to further their interpretation of Scripture, and it was also claimed that the pursuit of "natural knowledge" led to the abandonment of a correct, literal understanding of Scripture.

The early Protestant reaction to the concept of immortality was exemplified by Martin Luther's reaction to the Fifth Council of the Lateran, initiated by Pope Julius II and concluded by Pope Leo X. The Council defined the Catholic Church's position on the immortality of the soul: "according to the canon of Pope Clement V the soul is immortal, and we decree that all who adhere to ... erroneous assertions shall be shunned and punished as heretics." Martin Luther issued his *Ninety-five Theses* seven months after the end of the Council, and was particularly incensed by the declaration on immortality, as he believed that the human soul was not naturally immortal, a position known as Christian mortalism. Luther exclaimed: "he [the pope] is emperor of the world and king of heaven, an earthly god; that the soul is immortal; and all these endless monstrosities in the Roman dunghill of decrees."

Mortalism

In Christianity there is a concept called mortalism that states that the soul is not 'naturally' immortal. After death the body enters an intermediate state like a coma waiting for the day of Judgement when it will be resurrected. This opinion is based on a passage in the Bible where the Apostle Paul describes the dead being asleep.[211] People who did not agree with this used the term "soul sleep" pejoratively when talking about mortalism.

In Christian denominations, as well as Judaism, the souls of the departed are said to "Rest in Peace," based on a passage in the Book of Matthew.[212] Calvin also believed that the soul was not naturally immortal, and that immortality was something that could only be received from God.

Attached to the image of *The Catalogue of the several Sects and Opinions* (p.138) are short poems for each image; about "Soule Sleepers" it states:

> That souls are mortal, some have dar'd to say,
> And by their lives, this folly some bewray;
> Whilst (like the beast) they only live to eat,
> In sinfull pleasures wast their time and state:
> Meantime forgetting all immortality,
> To woe or joy for all eternity.

A second popular concept, that was championed by Milton, used the Greek term "thnetopsychism" meaning "mortal soul." This stated that when the body died, so did the soul, and on the day of Judgement both would be brought back to life, based on a passage in the Book of Timothy.[213] However, in a later unfinished religious manifesto, *De Doctrina Christiana*, Milton contradicted himself referring to the dead as asleep. Thnetopsychism appealed to many of the intelligentsia of the time such as Thomas Hobbes, John Locke and Isaac Newton.[214]

Together with the concept of mortalism, was the other side of the coin, annihilationism, a Christian belief that at the Last Judgement the souls of those people who are not saved will be annihilated, without the state of purgatory, leaving only the righteous to live on in immortality. This theory is found in the Book of Revelation and evangelical Christianity starting from the 1800s.

In Catholicism it is part of the catechism that after death souls enter purgatory for purification before entering heaven. This belief is based on a disputed verse in Corinthians,[215] and so for the Catholic Church soul mortality was a serious heresy, based on the edict of the Fifth Council of the Lateran. Opponents of Catholicism used arguments based on mortalism to challenge Catholic doctrines such as purgatory and holding masses for the dead.[216]

In Judaism the concept of mortalism did not exist, rabbinical teaching insisted that the dead were not saved by God. Jews were more concerned that their descendants flourished, and the dead just ended up in a dark underworld, Sheol. In Genesis, Jacob thought he had to descend into the underworld to find his son Joseph. The prophets Enoch and Elijah entered heaven "without experiencing death," and the ghost of Samuel is summoned up from the dead by the Witch of Endor.[217] In the Hebrew Old Testament, the soul (nepes) or spirit (ruah) were not portrayed as immortal substances, but rather as life-forces associated with breath. The idea of a soul entering Paradise was a post-exile concept, and even the idea of resurrection is only found in the last-written books of the Old Testament."[218] After 167 BC, following the slaughter of the Maccabees who were hiding in the desert and refused to defend themselves on the Sabbath, [219] the idea of resurrection started to be accepted so that the martyrs would not be left unvindicated.

Though much was written on the subject of mortalism, two publications of the period just before the Revival of Freemasonry gained considerable attention. The first was a series of pamphlets that was published between 1692 and 1704, where the author, Henry Layton, a not so well-known philosopher, negated the concept of immortality of the soul. Taking the opposite view was Thomas Browne, a doctor, who like so many of the era, was interested in both theology and the occult. He published a book in 1642, in the time of Charles I, called *Religio Medici* (The Physician's Religion) which he intended that only a few friends would read, but it was published without his knowledge and became very popular. In it, Browne analysed many Protestant concepts about the Last Judgement and the Resurrection, and also affirmed the existence of angels, as well as supporting the idea of mortalism, that the soul was not naturally immortal. Though Browne later published an edited edition in 1645 taking out some of his more controversial ideas, the book still ended up on the Catholic *Index of Prohibited Books*, which probably increased its popularity among

Protestants in both England and Europe. Surprisingly, both the unauthorized edition of *Religio Medici*, and the later authorized edition, were both published by the same man, Andrew Crooke. By the reign of King Charles II, Browne was very much in favour with the king, who saw fit to knight Browne in 1671.

Heaven and the Afterlife

Christianity's emphasis on the quality on one's soul and the possibility of immortality changed people's understanding of an afterlife. Bacon is quoted as saying, ""I have often thought upon death, and I find it the least of all evils."[220] Another contemporaneous writer, Henry King, the Bishop of Chichester, wrote a poem for the funeral of his wife, mourning her loss and hoping to meet her again in the afterlife, writing that she would know when he was there as:

> my pulse, like a soft drum, beats my approach, tells thee I come.[221]

Though hell and purgatory were disputed, no-one disagreed that Heaven existed. The proof could be found in the first chapter of Genesis, where Heaven in Hebrew was called Shamayim שָׁמַיִם The name is made up of the two words: "sky" שָׁם which itself was derived from the Assyrian word for fire, and "water." מַיִם

ref. [222]

A common medieval concept of entering Heaven was that of ascending a ladder, similar to Jacob's ladder. The theologian Thomas Aquinas wrote that language was not sufficient to be able to describe Heaven, it could only be inferred. The Bible was also ambiguous concerning Heaven, as Paul wrote in Corinthians:

> I knew a man in Christ above fourteen years ago, (whether in the body, I cannot tell; or whether out of the body, I cannot tell: God knoweth;) such an one caught up to the third heaven.[223]

Medieval theologians taught of three heavens; the first was the physical experience of the vault of Heaven and included the influence of celestial objects, the second was the realm of the righteous and sages, and the third was the Imperium and the *experience* of the blinding presence of God, but even then, the soul would not be able to see God. Though Catholics taught that the faithful were all part of the family of the Church, and that just by being a member of a church they would be eligible to enter Heaven, by the doctrine of Sola Fide, or justification by faith alone, Protestants however, believed that each was accountable for his or her actions and would have to come to terms with God at the final judgment. During the reign of the Stuarts, following the repeal of Elizabeth I's Act of Uniformity in 1650, various dissenters promoted a different form of Heaven, probably based on Marcello Ficino's ideas, that Heaven was within one. On this Milton wrote, "the mind is its own place, and in itself can make a Heaven of hell, a hell of Heaven."[224]

Prayer Book

The Book of Common Prayer was first written in 1549 following the English Reformation of 1534, that had been initiated by the Act of Supremacy. However, several changes had been made to the Prayer Book by the time James I decided to update it in 1604. It was only in 1662 after the Restoration that more Protestant demands, and especially some Presbyterian ones, were included; this Prayer Book was in use in Great Britain until 1928. The result of the revisions was that there was a greater appreciation of the cooperative role of the monarch and the Church in the Christian state of Britain.

From the start of editing the Prayer Book in 1662 there were controversies. The Presbyterians argued that the congregation should not be allowed to say prayers, and that they should only be allowed to say the refrain "Amen." Also, among other demands, any vestige of Catholic ceremony had to be expunged, such as the prayer for the dead. In the end about 600 changes were made to the Prayer Book, mostly in favour of High Church Anglicans. [225] Another area of contention was about the "Black Rubric;" originally directions, called rubrics, in the Prayer Book such as "kneel" where printed in red ink, but in the revised Prayer Book one important rubric was printed in black. It was the requirement that recipients of Holy Communion should kneel to receive the Host. It centred on the argument whether kneeling to receive the Host was adoration of the bread and wine and therefore acknowledging transubstantiation, which was in contradiction to the Test Act.

Though the language of the 1662 Prayer Book had not changed much, the fact that the Black Rubric was included meant that 936 lay ministers who did not accept the revisions, had to leave the ministry. Following the publication of the new Prayer Book, there were still attempts by various factions to implement further changes. In the 1690s one of the more interesting proposed changes was the attempt to include a prayer, called a collect, for the Fifth of November to remember the Gun Powder Plot; a part of the prayer read, "God...who didst miraculously preserve our Church and State from the secret Contrivance and hellish Malice of Popish Conspirators;" obviously sentiments still ran strong more than eighty years after the event. William III landed on the shores of England on the anniversary of the Gunpowder Plot, but eighty years later he is fondly remembered in the collect as, "[he] didst give us a mighty Deliverance from the open Tyranny and oppression of the same Cruel and Blood-thirsty Enemies."

In 1689, King William III asked John Tillotson, the Dean of Canterbury Cathedral, to set up a commission to consider further revisions that would allow for more latitude to incorporate some Presbyterian requests. Tillotson headed the *Liturgy of Comprehension* committee, but the committee members did not even bother to meet to discuss the appeals, and the Book of Common Prayer remained without change.

A Touch Piece

Despite the posturing and arguments over the nuance of religious texts, in England there still lingered a touch of superstition, not only that but the "King's Touch" was seen as the miracle of the Stuart era. Shakespeare refers to it in Macbeth, first performed in 1606:

> The mere despair of surgery, he cures,
> Hanging a golden stamp about their necks,
> Put on with holy prayers.
> And, 'tis spoken,
> To the succeeding royalty he leaves
> The healing benediction.[226]

The idea that a monarch could heal with his touch came from the idea that a king was sacred. The kings of England gave out coins to the sick that they had blessed in the belief that the coins ("golden stamp") could cure people of illness. Though a similar thing had been done in ancient Rome, in Britain it had started in 1206, when William the Lion, King of Scotland, purportedly healed a child with scrofula (tuberculosis) by touching him, the so-called "King's Touch."[227] Scrofula became known as "Morbus Regius" or the King's Disease, and in France, "Le Mal de Roi"[228] – coffee, that was imported for the first time in the 1660s, was once thought to relieve the symptoms of this disease.

The Royal Gift of Healing

These coins or amulets were given out at Holy Communion, and were especially minted for that purpose, some carrying the inscription "diabolus vicit" (devil defeated) on them.[229] The idea that monarchs had a God-given power to heal was an extension of the idea that they had been appointed by God, their "Divine Right." The ceremony had at one time also been included in the Book of Common Prayer. The expression "touch-and-go" was first recorded in 1645, and probably meant that even after receiving the King's Touch it was not certain that the patient would survive.

Like many things in the 17th century, the superstition of the king's healing power ended with Queen Anne, and was last performed in 1714. When George I ascended the throne, he stopped the practice calling it "too Catholic." In Britain, the monarch still gives out specially minted coins on Maunday Thursday, a tradition that was started in the 1200s, but these are viewed more as alms than amulets, and the coins are legal tender. The idea of a lucky coin still survives with the traditional English Christmas pudding, a steamed fruit cake with a small coin hidden inside. It seems that reason will never win out over superstition.

160

Summary

The Reformation started with Martin Luther in 1517, but rather than being reformed, the Catholic Church was split up, leading to Protestants feeling they were free from the corrupt and controlling Church of Rome. New Christian denominations had come out of the darkness into the light and thought they were in a better position to teach the authentic word of God.

During the Stuart era we see a change in attitudes concerning religion, where Catholics were willing to pretend to be Anglicans to save their skin, whereas Dissenters were still persecuted for their beliefs and either voluntarily exiled themselves or lost their lives for their cause. Religious freedom, that was won at such a great cost, encouraged Dissenters to demand equal rights and push for reforms, such as a new Book of Common Prayer.

In the latter part of the Stuart era, we also see elements of Freemasonry starting to develop, such as Calvin and the Architect of Universe, the abhorrence of atheism, the importance of Geometry in Deism, and the argument about immortality.

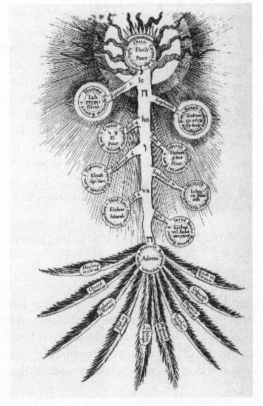

Sephirothic Kabbalah: Tree of Life by Robert Fludd drawn c1620

Ch. 5 Lodge, Laboratory and Temple

The performance of the three degrees does not happen in a vacuum, and though there are no backdrops or props used in the ritual, the Lodge itself contains important lessons for Masons. The First Degree is set in the outer chamber of King Solomon's Temple, the Second Degree in the middle chamber but the Third Degree actually takes place as "Hiram" is leaving the Inner Chamber.

I believe that Michelspacher's etching *Conjunction* (see *Freemasonry: Spiritual Alchemy*) was the template for the Lodge design; we can see many similar elements such as stars on the ceiling, the movement of the sun through the Lodge and a blindfolded man. Before the Revival in 1717, and for a long time afterwards, Lodge meetings were held in taverns, and as we can see from the Palser Plate,[26] some changes such as the designs on aprons, were introduced at a later date. Unlike the First and Second Degrees, there are no steganographic Signposts in this degree. They are summarized in *Freemasonry: Royal Arch*.

The Situation of a Lodge - Four Cardinal Directions

Here I wish to consider the alignment of the Lodge. A candidate joins Freemasonry in a state of darkness, what we term "spiritual poverty," and is first placed in the north. The north is a place of darkness, meaning unenlightenment. This is where the candidate starts his Masonic Journey.

This idea comes from the fact that in the past, suicides, executed criminals, and children who had died unbaptized, were buried in the north outside the churchyard, or on the sunless side of the church. So, the new candidate is seated in the north to show that he is spiritually unenlightened. In contrast to this, the east represents wisdom and spirituality, and the west, strength and reason.

---

[26] See *Freemasonry: Spiritual Alchemy*

The south epitomizes beauty and enlightenment, the mid-point between the spiritual intuition of the east and the rational understanding of the west. This balance is what all Masons aim to achieve.

The Kabbalah was a major component of Renaissance thought, and the three pillars of the *Tree of Life* in the Kabbalah similarly represent Severity and Mercy, with Balance in the middle. When the candidate stands in the south, the west pillar on the left would represent Severity (male), and the east pillar on the right, Mercy (female).[230] The middle pillar is also associated with holism and integration, and at the same time represents the alchemical balance between the Kabbalistic male and female pillars.[231] The pillar in the south is diametrically opposite the north, the place of ignorance, as those who are unenlightened receive information based on their five physical senses alone.

A candidate's journey in the Lodge also indicates a progressive mode of consciousness. In the north the candidate starts out by relying on impressions from the five senses, in the west he learns about intellectual reason, and in the east about spiritual intuition, arriving at a position of balance in the south, what we term enlightenment.

The candidate's education is not just about cardinal points. In each degree the Lodge represents a different part of the Temple of Solomon; like a theatre without backdrops or props, it changes in our mind's eye to align with the ritual. The important thing to remember is that the Lodge has been designed as a "power centre" or as we call it now, a "power spot," that empowers the ritual work that we do.[232] This adds not just energy, but also a degree of spirituality, to the performance of the degrees, through the use of several simple methods, such as sensory deprivation, circumambulation and the use of darkness and light.

Kabbalah - Stage Directions

The movement of Hiram's body to three positions in the Lodge is not arbitrary; with all the thought that has gone into constructing the three degrees, this had to have an important significance. I believe the first three Grand Masters used the elements of the Kabbalistic *Tree of Life* to both use as stage directions for the ritual and to spiritually tie the Christian mystery play to a Jewish philosophy.

As is given in the Scottish Rite Lodge of Perfection (4th Degree), "The early ritualists, whoever they were, adapted the symbolism of this system (Kabbalah) and used it to conceal some of the deeper truths which lie within the fertile fields of Masonic thought. They borrowed so heavily from this tradition that a complete understanding of Freemasonry is impossible without some familiarity with the Kabbalah."[233]

The Tree of Life

The word "Kabbalah" has its root in the Hebrew word "Qibel" meaning "to receive by oral tradition." So, whereas the Torah teaches the Law of Moses, and is a tenet of Judaism, the Kabbalah is a secret knowledge that showed a way to communicate directly with God, and was only taught orally to men of a certain age.

In the 16th century, Rabbi Isaac Luria, (1534-1572) known as ARI, redacted the *Sefer Yetzirah*, the Book of Creation, the earliest book on Jewish esotericism, to harmonize it with another sacred Jewish book, the *Zohar*, known in English as the Hebrew Book of "Splendour" or "Radiance" that is the essential work on Jewish mystical thought that we know as Kabbalah.[234] The *Zohar* introduced the concepts of the "Tree of Life" and the "Lightning Strike." ARI realized that man had alienated himself from God (known in Christianity as "the Fall of Man") so he drew the pattern of the Tree of Life to reflect this. The Lightning Strike shows the order in which God created the world, and conversely the order that spiritual work (known as "pathworking") should be done for man to return to God.

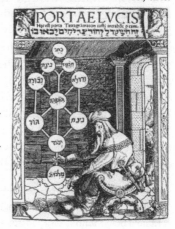

One of the earliest images of the Tree of Life comes from the 1516 edition of *Portae Lucis* by Paolo Riccio (right), a Latin translation of Gikatilla's *Gates of Light*. This was expanded on by Robert Fludd in his *Sephirothic Kabbalah: Tree of Life* drawn c1620 (see p. 160). As can be seen, the mystical sephirah "Da'at" is not evident in either drawing.

There are ten positions ("sephirah," plural is "sephirot") on the Tree of Life, but only seven Lodge officers occupy positions that match the sephirot when the Tree of Life is mapped on to the floor of the Lodge - it is the empty sephirot that are of interest to Freemasons.[27]

The Tree of Life is formed from three triangles, one on top of the other, with a single point at the bottom. The first triangle is Aziluth, the world of archetypes, made by the positions of the Master, Secretary and Treasurer. The second triangle, Briah the world of creation, is inverted and joins the altar, the Junior Warden and a "Warden in the north." When the triangle was inverted a hidden sephira, Da'at, meaning "knowledge," was exposed.

In most constitutions of Freemasonry, we understand there is no such position as a Warden in the north, though in some European constitutions there is, but more importantly, the position is important for the Hiramic Tragedy. The third triangle, Yetzirah, the world of formation, is also inverted and is created by the Inner Guard, the Pursuivant[28] and a point between the Senior Warden and the altar known as Yesod. The single sephirah, Malkhut, represents the material world (Assirah) and the Senior Warden. The positions of the officers and the sephirot are not just coincidental, they have a meaning that relates to the Ritual (see below).

---

[27] There is no consensus on the Anglicized spelling of the ten sephirot.

[28] Mainly only found in Grand Lodges

The Tree of Life depicts the situation of the Jews during the Diaspora, who felt they were separated from their Maker due to their transgressions, as recorded in the Bible. This is represented by an impassable gap between the first and second triangle, Da'at, which is the point of the higher consciousness, a great abyss that is the gateway into the afterworld.[235]

The Tree of Life is also known as the Ladder, which appears as Jacob's Ladder in the Bible, as well as in the Blue Lodge and in a different form in both Scottish and York Rites; this is an extremely important symbol that so few Masons truly understand. We can see from the Tree of Life, when overlaid on the Lodge, that the sephirah of Tipareth, representing spirituality, balance, integration, beauty and compassion, is at the position of the altar and Bible, and I believe that this is another reason why the altar is generally in the middle of a Lodge, not in the east as in Christian churches.

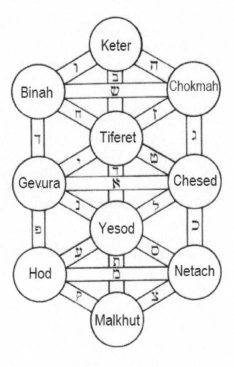

In the 18th century, Rabbi Vilna Gaon, (1720-1797) known as GRA, further edited the Tree of Life to show its perfected pattern where the lower two worlds of Briah and Yetzirah are inverted, and Da'at displaced. This was to give the exiled Jews hope that through their spiritual labours they would be able to restore man to his rightful position next to the Creator. However, this teaching would not have been known at the time of the Revival.

166

The Hiramic Tragedy on the Tree of Life

Though all the ten positions are important, the Hiramic Tragedy centres on three positions; interestingly, these sephirot are purposely not occupied by Lodge officers. This is important as it shows that the correlation is not coincidental but deliberate.

Gevura is where the Grand Master was slain. Gevura is about judging humanity in general. It is the foundation of the absolute adherence to the letter of the law, and strictly meting out justice.

Da'at is a sephirah that is only exposed in the ARI Tree of Life. It is where the Ruffians temporarily concealed their crime. It means "knowledge" and is the mystical state where all ten sephirot in the Tree of Life are united as one. Here it represents the death of the consciousness, a period of darkness (Dark Night of the Soul) followed by a rebirth into a higher consciousness with the Word (Logos) at Yesod.

In many Lodges, Masons are not allowed to cross "between the Lights," in other words between the VSL and the Master, and refers to the sephirah Da'at. It may be based on an ancient superstition that it is unlucky to walk over a dead man's grave. Secondly, it may be that the Brother would temporarily block the Worshipful Master's view of the Three Great Lights.

Yesod is where the Ruffians thought they had successfully hidden evidence of their crime, that is on the brow of a hill west of Mount Moriah. In the Kabbalah, Yesod is the foundation

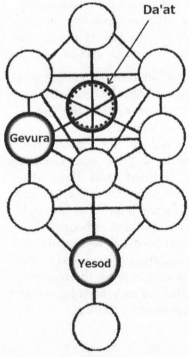

The Hiramic Tragedy

upon which God has built the world, which in Christian terms is Christ. Later the Brethren gather here before raising the Grand Master, in the same way that the disciples mourned at Christ's grave, prior to his Ascension.

Finally, it would not have been lost on the Grand Masters that the three sephirot Da'at, Gevurah and Yesod join up to form Kepler's Triangle and the triangle of the Pythagorean Theorem. So, we can see that a lot of thought was given in how to arrange the Lodge to perfectly fit the ARI Tree of Life. As the teachings of the Tree of Life are harmonious with those of Freemasonry, it was in this way that the first three Grand Masters were able to make the Lodge a bridge between Christianity and Judaism. Similar goals were being sought by Wren with his "ghost geometry" for St. Paul's Cathedral, John Evelyn's plan for the new City of London that also incorporated the Tree of Life,[29] as well as the mission of Christian Knorr von Rosenroth.

Francis Bacon's *New Atlantis*

I believe that to appeal to intellectuals, especially members of the Royal Society at that time, the first three Grand Masters included in the ritual certain hints that allude to Bacon's dream of building a college of sages. Bacon called this Salomon's House, "the very eye of the kingdom," represented by the "All Seeing Eye." To which order "God of heaven and earth had vouchsafed the grace to know the works of Creation, and the secrets of them," that is, by the use of alchemy, as well as "to discern between divine miracles, works of nature, works of art, and impostures and illusions of all sorts." [236] It is now understood that Bacon's story of Atlantis is based on an earlier work, Plato's myth of Atlantis in *Timaeus* c.360 BC.

Salomon's House

Bacon's *New Atlantis* is on a mythical island, Bensalem, which was supposedly discovered off the coast of Peru by the crew of a European ship after they got lost in the Pacific Ocean. Salomon's House was to Bensalem what Solomon's Temple is to Freemasonry.

---

[29] For these references please see *Freemasonry: Initiation by Light*

There are at least seven correspondences with Speculative Free-masonry:[237]

1   Salomon's House had three Masters who ruled it and made decisions. "Then after diverse meetings and consults of our whole number, to consider of the former labours and collections, we have three that take care out of them to direct new experiments, of a higher light, more penetrating into nature than the former. These we call lamps."

2   Visitors were not allowed to go more than one and half miles from the city "within their tedder," which meant within their cable tow. (The word tedder is related to "tether").

3   The inhabitants of Bensalem were very careful about allowing strangers onto the island. They had "Interdicts and Prohibitions" on how they could gain entrance.

4   The college sent out missions of three members for research, the same way that three Craftsmen went in search of Grand Master Hiram.

5   Members of Salomon's House were called "Merchants of Light." In a similar way Freemasons are "Sons of Light."

6   Special members in Bensalem wore a Jewel of an Ear of Wheat, which relates to the Fellow Craft degree.

7   Salomon's House was "an ideal government based on the brotherhood of man," Freemasonry as well.

In *New Atlantis*, the European visitors are received by the Father of Salomon's House who shows them around Bensalem. There were three examiners at the college; the governor of the House of Strangers, the Head of Salomon's House, and Joabin the Jew. Considering the times and the widespread prejudice against Jews, this last examiner was an interesting choice, though he appears to be a Christianized Jew.[238] Some have suggested that, as Joabin is educated in matters of government, he might be the ruler of Bensalem, [239] others have suggested that Joabin may have been the model for Hiram Abif.

Bacon saw Salomon's House as the ideal scientific research establishment, where people could concentrate on a subject without worrying about money, grants, or rivalry. In a similar way, I believe, the first three Grand Masters devised the Lodge to be an institution for experimental spiritual alchemy.

Another Point

Squaring Stones to Construct King Solomon's Temple

The reason that tools of metal were not used in the construction of the temple was because in the Bible Moses was told to build a temple on Mount Ebal, "And there shalt thou build an altar unto the Lord thy God, an altar of stones: thou shalt not lift up any iron tool upon them," [240] and King Solomon extended this command to mean any and all temples. However, that requirement makes it very difficult to square the stones.

In the Middle Ages there was a story about a Schamir, also known as Samur, a mythical worm that eats stone.[241] The story may have been invented by ecclesiastic authorities to explain this quandary, as reputedly the worm showed King Solomon how to prepare the stones for his temple without using tools of iron. The Schamir itself had been called the Philosophers' Stone, though these medieval stories were probably derived from a passage in the Bible.[242]

In the Third Degree we learn that there were 153,303 workers on King Solomon's Temple. 153,303 is an odd composite number, it is composed of three distinct prime numbers multiplied together: 3 x 137 x 373, and each number uses only three prime numbers, 1, 3 or 7. When we read I Kings chapter five, we see that the number of people employed was slightly different:

> [13] And King Solomon raised a levy out of all Israel; and the levy was <u>thirty thousand men</u>. [14] And he sent them to Lebanon, ten thousand a month by courses: a month they were in Lebanon, and two months at home: and Adoniram was over the levy. [15] And Solomon had <u>threescore and ten thousand</u> that bare burdens, and <u>fourscore thousand</u> hewers in the mountains; [16] beside the chief of Solomon's officers which were over the work, <u>three thousand and three hundred</u>, which ruled over the people that wrought in the work.

There were 153,303 workers at the temple (including three Grand Masters), and in the mountains, but also another thirty thousand helping to cut trees in Lebanon, so 183,303 men in total were employed in building the temple. However, this number does not have a unique mathematical property.

Summary

In this chapter we saw that the Lodge has been overlaid on the Tree of Life to incorporate the wisdom of the Kabbalah.

Added to this are the alchemical teachings; the First Degree lights the fire in the furnace; it awakens the spiritual spark in the candidate. The Second Degree helps us find the secret elixir – the dew – and shows us how to purify it. The Third Degree introduces us to the two main elements of alchemy, Mercury (King Solomon) and Sulphur (King of Tyre), then the third, Salt (Hiram Abif), has to be "killed" in the black stage of alchemy so that it may be purified and then resurrected. The salt is now converted into "spiritual gold."

The candidate is resurrected with the aid of the Lion's Paw of Judea, and together with the elixir as explained in the Second Degree, the candidate can complete the Great Work. It is said in the Bible that "except a man be born again, he cannot see the kingdom of God."[243] In alchemy it is similarly explained that "without putrefaction the Great Work cannot be accomplished."[244] As Pike explained,

> As to the Salt, it is Absolute Matter. Whatever is matter contains salt; and all salt (nitre) may be converted into pure gold by the combined action of Sulphur and Mercury. [245]

So, we now find that the purpose of Freemasonry is, as Pike states, "The Great Work is, above all things, the creation of man by himself; that is to say, the full and entire conquest which he effects of his faculties and his future" [246] - and this we explore in the final chapter.

Ch. 6   Quest for Immortality

The conclusion we reach from researching the degrees is that the hidden Signposts in the three degrees point towards immortality, "the full and entire conquest which he [a Mason] effects of his faculties and _his future,_"[247] and the lessons of the three alchemical texts that underpin the degrees also refer to the search for immortality. The Third Degree makes this very clear by "resurrecting" the substitute for the murdered Hiram.

The Masonic scholar Macoy is quoted as saying that both alchemy and Freemasonry have similar objectives, "immortality,"[248] but what is the reasoning behind this statement? It must be obvious to anyone who has taken the three degrees that the concept of immortality was important to the first three Grand Masters, but why? The subject is not even raised in the Bible, which led to divisions within Christianity. Why did the first three Grand Masters think it was important to teach people about immortality when all Britons were members of the Church of England, church attendance was compulsory, and everyone knew (in general terms) about life after death? Unless the Grand Masters had a very different message to teach, one that would also be of interest to the aristocracy.

I will approach this subject by first looking at what the Bible teaches us concerning immortality, then the controversy surrounding immortality, as well as what we can learn about it from Freemasonry, Daoism[30] and alchemy. As I outlined in a previous chapter on the religious beliefs of the 17th century, the English of that time were very religious and knew their Bible very well, but it is surprising that the issue of immortality was also debated in Parliament!

Though the subject of reincarnation in Christian theology, also known as the Transmigration of Souls and metempsychosis, is an interesting and pertinent topic, it is outside the scope of the teachings of Freemasonry.

---

[30] See _Freemasonry: Initiation by Light_

The Valley of Dry Bones

Over the centuries, many Christians have staked their lives on the belief that on death souls go straight to Heaven where they will meet God and Christ, while the souls of the evil go to hell.[249] Christ told his disciples, "I will show you whom you should fear. Fear Him who, after He has killed, has power to cast into hell; yes, I say, fear Him!"[250] However, despite this admonition, I believe that the God of Freemasonry is the God of the New Testament, "loving and kind,"[251] not that of the Old Testament, "wrathful and punishing."[252]

We need to look again at the subject of immortality, because it was important to both the first three Grand Masters and an essential lesson in the early days of Freemasonry. Ironically the argument focuses on Christians getting into Heaven rather than the Christian dogma of doing good deeds without thought of reward.[253] In Christian denominations, as well as in Judaism, the souls of the departed are said to "Rest In Peace" based on a text in the Bible,[254] as we see below, this phrase is the centre of a theological dispute that lasted centuries.

The Soul

In Greek philosophy there were two ideas about the soul, which was known as *psychi* ψυχή meaning breath, as in "breathing life into someone." Earlier Platonic philosophy taught that the soul had three parts; an oppressive part, a lower appetite part and the reasoning part, and that each part had to be looked after, but only the reasoning part was immortal. The soul was thought to have a morality, and the individual was responsible for his or her soul, a moral imperative, which was taught by Plato and Pythagoras, and for the soul to survive and enjoy the afterlife it had to be purified, and its morality raised. Like Pythagoras, Plato also believed in reincarnation; they also believed that animals were reincarnations of humans who did not use their reason well. Plato thought that plants had a form of soul, though they could only feel but not reason. Aristotle, on the other hand, believed in a biological function for the soul, that it manifested life, and as it was so integral to the body it perishes when we die. As Aristotelian thought predominated at universities across Europe, this idea was a challenge to medieval theologians.

According to the 18th century English theologian and scientist, Joseph Priestley, the first Christians did not believe in an immortal soul. Later, Church fathers, such as Irenaeus and Augustine, then incorporated the Greek idea of an immortal soul with the Biblical promise of resurrection, probably inherited from ancient Egyptians, to arrive at a Christian doctrine of immortality. However, the concept of immortality was not consistent in the Scriptures, though now the three Abrahamic faiths believe that immortality is attained when the body is resurrected and stands before God at the time of the Final Judgment.

When we read the Bible, we see several different opinions: in the Old Testament, Solomon did not believe in an immortal soul, writing, "For the living know that they will die; but the dead know nothing." [255] The prophet Isaiah recognized only the resurrection of the dead, but not an immortal soul, "Your dead shall live; together with my dead body they shall arise. Awake and sing, you who dwell in dust; for your dew is like the dew of herbs, and the earth shall cast out the dead." [256] The prophet Ezekiel had a vision of a Valley of Dry Bones. In it, God shows the bones to the prophet as the people of Israel in exile, and attested that they would be resurrected and enter the Land of Israel.[257] Though the vision refers to the Hebrews, it implied that all of mankind would be resurrected at the End of Days. Another prophet, Daniel, believed in a different type of immortality for some, "And many of them that sleep in the dust of the earth shall awake, some to everlasting life, and some to shame and everlasting contempt." [258]

In the New Testament, we have more inconsistencies; Peter says of King David, whom God called "a man after mine own heart," [259] that his death was final. "Men and brethren, let me freely speak unto you of the patriarch David, that he is both dead and buried, and his sepulcher is with us unto this day."[260]

The most disputed passage in the New Testament can be found in I Corinthians, often called the "resurrection chapter." Paul, talking of the resurrection of the dead, says that "some are fallen asleep."[261] Then those that are asleep shall be resurrected, "For as in Adam all die, even so in Christ shall all be made alive."[262] Paul explained it thus:

> Behold, I shew you a mystery; we shall not all sleep, but we shall all be changed, in a moment, in the twinkling of an eye, at the

last trump [trumpet]: for the trumpet shall sound, and the dead shall be raised incorruptible, and we shall be changed. For this corruptible must put on incorruption, and this mortal must put on immortality. [263]

Christianity: Immortality and Mortalism

Some of the most astute minds in Europe during the 17th and 18th centuries were involved in trying to understand what was implied by immortality as given in the Bible. Belief in a just God and personal immortality had been shaken by calamitous events throughout the 17th century, the Civil Wars, the Fire of London, plagues and threats from the sky. The predominant theology of the Middle Ages was Catholic, and this came under attack by theologians who "protested" that dogma, thus starting the Protestant movement.

Priestley's book *History of the Corruptions of Christianity* delineates the history of the concept of mortalism, maintaining that early Christians did not believe in the immortality of the soul, that it was "originally a doctrine of Oriental philosophy," that later spread to the West.[264] The early Church fathers added to that idea Greek Platonism, resulting in a combined concept of a Last Judgement, with that of an immortal soul. Pope Gregory the Great wrote in around 590 AD, "And yet is it more clear than day that the souls of them that be perfect, do, straight after death, possess the joys of heaven."[265]

Later a doctrine of purgatory came to dominate medieval eschatology. The Catholic Church had changed its stance on immortality at the Council of Florence in 1439, introducing the doctrine of purgatory, dictating that the souls of the dead were conscious and "capable of pain or joy even prior to the resurrection of their bodies," [266] which was again endorsed at Fifth Council of the Lateran 1512–1517. At this council it was decreed that "souls stay in purgatory temporarily to be purified for entering heaven," based on the disputed verse in Corinthians,[267] which had so incensed the Protestant reformer Martin Luther.

Luther's Protest

The idea that souls had to be purified and/or punished before being resurrected was part of Luther's complaints, that included indulgences and simony, which he addressed in his Ninety-five Theses in 1517. This vehement attack on the Catholic Church divided religious thought in Europe and started the Reformation movement. Luther believed that the soul existed separately from the body and was in an unconscious sleep after death.[268] Luther explained that at the resurrection - the "chief article of Christian doctrine" [269] - the body and soul would be reunified on the Last Day and then enter into heavenly bliss, saying:

> Salomon judgeth that the dead are asleepe, and feele nothing at all. For the dead lye there accompting [counting] neyther dayes nor yeares, but when are awaked, they shall seeme to have slept scarce one minute. [270]

The English Reformation started seventeen years later with Henry VIII breaking from Rome, as we saw in an earlier chapter. It was his son, the child monarch Edward VI, who introduced into England many protestant reforms such as the abolition of the Latin Mass and the prescript of compulsory services in English, as well as the repeal of clerical celibacy. However, there was no decision on what Anglican immortality meant.

Tyndale's Bible

In England in 1526, eight years before the start of the English Reformation with the Act of Supremacy of 1534, William Tyndale completed the translation of the New Testament into English, which was smuggled into England from Germany where it had been printed. This controversial Bible was not only responsible for the development of the English language and English Protestantism, but also added to the immortality argument.[271]

Naturally the Catholic Church came down hard on Tyndale's Bible, claiming that there were over 2,000 errors in it, hoping to maintain their hold over the "Latin litany with a Latin Bible." Three years before Tyndale's Bible was printed, the Catholic bishop Cuthbert Tunstall had denied Tyndale permission to translate the Bible into English, as required under the Constitutions of Oxford of 1409 concerning censorship, which were still in force. That is why it had to be printed in Germany and smuggled into England.

The Protestant priest and translator, George Joye [272] had, without Tyndale's permission, revised Tyndale's 1526 New Testament, which he published in 1534. [273] Joye redacted passages that referred to "resurrection" to read "the next life" or "the life after life" to avoid the "Lutheran idea" that the soul sleeps after death. Tyndale was upset that Joye's editorial interference would change the meaning of resurrection and reprinted his Bible the same year, replacing the changes, writing this about souls in the introduction:

> And we shall all both good and bad rise both flesh and body and appear together before the judgement seat of Christ, to receive every man according to his deeds. And that the bodies of all that believe and continue in the true faith of Christ, shall be endued with like immortality and glory as is the body of Christ. [274]

Since this time, in many versions of the Bible, the following important passage in Matthew has been changed to avoid the immortality problem. "And whosoever speaketh a word against the Son of man, it shall be forgiven him: but whosoever speaketh against the Holy Ghost, it shall not be forgiven him, neither in this world, neither in the world to come." [275] Similar to Joye's edits, the last line has been changed to "neither in this age nor in the age to come," which also changes the meaning.

An interesting aside: because of rudimentary printing techniques, typesetters often made typographical mistakes. Surprisingly, each proof sheet was not read for errors before printing hundreds of pages. This resulted in some strange Bibles being printed, such as: the 1612 "Printer's Bible," where a passage from Psalms reads "Printers have persecuted me without a cause," instead of "Princes have persecuted me." [276] A misplaced comma seriously changed the meaning of a passage in Luke, in the "Blasphemous Bible," to insinuate that Christ was a "malefactor." [277] The "Vinegar Bible," from 1717, replaced the "Parable of the Vineyard" with "The Parable of the Vinegar." A last example, out of many, was the "Adulterous Bible," also called the "Wicked Bible," of 1631, where "not" was left out of the seventh commandment "Thou shall not commit adultery." This time, the printer was fined heavily for his error.[278] Obviously, the Stationer's Company must have been kept very busy, as Parliamentary records state that thousands of Bibles were confiscated and destroyed in 1653 alone.

Mortalism

In Europe, following Luther's remonstration, a concept called "mortalism" became popular, stating that the soul was not "naturally" immortal. It was based on the passage in the Bible where the Apostle Paul talks of the dead being asleep,[279] what mortalists termed "soul sleep," waiting for the day of Judgement when the soul and body would be resurrected. This idea that the soul separated from the body and slept until the day of resurrection was known by the Greek word "Psychopannychiasm," literally "soul all-night sleep." However, there were several variations on the theme, such as "thnetopsychism," [280] meaning "mortal soul," that when the body dies, so does the soul, but on the day of Judgement both are brought back to life, based on a passage in the Bible in Timothy. [281] A third variation, known as Conditionalism, believed that only God could bestow immortality, which was only attainable by humans through a belief in Christ and resurrection on the Last Day. Later, in the 1800s, a fourth way of thinking, Annihilationism, was introduced saying that at the Last Judgement the souls of those people who are not saved would be annihilated without experiencing purgatory, or suffering everlasting torment in hell, leaving only the righteous to live on in immortality, as given in Luke.[282]

Following the Interregnum, some dissenters such as the Levellers and Ranters started pamphleteering a message that rejected the concept of immortality. Intellectuals in England argued the nuances of Biblical hermeneutics, with some such as Thomas Vaughan favouring Psychopannychiasm in his 1650 book on mortalism, *The Nature of Man and his State After Death* and Thomas Hobbes, John Locke and Isaac Newton arguing for thnetopsychism. Each camp quoted scripture as the final authority, emphasizing a literal interpretation of the Bible, and that the whole weight of Biblical evidence needed to be taken into consideration before any doctrine was established, as it was important that reason should be used in interpreting scripture, not revelation.

The mortalists' position often put them in theological conundrums, such as the argument of the Swiss Anabaptist Michael Sattler, who denied the Catholic dogma that the Virgin Mary or other saints could intercede for the living, which was deemed heretical. He claimed that they could not intercede because as they were dead, they were also asleep awaiting resurrection; this line of thought led to Sattler being burned at the stake in 1527.

Another example of the difficulty that theologians had in explaining immortality can be found in a passage from Matthew, called the "zombie verses":

> And, behold, the veil of the temple was rent in twain from the top to the bottom; and the earth did quake, and the rocks rent, And the graves were opened; and many bodies of the saints which slept arose, And came out of the graves after his resurrection, and went into the holy city, and appeared unto many. [283]

The growth of mortalism in Europe was seen as a threat by more traditional Protestants, such as John Calvin who attacked mortalist theology in his book written in 1542, *Psychopannychia*, about which it is said his doctrine had "enormous and lasting implications for the future of Protestantism." [284] Despite this, Baptists in England quickly adopted the mortalist theology and by 1660 it was claimed that there were 20,000 believers in mortalism in the southern counties of England alone, and recently discovered documents suggest that the followers were still going strong in 1745.[285] To return to my opening statement, "Rest In Peace" infers mortalism, and its popularity on graveyard headstones suggests that the argument still has not been decided.

The Protestant Response to Mortalism

In 1646, during the Civil War, Parliament summoned a council of theologians called the "Westminster Assembly of Divines" to re-examine the Forty-two Articles, the doctrinal standard of the Church of England, that was current at the time and which had been drawn up by Archbishop Thomas Cranmer in 1552. Article 40 reads:

The soulles of them that departe this life doe neither die with the bodies, nor slepe idlie, thei which saie that the soulles of suche as departe hens doe sleepe, being without al sence, fealing, or perceiving, until the daie of judgement, or affirme that the soulles die with the bodies, and at the laste daie shal be raised up with the same, do utterlie dissent [31] from the right beliefe declared to us in holie Scripture. [286]

Parliament may have had its hand forced to make a judgement on the issue of immortality by the writing of the Leveller, Richard Overton, who three years before had published the first statement on mortalism in his book *Man's Mortality*, in Amsterdam in 1643. Overton believed that the existence of the soul as an entity distinct from the body, able to think and feel separately, which on death goes to either heaven or hell, was "contrary to reason." He gave the example of God breathing life into man who had been formed from dust "and man became a living soul."[287] Overton said that before that, man was not a living soul as:

That which was formed or made of the earth became a living soul, or creature, by breathing . . . the breath of life that lifeless lumpe became a living soul.[288]

In the same way, when a person dies, thought Overton, the soul is no more because the living person is no more, so death "returns man to what he was before he was, that is, not to be." On death, Overton stated, "man is void of actual being . . . he absolutely IS NOT." [289]

The Assembly of Divines rewrote the Forty-two Articles, drawing up the "Westminster Confession of Faith" in 1658 which set a new definition of life after death, that left no place for the contentious Catholic idea of purgatory.

The bodies of men, after death, return to dust, and see corruption: but their souls, which neither die nor sleep, having an immortal subsistence, immediately return to God who gave them:

---

[31] As we have seen, following the Commonwealth and King William III's Toleration Act of 1689 religious dissention grew - the word "dissention" comes from this last line of Crammer's Forty-two Articles.

the souls of the righteous, being then made perfect in holiness, are received into the highest heavens, where they behold the face of God, in light and glory, waiting for the full redemption of their bodies. And the souls of the wicked are cast into hell, where they remain in torments and utter darkness, reserved to the judgement of the great day. Besides these two places, for souls separated from their bodies, the Scripture acknowledgeth none.[290]

Pre-Revival Mortalism

Prior to the Revival of Freemasonry, the main proponents of mortalism were Tyndale and Overton, and though the growth of dissention following the Toleration Act, together with the rethinking of the concept of immortality, might have been put aside as "enthusiasm" by the government, when influential thinkers such as Thomas Hobbes and John Locke weighed in on the argument, the authorities took notice.

Hobbes, who has been called the greatest political philosopher to have written in the English language,[291] wrote his most important work *Leviathan*, in 1651. It discusses the structure of society and legitimate government, arguing for rule by an absolute sovereign, "His heart is as firm as a stone,"[292] to end the Civil War, "the war of all against all," that was being fought in England at the time. In *Leviathan* can be found references to mortalism as well as the famous quotation, "the danger of violent death, and the life of man, solitary, poor, nasty, brutish, and short."

Locke approached the subject of mortalism directly in his book concerning the use of reason in theology. In *The Reasonableness of Christianity*, written in 1695, he argued that true Christian faith is always consistent with reason. It is said that Locke's Biblical exegesis of divine revelation led him to a belief in thnetopsychism.[293]

John Milton's position on mortalism was less clear at the time. Milton had been a strong supporter of the Commonwealth, writing a tract *Defensio Secunda* in its defence, so, following the Restoration in 1660, his position was difficult. His books were burned, and he went into hiding, later turning his attention to less political subjects. Milton died in 1674. In an unfinished religious manifesto, *De Doctrina Christiana*, published one hundred and fifty years after his death, Milton set out his argument for mortalism, referring to the dead as "asleep," and also emphasized that Biblical doctrine needed to be confirmed by "arguments from reason." [294]

By the time of the Revival of Freemasonry, the subject of mortalism had again been resurrected, this time by a lawyer, Henry Layton (1622–1705), who wrote dozens of pamphlets on the subject between 1691 and 1704. These were collated and republished in 1706, after his death, as *A Search after Souls, or the Immortality of a Humane Soul, Theologically, Philosophically and Rationally Considered.* In it he stated that the soul is a function of body, and thus dies with the body awaiting resurrection (thnetopsychism), based on his interpretation of scripture.

The Three William Cowards

Around the end of the seventeenth century there were three prominent men named William Coward in England. In 1689 the pirate William Coward was captured off the coast of Massachusetts, but he was able to avoid punishment and regain his freedom. The second William Coward, a merchant, had made his fortune in investing in Jamaican sugar plantations, he later became a dissident and left his wealth to support the cause.

However, for our narrative, it was the third William Coward (1657?–1725), a doctor, who had an important role in the argument. In 1702 Coward published *Second Thoughts concerning Human Soul*, under the pseudonym "Estibius Psychalethes," claiming the idea of a soul was "a plain heathenish invention," and "derogatory in general to true Christianity." Coward argued that the idea that an immaterial substance called a soul has existence is contrary to reason saying, "I can as soon conceive a black whiteness as frame such a concept in my mind."

Coward's pseudonym may be a play on the name "Eugenius Philalethes" the nom-de-plume of the alchemist Thomas Vaughan, which means "noble lover of wisdom" or even George Starkey's Greco-Roman pseudonym "Eirenaeus Philalethes," meaning "peace lover of wisdom," as all three have the same initials, E.P. William Coward, called himself "Estibius Psychalethes." Estibus is Latin for "witness" and Psychalethes is a play on the Greek "philalethes" a lover of truth, as psychi (ψυχή) means "soul" and alitheia (αλήθεια) "truth" and put together, Estibius Psychalethes means "the witness for the truth about the soul."

The resulting furor over Coward's book even drew the attention of Parliament. Though it might seem strange to us now that Parliament would involve itself in such matters, but because of the uncertain situation of the law concerning censorship at the time, *Second Thoughts concerning Human Soul*, was debated on in Parliament and found to be blasphemous. The book was burned in Coward's presence by the hangman which, as mentioned before, paradoxically just increased the popularity of the book. Coward then wrote a second book on the same subject, which was ridiculed by Locke, followed by several other books, including *Ophthalmoiatria* in 1706, in which he derided the Cartesian notion of an immaterial soul residing in the pineal gland.[32]

Post-Revival Mortalism

After the Revival of Freemasonry in 1717, the argument over the nature and destiny of man continued and, two hundred and twenty-five years after Tyndale's bible, there appeared three apologists for mortalism, Edmund Law, Peter Peckard and Joseph Priestley.

Certain passages in the Bible deal with the resurrection on the Last Day, and these caused problems as they were seen to undermine the redemptive work of Christ.[295] Edmund Law was bishop of Carlisle and professor of moral philosophy at the University of Cambridge, and his doctoral dissertation in 1749 had been on thnetopsychism, where the dead await resurrection.[296] In 1756, Peter Peckard, dean of Peterborough and vice-chancellor of the University of Cambridge, wrote *Observations on the Doctrine of an Intermediate State*. In the book he reiterated that the soul's immortality negated the redemptive work of Christ, which would then be superfluous and unnecessary, writing,

---

[32] see *Works of God* in *Freemasonry: Spiritual Alchemy*

"Scripture expressly asserteth the mortality of man, and the restoration to life from that mortality by Jesus Christ," [297]

Joseph Priestly is now better known for his discovery of oxygen, but he was also a scholar of theology, and a mortalist. Priestley believed that the resurrection on the Last Day was the key to immortality, as it reverses death. He explained it in terms of extinguishing a candle, "we surely do not mean it is annihilated, that there is nothing left to light again." [298]

Importance of Mortalism to Freemasonry

Though Freemasons refrain from getting involved in debates on politics or religion, the first three Grand Masters had strong views on the subject of immortality. We can see from the Ritual that there are five heavily emphasized passages in the Ritual stating the soul is immortal. As we will see, this was probably related to the theological position of John Calvin and thus that of John Desaguliers (see below).

I believe that the first three Grand Masters understood that through alchemy "resurrection in one's lifetime" was a real possibility though, as explained in the previous chapter, it was a rebirth in Christianity, a spiritual experience not a physical one. This teaching was also to be found in the apocryphal text of the Gospel of Thomas that was discovered in 1945 in Nag Hammadi in Egypt among old parchment copies of the Bible. In this gospel, Thomas explains resurrection as a form of spiritual attainment, based on a certain discipline or asceticism and, concerning the teachings of Christ, "Whoever finds the meaning of these words will not taste death," suggesting a salvation by secret knowledge, as echoed in the Book of Lambspring. [299] Though the Gospel of Thomas would not have been known to the first three Grand Masters, the teachings of alchemy offered something very similar.

Immortality in the Degrees of Freemasonry

One of the Landmarks of the Grand Lodge of Massachusetts is a "Belief in immortality, the ultimate lesson of Masonic philosophy." This lesson was deemed to be a secret of great worth, as Pike says, "The truth must be kept secret, and the masses need a teaching proportioned to their imperfect reason." [300]

In the First Degree, the Entered Apprentice learns the lesson of the movable jewels, that humans are in a "rude and imperfect state" and that "by a virtuous education, our own endeavors, and the blessing of God" we hope to arrive at a "state of perfection." Secondly, that we should "erect our spiritual building agreeably to the rules and designs laid down by the Supreme Architect of the Universe, in the great book of (nature and) revelation, which is our Masonic Trestle Board;" interestingly, the passage does not expressly say "the Volume of Sacred Law." Again, the Working Tool lecture of the First Degree says we should be as "living stones... eternal in the heavens."

Throughout the three degrees there are references to immortality. The lecture in the First Degree includes immortality in the tenets, "Jacob's Ladder... teaching Faith in God, Hope in Immortality," and the Lesson from Psalm 133 teaching, "for there the Lord commanded the blessing, even life forevermore." However, most of the references are to be found in the lecture of the "Christian" Third Degree: "Three steps in a Lodge... as Master Masons, we may enjoy the happy reflections consequent on a well-spent life, and die in the hope of a glorious immortality." Two more references are to be found at the end of the lecture, "Acacia... reminds us of that far better and immortal part which survives the grave," and "it being the inspiration of that Divinity whom we adore, and bearing the nearest resemblance to that Supreme Intelligence which pervades all nature and which can never, never, never die." In Duncan's ritual the wording is even more emphatic: "acacia... is an emblem of our faith in the immortality of the soul, which never! Never - no, never dies."

In the Second Degree, in the Working Tools lecture, there is a quotation from Shakespeare's play *Hamlet* citing, "that undiscovered country from whose bourne no traveller returns" – "bourne" is an archaic word meaning realm or destination. What the text is saying is that after death the body does not return, there is no physical reincarnation, but *there is life* after death. This would have been important rider to add, as the "resurrection" in the Third Degree could be misconstrued; the resurrection was a spiritual experience not a physical one. This was also emphasized at the end of the First Degree lecture, where the Ritual describes the finality of death, "we come from earth (clay) and to it we will return!" Again, in the Third Degree lecture, concerning the scythe: "we must soon be cut down by the all-devouring scythe of time, and be gathered into the land where our fathers have gone before us."

There might have been pressure on the first three Grand Masters to explain their position on immortality, as many thought that the "Revival" Freemasons were Deists who were known for either doubting or even denying the immortality of the soul, especially as there was no mention of Christianity in the *Constitutions* of 1723. However, as both Desaguliers and Anderson were Christian ministers, it is probable that they were responsible for including in the *Constitutions* of 1738 the reference to Christ rising from the dead "for the Justification of all those who believed in him."

Resurrection in Freemasonry

The first three Grand Masters emphasize the point that the soul is immortal, but do not explain what will happen at the End of Days. We can only assume that they believed that a final Judgement was inevitable, and at that time the body would be resurrected in a spiritual form of the same body. The body that was resurrected would be the exact body that died, the difference being that it was "perfected" and no longer subject to frailty and death, but would be imbued with life, (this is why the Third Degree is "True and Perfect.") This was very different from the Jewish Sheol where the souls of the dead dwelled in a gloomy underworld, becoming dulled, miserable remnants of their former selves. The Bible supported the belief that the resurrected body looked the same as that in life: after the resurrection, Christ said: "Behold my hands and my feet, that it is I myself: handle me, and see; for a spirit hath not flesh and bones, as ye see me have." [301] It may be this idea of a physical reincarnation that the quotation from *Hamlet* was trying to negate.

This idea of a spiritual resurrection is also explained in detail in *I Corinthians*:

> So also is the resurrection of the dead. It is sown in corruption; it is raised in incorruption: It is sown in dishonour; it is raised in glory: it is sown in weakness; it is raised in power: It is sown a

> natural body; it is raised a spiritual body. There is a natural body, and there is a spiritual body. [302]

Due to the deep faith of Christians in those days, it is doubtful that they would have believed otherwise. They had faith in Christ, and that "For by grace are ye saved through faith; and that not of yourselves: it is the gift of God." [303] As the most famous passage in the New Testament emphasizes: "For God so loved the world, that He gave His only begotten Son, that whosoever believeth in Him should not perish, but have everlasting life." [304]

However, there is a caveat. I believe that the Grand Masters thought that immortality had to be earned, in a Conditionalist sense – it was not a right granted to all and sundry;[305] as is given in John: "... know that no murderer has eternal life abiding in him."[306] This then explains the lectures about virtue and Masons becoming "perfected."

> As smoke is driven away, *so* drive them away: as wax melteth before the fire, so let the wicked perish at the presence of God.[307]

Secondly, the Bible introduces an interesting requirement for entry into Heaven, "Verily I say unto you, except ye be converted, and become as little children, ye shall not enter into the kingdom of heaven." [308] We saw this before in the steganographic Signpost in the First Degree, the missing section from Corinthians, which enjoins us to "become as a child." [309] These references are not implying that Christians should be childish, but rather that they should be virtuous and innocent like children.

Lastly, in Duncan we read the following passage, which is no longer included in the ritual of most Third Degrees, but is a fine summary of how Freemasons of the time thought about death and dying:

> Thus, brother, we close our lecture on the emblems with the solemn thought of death. We are all born to die; we follow our friends to the brink of the grave, and, standing on the shore of a vast ocean, we gaze with exquisite anxiety until the last struggle is over, and we see them sink into the fathomless abyss. We feel our own feet sliding from the precarious brink on which we stand, and a few more suns, and we will be whelmed 'neath

death's awful wave, to rest in the stilly shades and darkness, said silence will reign around our melancholy abode. But is this the end of man, and of the aspiring hopes of all faithful Masons? No! Blessed be God, we pause not our feet at the first or second step; but, true to our principles, look forward for greater light. As the embers of mortality are faintly glimmering in the sockets of existence, the Bible removes the dark cloud, draws aside the sable curtains of the tomb, bids hope and joy rouse us, and sustains and cheers the departing spirit; it points beyond the silent grave, and bids us turn our eyes with faith and confidence upon the opening scenes of our eternity. [310]

Desaguliers's Immortality

As mentioned before, I believe that Desaguliers was responsible for not just including the "Christian" Third Degree, but also rewriting the Ritual, and that he emphasized the argument for immortality while denying a physical reincarnation. Naturally, as a Protestant, he also denied purgatory. The background to his position on immortality, which denied all forms of mortalism, is that as he was brought up a Huguenot, his faith would have been closely aligned to that of Calvinism. As we saw, Calvin believed that the soul was not naturally immortal and that it was something that could only be received from God, prompting him to write his theological position in *Psychopannychia* to counter the arguments supporting soul sleep, as promulgated by Anabaptists.

John Calvin, a Frenchman, taught a doctrine of Christian worship that was a personal relationship with God, focusing on the importance of Biblical texts. In the 16th century, due to Calvin's influence, many, especially from the French middle class and skilled artisans, left the Catholic Church to join his Reformed Church of France, becoming known as Huguenots. At the time Huguenots represented nearly ten per cent of the population of France, which was around twenty million. During the French Wars of Religion that raged between Catholics and Huguenots for more than thirty years (1562-1598), more than three million people died. In one infamous incident, the St. Bartholomew's Massacre of 1572, two thousand Huguenots were slaughtered in Paris on the saint's day, August 23rd, and another ten thousand across France. This act essentially helped to divide Europe into Protestant countries to the north of France, including England, and Catholic countries to the south, including France.

The Protestant king of France, Henry IV, the son of a Huguenot, ended the fighting by giving the Huguenots protection to worship freely, issuing the Edict of Nantes in 1598. However, this did not end the hostilities, and when he was assassinated in 1610, a Catholic king, Louis XIII, ascended the throne. The conflict between Catholics and Huguenots intensified, and the Huguenots' hopes of peace were dashed after their stronghold of La Rochelle fell in 1628, causing many to flee the country, though a small enclave was allowed to live in northern France. The next king, Louis XIV, also Catholic, intensified the campaign against the Huguenots, using "Dragonnades" (intimidation by unruly soldiers) to intimidate Huguenots into either leaving France or converting to Catholicism. Desaguliers's father was evicted from France following Louis XIV's Edict of Fontainebleau in 1685, also known as the "Revocation of the Edict of Nantes."

Desaguliers was born in 1683, so he would not have experienced the fighting, but living in a Huguenot community in England, he would have known about it. This background, together with a grounding in Calvinism – his father was a minister – would have convinced Desaguliers the necessity of a correct understanding about life after death. Secondly, the phrase "The Architect of the Universe," was used by Calvin to refer to God; this may be where Desaguliers first heard it and decided to use it in the ritual of Freemasonry. The phrase was not unique to Calvin, as we have seen, it was used for the 13th century painting called "God the Architect of the Universe" and Leibniz also talked of "God as the architect" in his Two Kingdoms theory. However, the phrase "The Architect of the Universe," including "Supreme" and "Great," is not to be found in any exposés before Pritchard's *Masonry Dissected* of 1730, so I believe that Desaguliers introduced this unique phrase into Freemasonry, based on his Calvinist beliefs.

Symbols of Immortality

There are two symbols in the degrees to remind the Mason of the lesson of immortality, the Tau cross and the Sprig of Acacia.

The Tau Cross

The first symbol is very subtle, it is the Tau cross that is formed by the feet, the "first lesson in Freemasonry," which later, as a Past Master, is seen as the "last lesson" as well.

In the mythology of Freemasonry, we hear that Hiram Abif was given a hammer by his ancestor, Tubal Cain, which was shaped like the letter "Tau" and is represented in the Lodge by the gavel. A second myth is that where the Christian cross symbolizes the teachings of the New Testament, the Tau cross symbolizes those of the Old Testament.

The Tau has been called the "Philosophical Cross," the two lines running in opposite directions, the horizontal and the perpendicular, the "Alpha and Omega of secret divine Wisdom." [311] It was also the symbol of immortality for the first two degrees, indicated by the position of the feet, [33] however for the Third Degree the first three Grand Masters realized that they needed a more visible symbol, and chose the "Sprig of (flowering) Acacia."

Acacia

In the Ritual we are told that acacia is the symbol of immorality, the reason being that it was an evergreen plant in an arid environment. The wood is very hard and durable, and as the trees grew to a great age, they were considered immortal, so that sacred objects were made with acacia wood. Isaiah, describing God's promise of mercy for the Israelites on their return from captivity, told them that God would plant acacia in the wilderness as a sign that Israel had been created by God.[312] God also ordered Moses to use acacia to make the Tabernacle, the Ark of the Covenant and the table for the Shew Bread.[313]

Another reason for the use of acacia as a symbol of immortality was more metaphysical; the wood being very hard was free from attack by

---

[33] see *Freemasonry: Spiritual Alchemy*

insects and animals, so it also symbolized the incorruptible nature of the soul. As acacia is found in arid land, its roots grow deeply, and thus suggests that, in a similar fashion, our lives should be deeply rooted in God.

Many have commented that in the exposé *The Grand Mystery of Free Masons Discover'd* Pritchard refers to "cassia," which they believe is a corruption of acacia, though it might mean cinnamon.

Forget-me-not

In 1925 Adolf Hitler published *Mein Kampf* (My Struggle) in which he outlined his political ideology and future plans for Germany. In it he claimed that Freemasons, as well as communists, were part of a greater Jewish conspiracy to overthrow the German government, and he also blamed both the Jews and Freemasons for Germany's defeat in World War One.

In 1933, when Hitler became Chancellor of Germany, he prohibited Freemasons from holding office in the Nazi party or in the army, and they were also ineligible for public service. He established a special section of the Security Service to prosecute Freemasons, sending Masons to concentration camps reserved for political prisoners, and they were obliged to wear a red triangle on their coats. Then in January 1934, the German Ministry of the Interior ordered the disbandment of Freemasonry and confiscated the property of every Lodge.

In August 1934 the President of Germany, von Hindenburg, died and Hitler became both the Führer of Germany, meaning the head of state, as well as Chancellor. One week later German military forces were obliged to swear a personal oath of loyalty to Adolf Hitler. Between 1933 and the fall of Nazi Germany in 1945, more than 3.5 million Germans were forced into concentration camps. Freemasons were put in political prisons, which included not just communists but Polish Jews and Soviet prisoners of war as well.

After Hitler's rise to power, it was obvious that Freemasons in Germany were in danger, so they adopted the forget-me-not, the "Vergissmeinnicht," to use to replace the square and compasses as a sign of recognition. As the flower is in the shape of a pentagram, it is also based on the

Golden Ratio, and appropriate for Freemasonry, the colour blue signifying "Blue Lodge Masonry." There was also a tradition in Germany in the Middle Ages, that men would wear the flower so as not to be forgotten by their loved ones, from which the flower's name derives.

The "forget-me-not" is the lapel pin favoured by British Masons because of its many associations. Nowadays the forget-me-not pin is worn by Masons to remember those Brethren that died at the hands of the Nazi regime, when in excess of 80,000 Masons were executed.[314] It is also worn to remind us that though a person's body is mortal, the memory of them is immortal. In recent years, the pin is often used as a symbol of friendship and the importance of free speech.

According to the Masonic scholar James Godley, the forget-me-not may be based on the story of another flower that was used by a band of gentlemen for recognition, the scarlet pimpernel.[315] The historical fiction novel *The Scarlet Pimpernel* was written by Baroness Orczy in 1905. It gives the story of a chivalrous Englishman who rescues aristocrats from the guillotine during the Reign of Terror that followed the start of the French Revolution. The hero leaves a pimpernel as his calling card.

Other Images of Immortality in Freemasonry

The coffin has always been a symbol of man's mortality; however, Freemasons have also alluded to mortality by using the symbol of a skull inside the square and compasses, similar to the skull and crossed-bones seen on one of George Washington's aprons.

When we look at the Palser Plate of 1812 we can see that Masons did not have decorations on their aprons at that time, and the aprons were not even square. So, the Triple Tau on the Past Master's apron is a later invention.

In Europe however, aprons were more decorative, for example one of three aprons George Washington is said to have owned.[34] The apron was made in France and is believed to have been presented to Washington at Mount Vernon in 1784 by the Marquis de Lafayette, a former general and close friend of his, and also a Freemason.

The apron is decorated with a flag of thirteen stars and stripes, which was the flag of the United States at that time. The flag is crossed with another pennant, and superimposed on these are the square and compasses, inside of which is a skull and crossed bones, except one of the bones has been replaced by a poniard. The square and compasses are entangled in branches of acacia. In England sepulchral images have been largely avoided in Freemasonry, with the exception of the Trestle Board of the Third Degree, as they can be misunderstood by non-Masons.

Following the end of the War of Spanish Succession in 1714, there was a growth in piracy. Though most pirates flew British Naval colours to enable them to get close to their prey, some flew black flags.[316] The designs of these flags were not always the skull and crossed-bones; skeletons, swords and even an hourglass (your time is up!) were used

---

[34] Now in the possession of Mount Nebo Lodge #91 in Shepherdstown, West Virginia. Image used with permission.

as symbols. However, as the notorious pirate Blackbeard used a skull and crossed-bones for his motif, it probably came to symbolize pirates in general.[317] The fact that this "memento mori" is used by both Freemasons and pirates does not constitute a relationship between the two.

Symbolism in Paintings

Allusion to immortality in allegorical paintings can be very subtle, such as this etching that has been suggested as evidence that Christopher Wren was a Mason, though the subject was probably King Solomon.[318] The etching is a work by William Tringham, a London engraver (and Mason) who lived 1723-c.1770. It is titled *The Mysteries that here are Shown are only to a Mason Known*, and is dedicated to "The Ancient and Honourable Society of Free and Accepted Masons," dated 5755 A.L. (see detail on p.196). Tringham is also famous for his caricature "*A Free Mason Form'd out of the Materials of his Lodge*" of 1754.

The image shows a combination of Masonic and alchemical themes, such as a skull and crossed-bones, a square and compasses, the scythe of death and even a pyramid. In the bottom right corner can be seen a coat of arms, that has Operative symbols on it, but is not that of the Premier or Antient Grand Lodges nor that of Operative Masons, (see *Freemasonry: Initiation by Light*). Finally, there is an interesting clue hidden in the picture. In the top left corner is a goddess-like queen who is holding in her right hand a scroll which reads "Hic Labor Hoc Opus." This is another steganographic hint that points to something else. The quotation is in fact written in reverse, the correct quotation comes from book six of Virgil's *The Aeneid*, "Hoc opus, hic labor est." It is the last line of a speech by the Sibyl:

The way downward is easy from Avernus.
Black Dis' [underworld] door stands open night and day.
But to retrace your steps to heaven's air,
There is the trouble, there is the toil.

Avernus, a lake near Naples, was thought to be the entrance to Hell, and the full quotation itself refers to immortality. Interestingly, on the king's easel we can see that he has drawn Pythagoras's Theorem, suggesting that the link between immortality and the Philosophers' Stone was quite widely known by that time.

Summary

The first three Grand Masters intended to prove to Masons from the standpoint of scientific knowledge and reason, rather than that of blind faith or emotion, that immortality was a fact. The three degrees combine to make a Perfect Master and give the Mason the tools to help him find the Twenty-fifth Signpost. We now think of the degrees as a moral philosophy teaching cardinal virtues, but there is so much more to the degrees than this. The inquisitive Mason should not be fooled by the apparent simplicity of Freemasonry's ritual, it is deep. Now we can understand the simple prayer used in Yorkshire Lodges, which is based on the *Upanishads*, in a different light:

> From the Unreal lead me to the Real;
> From the Darkness lead me to Light;
> From the Mortal bring me to Immortality! [319]

With the public debate about immortality, the various scandalous and blasphemous books that were being printed, the publication of *Long Livers* and even the Gormogons who also ostensibly engaged in the search for the Philosophers' Stone, and thus immortality, the subject must have been a cause célèbre at the time.

The concept of immortality in the 17th and 18th centuries was based on the Bible, "For God so loved the world that he gave his only son, that whosoever believes in him will not perish but have eternal life." [320] However, there was much debate as to what that "eternal life" meant. For the Catholics it included purgatory, for some it meant "soul sleep," waiting to be chosen for immortality, for others it meant after death immediately meeting God, or for some, even extinction of the soul. Immortality was so central to the teachings of Freemasons, that it also explains why Masons despised atheists, though Catholics were welcome in Lodge, whereas in England generally at the time it was the Catholics that were reviled, not atheists.

The first three Grand Masters, Sayer, a possible alchemist, the antiquarian Payne, together with the "spiritual scientist" Desaguliers, seeing the word becoming too materialistic, rewrote and expanded the degrees to restore spirituality to the ritual, and move away from the search for gold towards the search for immortality through spiritual alchemy.

So now we are able to identify the objective the first three Grand Masters had in rewriting the three degrees; by the Revival they gave people a practical way to ensure the promise given in the Bible of a wonderful life after death. The "Light Transmission" in the First Degree was added, a spiritual alchemical practice was hidden using steganography, and a Christian mystery play was included to complete the transformation. Though the Royal Society had hammered a nail in alchemy's coffin, few realize that thanks to Freemasonry the practice of spiritual alchemy has survived for over 300 years!

There are three other levels to the Ritual; the encoded cipher to hide the teachings from prying eyes, the esoterica to pique the curiosity of the Brethren, and the "Hidden Mysteries," which are or should be the journey of all Masons, but there is still further to go, "And ye shall know the truth, and the truth shall make you free." [321] I hope this adds to the Brethren's understanding and enjoyment of finding what Kepler called "the wonderful jewel," the secret key of Freemasonry, the Kepler triangle that incorporates both Pythagoras's Theorem and the Golden Ratio.

I understand that the information in this book is a lot to take in, so I have summarized it in the Epilogos, the last chapter. As the entomologist and novelist Vladimir Nabokov once observed, "Life is a great surprise. I do not see why death should not be an even greater one."[322]

196

The Mysteries that here are Shown
are only to a Mason known.

Price 6^d Plain

To the most Ancient and Honourable Society of Free and Accepted Masons this Plate
is most humbly Inscribed by their most Affectionate Brother Willm Frenchton

Epilogos

As I mentioned at the beginning of this narrative, to understand the objectives of the first three Grand Masters at the start of the Revival, we have to "walk in their shoes" to appreciate, not just the first Speculative Freemasons' culture and environment, but also their concerns and aspirations. We need to understand the realpolitik of that period, cutting through the myth, and understanding the processes of power in that period, the geopolitics, and the very real threats Freemasons faced.

Freemasonry is now understood to be a syncretic charity, promoting the universality of brotherhood and "making good men better," but it was not always so. *Freemasonry at its core is a quest for immortality.*

A Summary of the Book

With the dissolution of the Monasteries, Henry VIII changed the course of English history. Instead of becoming a feudal state in the Holy Roman Empire, England, and later Great Britain, took back its sovereignty. In 1534 the Church of England was established, and it gave England the opportunity to recreate Christendom based on London, not Rome, though it took 180 years to complete.

The Reconquista of 1492 had forced spiritual teachers and Kabbalists into northern Europe and England, and along with the new teachings came the excitement of alchemy. In 1547 most guilds were forcibly closed, and many stonemasons lost work following a decline in building large cathedrals and abbeys.

With the coronation of James VI of Scotland in 1603 to become King James I of England the Stuart dynasty started, but from the beginning the Catholic minority in England continued to cause problems, such as the Gunpowder Plot, among several others.

In Freemasonry's first *Constitutions* of 1723 there is no mention of Templars or any other knights, so the Templar connection was probably a Victorian invention. As Victorian historians researched the roots of Operative Masonry in Scotland, they discovered Rosslyn

Chapel and put two and two together. Rosslyn was visited by Queen Victoria in 1842 who asked for it to be restored. In the 1880s the Fourth Earl of Rosslyn, who was a Freemason, made subtle changes to the chapel during the restoration, in line with his beliefs.

With the first *Constitutions*, the history of Freemasonry was rewritten and expanded to include a glorious legend. The first Grand Masters, George Payne, John Desaguliers, together with Anthony Sayer and possibly James Anderson, rewrote the three degrees with the objective of emphasizing the immortality of the soul, at a time when that concept was under attack. As the teaching of immortality was important to them, Freemasons were very opposed to atheism because it negated an afterlife. The two-degree ritual was rewritten by the first three Grand Masters and by 1725 a third degree was added. I believe Isaac Newton supported Payne and Desaguliers in their rewriting of the rituals, because the first three Grand Masters had no knowledge of alchemy, and Newton may have also suggested the use of Wilkins's steganography.

> It was into a somewhat analogous state that the whole ritual had fallen in the days of Anderson and Desaguliers, who after the founding of the new Grand Lodge set to work to bring order out of chaos.[323]

The Book of Constitutions for Free-Masons of 1723, which included a glorious history, was introduced by the first aristocratic Grand Master, the Duke of Montagu, helping to bring structure to the organization. This attracted many members of fashionable society to join the Craft, and the placement of aristocrats, and eventually royalty, as Grand Masters ensured Speculative Freemasonry's success.

Concerns and Fears

London in the early 1700s was a dirty city, and in places squalid and often dangerous. There were street gangs, highwaymen in the environs of the city and street urchins, orphans who robbed people just to survive. The rich rode around the city in carriages with footmen for protection, but as can be seen in Hogarth's etching *Night*, the carriages were often attacked. Metropolitan London was two cities, the city of Westminster and the City of London, each with a unique characteristic and different classes of people living there.

The leisured classes either lived off the revenues from their land and properties or had a profession. They had a deep knowledge of not just classical Latin and Greek, but also of the Bible. The majority were Anglicans, but wealthy Catholic families were also tolerated, though the laws prevented them from holding office. The leisured classes had time and money to pursue any interest that caught their attention, though they tended to follow the interests of the leading lights, as it was politic to keep company with them. The Royal Society was one such establishment; many of the early members were not scientists, but just people interested in new inventions. The Foundling Hospital was another; as soon as Royalty showed interest in the venture, then everyone supported it. In Georgian Britain there was an explosion of interest in England's ancient history, which led to a proliferation of antiquarians, and their attempts to recover and reconstruct England's "glorious past."

The intelligentsia liked to discover things for themselves, and many were accomplished mathematicians, scholars and alchemists. In the late 1600s books were not published so much as printed, with the costs borne by the writer. Censorship was in place until 1692, and as the Church and Parliament were concerned about publications that were blasphemous or attacked the king or government, they were monitored closely.

During the era of the Stuarts, elections were not free as many did not qualify to vote, [35, 324] and the House of Commons was mainly composed of aristocrats and intellectuals, such as Newton, so that laws tended to be created by the aristocracy, though the monarch also had the right to enact law. The House of Lords was abolished during the Interregnum, and groups such as the Levellers, Diggers and the Fifth Monarchy Men also started to call for the abolition of the monarchy. However, the Restoration not only restored the king, Charles II, but also the aristocracy, to power. Aristocrats in Parliament later invited the Dutch William of Orange to be king of England, so they were seen as the heroes of the Glorious Revolution and were well

---

[35] Even by 1832, only seven per cent of the population was entitled to vote.

rewarded with titles and land. The last Stuart monarch, Queen Anne, was only able to rule with the help of the aristocracy, which also took a more prominent role in government.

After the Glorious Revolution of 1688, King William III (and the first two Kings George) was to a large extent an "absentee monarch," as he also had interests in his own country abroad to attend to. Social life was important for the aristocracy. They became patrons of the arts and deserving causes, enjoyed the London Season, the Grand Tour and, as most went to either the University of Oxford or Cambridge, they also married into each other's families, leading to greater social cohesion.

Among the working classes, life was hard. Life expectancy was in the forties, infant mortality was high, and medicine was primitive. Living conditions in the City of London, which was built around the docks, was grim. As there was no sewage system, this enabled the quick spread of the plague, and wooden houses that were crammed together encouraged fire. After the Fire of London in 1666, the government started to rebuild the medieval city, this time out of stone, but there was little public money available as wars had drained the Stuarts' purse. Aristocrats made wealthy during the Restoration, bought up tracts of land around the City and in Westminster, built enormous mansions and palaces, as well as terraced housing for investment.

During all this growth, hundreds of masons and builders came to London looking for work. The work continued for decades, St. Paul's Cathedral was not completed until 1711. These masons formed Operative Lodges in Covent Garden, Drury Lane and St. Paul's Churchyard. In these areas brothels and slums quickly developed, bolstered by the influx of labourers with money to spend, and cheap gin was readily available. At the same time several groups of dissenters such as Baptists and Quakers formed temperance movements to battle these social issues.

Another aspect of life in London in those days was the sudden wealth that had entered the economy. Trade with the colonies was booming, and ships brought goods to London from as far away as India and China; one report states that in 1814 England was then even importing ginseng.[325] The development of the insurance industry would have been a tail wind for trade. Sudden wealth also brought with it "get rich quick" pyramid schemes, such as the Darien Venture and the South Sea Bubble, where many rich people lost fortunes.

War was an on-going fact of life during the Stuart and Hanover eras, putting a strain on the Exchequer. Following the end of the Civil War in 1651, the Commonwealth of England was still fighting the First Anglo-Dutch War which lasted until 1654, war was fought nearly continuously for another seventy years. In 1654, the Anglo-Spanish War started, continuing until 1660, and was only finalized by the Treaties of Madrid in 1667 and 1670, from which England gained acquisition of Jamaica, the Cayman Islands and Dunkirk. A second Anglo-Dutch War started in 1665, lasting two years, which is why the Dutch were also accused, together with Catholics, of starting the Fire of London.

In 1672 the third Anglo-Dutch War started, lasting another two years. English troops were stretched thin as they were also involved at the same time in the Franco-Dutch War which lasted for six years. James II then had to face an internal revolt with the Monmouth Rebellion in 1685. The Glorious Revolution of 1688, when William III entered England, started the Nine Years' War, pitting England against France and the Jacobites, and lasted until 1697. In Ireland, the new monarch was involved in the Williamite War, 1688–91, which included the Battle of the Boyne in 1690. This was the last battle between two rival claimants for the British throne.

War did not end with the beginning of the Hanoverian era, there was the War of Spanish Succession 1701-1714, after which Spain ceded Gibraltar to Britain. Then there were three further Jacobite Rebellions, 1715–16, 1719 and 1745–46, in England, Scotland and Ireland respectively. Stuart pretenders to the throne continued to threaten Britain, though it was not so much the Jacobites who represented the threat, but rather their Catholic allies, Spain and France.

On top of being in a constant state of war, there was the worry that the world may come to an end at any time; portents had been seen in the sky, such as Mirk Monday in 1652, and as the population was generally superstitious, this often caused much panic in the streets. Though by 1715, at the time of the next solar eclipse, which had been predicted by Edmond Halley to within 4 minutes accuracy,[326] the understanding of comet cycles and how to predict eclipses had advanced so much that, rather than being blinded by fear and superstition, the population was this time looking forward to the event and lined the streets in anticipation. This shows how much England had changed: at the beginning of the Stuart era, an astrologer was asked to predict the Roundhead victory at Naseby and a psychic was consulted by authorities at the execution of Charles I, but one hundred years later, following the founding of the Royal Society, superstition had been replaced by science.

It was during these turbulent times that the Lodge at the Rummer and Grapes Tavern (later moving to the Horn Tavern) was established. Its date is not recorded but it was probably sometime after the Glorious Revolution when Dutch rummer wine glasses became fashionable. It is quite possible that there had already been a meeting of a sorts there, but with the endeavours of George Payne, who was listed in the *Constitutions* of 1723 as the Master of the Rummer and Grapes, he was able to attract not just Desaguliers to join, but also a dozen influential nobles.

Aspirations: A New Jerusalem

St. Paul's cathedral 1896

King Solomon's Temple is very important to Freemasons for two reasons, first, it represents a metaphor for the Craft and secondly, it represents the aspirations of Freemasons. The number three is also important to Freemasons, representing among other things the Holy Trinity, the three degrees of the fraternity and also the three stages of life. As King Solomon's Temple was destroyed twice, the third temple is for Masons to build. This is not a physical place but rather a spiritual one, a place in a Mason's heart where he will meet God, as explained in the Bible.[327]

It is believed that Francis Bacon saw in James VI and I the qualities of Solomon, as in 1605 he dedicated his book *The Advancement of Learning* to the king stating that "there hath not been since Christ's time any king or temporal monarch, which hath been so learned in all literature and erudition, divine and human." [328] In 1620, John King (c1555-1621), the Bishop of London, read a sermon eulogizing the king from St. Paul's Cross, an open-air pulpit in front of the north-east corner of the charred structure of St. Paul's cathedral – the wooden spire had burned down and the structure was unsafe. It is now believed that this sermon was scripted by the king:

> If England bee the ring of Europe, your City is the gemme. If England the bodie, your City the eye; if England the eye, your City the apple of it. You, of all others, are neerest the heart, for care and protection Here hath the Lord ordained a lanthorne for his Anoynted. Here are the thrones of David, for judgement; and the chaire of Moyses, for instruction.

At the opening of Parliament in 1621 King James VI and I used the phrase "in multiloquio non deerit peccatum" (when words are many, sin is not absent),[329] a quotation from Proverbs reputed to have been written by Solomon, who also wrote the wisdom books of Ecclesiastes and the Song of Solomon.[330] Finally, at his funeral in 1625, James was called the "Solomon of Great Britain," showing how England in the 17th Century was seen by some Christians as "God's chosen country," with London its "New Jerusalem."[331]

The later Stuarts also identified themselves with King Solomon, as he was both head of Church and State and ruled by Divine Right. Their palace in Whitehall was their "King Solomon's Palace" and both Charles II and James II wanted the new St. Paul's Cathedral to be a new "King Solomon's Temple," resurrecting London from the ashes of the Great Fire as the New Jerusalem, where the Second Coming of Christ would occur.[332]

Axis Mundi

Charles II saw the Great Fire as an opportunity to rebuild London to match the splendor of Paris, with wide boulevards like the Champs d'Elysées. Starting as a Roman town in 50 AD, London had grown over many centuries, expanding organically without town planning. As a result, the streets were narrow and by the 1670s it was thought unfit to be the capital of England. Charles II envisioned London as not only being the governmental centre but also a spiritual center. He started renovations to the city to establish the ideal Christian City, the "New Jerusalem," with the centre of this spiritual city being St Paul's Cathedral, for the sole purpose of preparing the world for the Second Coming of Christ. The king wanted London to be redesigned not only on spiritual but also cosmic principles, with St. Paul's Cathedral as the Axis Mundi, as suggested in Bishop John King's sermon. This axis served as a celestial pillar, connecting Heaven and Earth, but had been destroyed with the collapse of the spire of the old St. Paul's Cathedral. By rebuilding the cathedral and the axis, man would then be reconnected to the greater consciousness of Heaven.

To the English, even now one of the most important pieces of religious music is the anthem *Jerusalem*. It was written in 1808 by William Blake, who lived during the monarchy of the House of Hanover. The last four lines of the anthem are:

> I will not cease from mental fight, Nor shall my sword sleep in my hand, 'Till we have built Jerusalem, In England's green and pleasant land.

So, it can be seen that the idea of making London a spiritual centre was still alive 150 years after the Great Fire of London.

A Peculiar System of Morality

Symbolism is everything in Freemasonry, as every symbol points to a deeper meaning. In *Esoterica*, Pike analyses five symbols that he believed were important; The Compasses and the Square [sic], The Weapons and Blows of the Assassins, The Three Grips, The Substitute for the Master's Word and the 47th Problem of Euclid. With the exception of the three grips, we have looked at two of these symbols in detail and two en passant.

Freemasonry in England as we know it today started with the Revival. Before that, there were Operative Masons' guilds with their sacred ceremonies and mystery plays. Later, the Rosicrucians probably tried to piggyback on to masons' guilds for quick growth. However,

Revival Freemasonry changed the ritual into an alchemical theatre that was centred on Metropolitan London. Then in Victorian times, moral education and the phrase "a peculiar system of morality" gained currency. The Victorians took their trains, education and trading to conquer the world and subjugate new colonies for the Empire, and with it they took the Craft. What they did not expect were Brethren, who had been raised in the colonies, returning to settle in England and wanting to continue in Freemasonry. So, in the 20th century, Freemasonry became pluralistic and more religious texts were added to the altar. Now in the 21st century, Freemasonry is opening itself up to be more inclusive and less secretive, but at the heart of the Craft still lies, nearly intact, a secret transformation through spiritual alchemy.

The Philosophers' Stone is Broken

It is a pity that the new logo of the United Grand Lodge of England is, knowingly or unknowingly, distancing itself from the alchemical roots of Freemasonry by separating the square and compasses, making it impossible for future Masons to discover the Philosophers' Stone.

Fraternization

Many still believe that following the dissolution of guilds in 1547, the number of working stonemasons dwindled, and following it, outsiders were allowed to join Operative Masons' Lodges. As a modern commentator stated, "This is like saying that the dockworkers union, finding itself shorthanded, let the king of England sign up."[333]

Britain is governed by a constitutional monarchy with a nobility comprising eight ranks, from baron to king. Britain is also a nominal social democracy, based on social status or birth, and has been since King John signed the Magna Carta on June 15th, 1215, which protected the rights of English Barons and the other large landholder, the Church. So, when British Masons read books that say, "the nobility sought membership in Operative Lodges which was the beginnings of Speculative Masonry..." they know it is incorrect. Even today the class structure in England is quite rigid, celebrities try to buy their way in, only to be shunned by "old money."

In all probability, what happened was that a gentleman - a rank of gentry - who had an interest in alchemy, paid to join a stonemason's guild, or Lodge, in order to learn the secrets of architectural alchemy that had been built into a few select cathedrals in Europe, such as Notre Dame or Chartres, which may have been financed by the Templars. As we saw in the section about Operative Masonry, the Dean of Worcester wrote in 1678, in a study of Operative Masonry, "the Lairds of Roslin have been great architects and patrons of building for these many generations. They are obliged to receive the Mason's word." This means that in order to be able to manage the workmen on his chapel, the Lord of Rosslyn had to join an Operative Lodge. This also explains the king's Principle Master of Work in Scotland, Sir Anthony Alexander's interest in Operative Masonry.

The Templars knew first-hand of Arabic-Egyptian alchemy, which flowed into Spain following its conquest by the Moors in 711. Jews who accompanied the Moors brought the Kabbalah, alchemy and the occult sciences with them into Spain. The Templars involvement during the Crusades of the 11th and 12th centuries would also have brought more information about alchemy to Europe. The Reconquista in 1492 then pushed this hidden knowledge into central Europe and later into England.

This was the era of the "puffers" who probably sought out these secrets from the people who had built the cathedrals. However, the only people who were likely to have had knowledge of these secrets would have been those who commissioned the buildings, as architecture as a discipline did not start until after the Great Fire in 1660. Gentlemen would have been invited to attend Operative Masonic meetings, though not the rituals, without having received the then two degrees, and these Masons became known as the "Acception" or Accepted Masons. It very unlikely that in the 1600s anyone remembered anything of what happened in the 1300s or before, particularly as so few people kept records.

Nobility would not deign to meet workmen - that was the gentry's job - but they would meet a person of the stature of Christopher Wren.

At the time of the building of St. Paul's Cathedral in London, Wren was not yet a knight, but probably he would have been invited to join the Lodge adjoining the cathedral in St. Paul's Churchyard, "The Goose and Gridiron," the tavern where stonemasons would meet in the evenings after working on the cathedral. This is not the same as nobility seeking membership in Operative Lodges, or these Lodges becoming the basis of Speculative Freemasonry.

Challenges Facing Freemasonry

One of the weaknesses of modern Freemasonry is that for the average Mason the element of research and discovery has been omitted, and that responsibility has been given to either Grand Lecturers or a Research Lodge. So that in many cases, as Laurence Dermott of the Antient Grand Lodge wrote, Masons have "given up geometry in favour of dining."

The Major Challenge

The author of a recent article on Masonic education said that people joined Freemasonry because they were seeking something, they wanted to join a Lodge that shared their values, and they also wanted to be active in the community, but instead the Lodge meetings were boring, they talked about trivia, as he wrote, "whether to repave the parking lot or just fill in the potholes."

Many Masons join a Lodge and attend for a while, then stop coming. Lodges get embroiled in detail, they have long, boring business meetings, and little time is spent on education, or finding interesting speakers.

> People join Freemasonry for different reasons: the camaraderie; self-improvement; charitable service —mostly to fill some void in their lives. Many today are looking for something deeper, but are not interested in the formal trappings of the various religions. Many of these are disappointed because they don't find what they are looking for in Freemasonry and, as a result, leave the organization. [334]

When we look to Masonic texts for information about Masonic education, we read in *Morals and Dogma*, by Albert Pike:

> The Blue Degrees are but the outer court or portico of the Temple. Part of the symbols are displayed there to the Initiate, but he is intentionally misled by false interpretations. It is not intended that he shall understand them; but it is intended that he shall imagine he understands them. Their true explication is reserved for the Adepts, the Princes of Masonry.
>
> The whole body of the Royal and Sacerdotal Art was hidden so carefully, centuries since, in the High Degrees, as that it is even yet impossible to solve many of the enigmas which they contain. It is well enough for the mass of those called Masons, to imagine that all is contained in the Blue Degrees; and whoso attempts to undeceive them will labor in vain, and without any true reward, violate his obligations as an Adept. Masonry is the veritable Sphinx, buried to the head in the sands heaped round it by the ages.[335]

Again, in *Liturgies, Legendas and Readings*, Pike states:[336]

> When the Knights of the Order of the Temple were multiplied until they became armies, that happened which at length comes to pass in all mysteries, orders and rites whatever. The large mass of the knights, mere soldiers and unlettered men, were unfit to be entrusted with the chief secrets of the order, and these were confined to only a select few, forming an inner circle in the order; and pains were taken, while seeming to make all known to all, to conceal them by symbols, by enigmatical expressions, by trivial explanations, which led away from the truth, instead of toward it. The same has occurred in Masonry, not only in that of the Blue Degrees, where no symbol receives its true explanation, the formulas have been reduced to the merest forms of words, and the most essential portion of the Third Degree has been wholly cut away; but also in the higher degrees.

So, what are we to understand by this? Obviously, Pike was keen to promote the Scottish Rite, but is what he said about the Blue Degrees correct? Has the most essential part of the Third Degree been cut away? Is Blue Lodge Masonry a sphinx buried up to its head in the sand?

As I have shown in the previous chapters, we can learn a lot just by analysing the ritual. It is easy to introduce an educational program into a Blue Lodge; a Master of the Lodge has a wealth of experience in the Past Masters, as well as the Grand Lecturers and Grand Historians of their respective Grand Lodges, whom they should be calling on for advice. Lodges should make education a regular item on the Trestle Board not a one-off event, and membership will increase. Do it properly, and not just fill in the potholes!

As Rev. George Oliver, quoting Preston, wrote:

> Many are deluded by the vague supposition, that our mysteries are merely nominal; that the practices established amongst us are frivolous; that our ceremonies may be adopted or waived at pleasure. On this false basis we find too many of the Brethren hurrying through all of the degrees of the Order, without advert- ing to propriety of one step they pursue, or possessing a single qualification to entitle them to advancement. Passing through the usual formalities, they consider themselves authorized to rank as Masters of the Art, solicit and accept offices, and even assume the government of the Lodge, equally unacquainted with the rules of the Institution that they pretend to support, and the nature of the trust which they are bound to perform.[337]

It is important to include the younger members in educational activities so that Lodges do not turn into a men's social club. Many men are searching for an esoteric education that introduces a non- religious spirituality. This should be an opportunity for Lodges to grow.

Misunderstanding Freemasonry

Freemasonry is part theatre, charity, chapel, fraternity and debating society that includes ritual, faith and esoteric knowledge. It can be boring, every business meeting is the same, and this leads to people dropping out. Many Masons feel that there is nothing more to learn once they become Master Masons, perhaps this is because the teachers themselves do not know.

Freemasonry is not a religion and its teachings are not contrary to anyone's religion, which may account for its appeal. Over the years many Anglican clergy have been members, and there has been a good rapport between clergy and Freemasons. For example, in 2013 Canterbury Cathedral marked the 200th anniversary of Royal Arch Masonry with a special service led by the Archdeacon of Canterbury, the Ven. Sheila Watson.[338]

Many writers attack Freemasonry as being un-Christian, but this is because they do not really understand the hidden symbolism. An example is one Brother, who progressed as far as the Chapter of Rose Croix in the Scottish Rite, later writing a denunciation titled *The Craft and the Cross.*

The Craft & The Cross

A former Freemason, Ian Gordon, wrote a book about his experiences in Freemasonry,[339] and how he had a crisis of faith, that led to him leaving the fraternity. I believe there are important lessons for Freemasons to learn from this former Brother's experience, so I am adding some details here.

When Gordon first joined the Craft, he felt as many men do:

> Freemasonry seems to represent different things to different people; in my case it combined the all-male camaraderie which I had enjoyed at public school and later in the regimental mess, with the esoteric enjoyment of an exclusive club, all tempered by a good helping of firmly-based, old-fashioned religion.

Gordon advanced to the Chapter of Rose Croix after a career of nine years, which included being the Master of a Lodge in London. Initially he was proud to be a member saying that "I would have given a lot to be able to tell him [his brother] about my Lodge, about the generosity shown towards charitable causes, the decency and integrity of its members, and the constant insistence on a moral code." He held off explaining to his brother anymore about the Craft, because of the Masonic oath he had taken, though he did tell him about the existence of Christian orders within the Craft.

However, Gordon became upset by the ritual of the degrees of an appendant body, which he felt was un-Christian, and started to re-examine his beliefs. He admits that his knowledge of the Bible was "scanty," and at the same time he was reading books by born-again Christians who lumped Catholic liturgy in with Satanism and New Age practices. Gordon came to the conclusion that Satan was planning world domination, and had prompted the founding of many cults and societies to keep their members in ignorance. That is an enormous leap from the "camaraderie of the regimental mess."

Later he makes a mistake that many people do in believing that "all Masonry was the one and same," as well as mixing Operative Masonry with Speculative Masonry. He also claimed that John Desaguliers was "head of the Rose Croix," which would have been impossible as Desaguliers died in 1744, the same year as Estienne Morin was envisioning high-degree Masonry in France, that later became the Scottish Rite. Gordon writes that the Rose Croix held a meeting in 1617 in Magdeburg in Germany, where it was agreed that it would destroy the Church of Jesus Christ, and that one hundred years later in 1717 the Rose Croix would transform the fraternity to carry out an overt campaign to that end. We know this is nonsense, but how did a Mason come to think this way? When I saw the bibliography at the end of the book, I can understand why Gordon came to these conclusions, as many of the books listed are anti-Free-masonry.

I believe that many Lodges leave Brethren up to their own devices once they have taken the degrees. "You're a Master Mason now. Well done!" and that is it. It is really important for education to be contin-uous in Lodges, so that there is a forum for questioning and discussion. Having been the Master of the Research Lodge for the Grand Lodge of Japan for several years, I can positively say that I would not have been able to write this book without the things that I learnt outside the Blue Lodge. Gordon's example is just one of many concerning peo-ple's confusion about Freemasonry. There are many such books and websites.

> The least initial deviation from the truth is multiplied later a thousandfold. - Aristotle

Is Membership Declining Worldwide?

According to the United Grand Lodge of England, as of 2017 there are approximately six million Freemasons worldwide, and under UGLE there are over 200,000 English Freemasons.[340] The Grand Lodges of Ireland (Northern Ireland and Eire), and Scotland have a combined total of approximately 150,000 members. The number of Lodges warranted by UGLE has gone down from 8,389 in 2006 to 7,401 today, which computes to nearly 100 Lodges closing every year for the past decade.[341]

In 2016, in the fifty-two states of America there was a combined total of 1,117,781 Masons, down from the 1960s when there were 4 million Masons.[342] The state with the largest number of Masons is Pennsylvania, with nearly 100,000. Unfortunately, nearly every state saw a decline 2016/2015, some in the thousands. A bright spot on a cloudy global horizon is the growth of Freemasonry in other countries around the world, such as India, Brazil, the Philippines, Singapore and Taiwan.[343]

The major reason for a decline in membership is that people have become busier, overtime is now de facto, and many families rely on two incomes. In the past, volunteering for a church or community was normal, now it is uncommon. People are more concerned with how membership of a Lodge will benefit them, such as its networking potential.[344]

However, there is some optimism, as the world is still interested in Freemasonry, as we have seen from best-selling books such as Dan Brown's books, *The DaVinci Code* and *The Lost Symbol* and the movie, *National Treasure*, though Freemasonry's "public identity is now positioned in the context of historical fiction."[345]

Does Freemasonry Conceal Secrets from Members?

Many Masons believe that there are higher grades within Freemasonry, besides Scottish and York Rites, that have access to information that is not available to the Brethren. In the public's imagination this is referred to as the "Illuminati." Unlike Weishaupt's group that died out after fourteen years in 1790, this theory, though misguided, persists.

> Masonry, like all the Religions, all the Mysteries, Hermeticism and Alchemy, conceals its secrets from all except the Adepts and Sages, or the Elect, and uses false explanations and misinterpretations of its symbols to mislead those who deserve only to be misled; to conceal the Truth, which it calls Light from them and to draw them away from it.

This quotation from *Morals and Dogma* is often quoted by conspiracy theorists, however it should be remembered that this is mixing apples and oranges. Blue Lodge Masonry is not the same as the Scottish Rite or the York Rite, though the roots maybe seen to be the same.

Part of the problem is due to the way Freemasonry is taught to new members; in many cases they are left to their own devices. Again, I quote from Albert Pike, who was influenced by the writings of the French occultist, Eliphas Levi:

> If you have been disappointed in the first three Degrees, as you have received them, and if it has seemed to you that the performance has not come up to the promise, that the lessons of morality are not new, and the scientific instruction is but rudimentary, and the symbols are imperfectly explained, remember that the ceremonies and lessons of those Degrees have been for ages more and more accommodating themselves, by curtailment and sinking into commonplace, to the often limited memory and capacity of the Master and Instructor, and to the intellect and needs of the Pupil and Initiate; that they have come to us from an age when symbols were used, not to reveal but to conceal; when the commonest learning was confined to a select few, and the simplest principles of morality seemed newly discovered truths; and that these antique and simple Degrees now stand like the broken columns of a roofless Druidic temple, in their rude and mutilated greatness; in many parts, also, corrupted by time, and disfigured by modern additions and absurd interpretations. They are but the entrance to the great Masonic Temple, the triple columns of the portico. [346]

Elsewhere in *Morals and Dogma* Pike discusses "concealed truth":

> These Degrees are also intended to teach more than morals. The symbols and ceremonies of Masonry have more than one

meaning. They rather conceal than disclose the Truth. They hint at it only, at least; and their varied meanings are only to be discovered by reflection and study. Truth is not only symbolized by Light, but as the ray of light is separable into rays of different colours, so is truth separable into kinds.

The answer to the problem is probably that the genuine secrets of Freemasonry cannot be taught; the symbolism must be meditated upon, the virtues lived, and the veiled allegory probed and experienced. The "quest" is in *quest*-ioning the ritual; that is one of the secrets that has been lost.

This is one reason that the ritual was taught by emulation – imitation – until the 1870s. Then rituals were printed for the first time as differences in words and even changes in meaning had crept into the ritual. In England in 1823, an Emulation Lodge of Improvement was established by the United Grand Lodge of England to preserve Masonic ritual as closely as is possible to that which had been formally accepted in 1816 by the newly formed United Grand Lodge of England, and to include any subsequent changes.

A Secret Society

As many Brethren affirm, *Freemasonry is not a secret society, but rather a society with secrets.* That is very natural, an individual's bank balance is likewise a secret. I believe it has more to do with privacy, like a private club, and that what we do or believe is none of anybody's business but our own. However, times have changed, and everybody wants to know everything about everybody. Unfortunately, as most people do not discriminate what news source they research, they tend to wander into the warren of conspiracy theorists.

Secondly, few people nowadays think that a spiritual quest is important, as can be confirmed by the number of empty churches being converted to secular uses. If a person is interested in the spiritual, they tend to relinquish that responsibility to a religion. Even so, most members do not see Freemasonry as a quest. So, an urgent imperative is to see how we can realign the Craft to meet modern needs, without destroying the Ritual and customs. Some ideas could include what day of the week or time is most convenient to meet. Could Lodges share the same premises to save on expenses? Should there be extracurricular activities that include the families of members?

Are Standards Dropping?

Three areas of concern are: first, how Masons present themselves in Lodge, and in society, secondly, their commitment to learning the Ritual and lastly, the non-ratification of Landmarks, which vary greatly from Grand Lodge to Grand Lodge.

A Masonic Dress Code

Many Masons do not think it is important what they wear in Lodge, and many Grand Lodges have made no pronouncement on a dress code. A few of the oldest Grand Lodges such as the United Grand Lodge of England,[347] the Grand Lodge of Scotland[348] and the Grand Lodge of Massachusetts [349] do have a dress code, but in hotter countries such as the Philippines or the State of Hawaii, obviously Brethren just wear shirts. However, many Brethren take advantage of this situation to attend Lodge dressed as they wish.

In my English mother Lodge, we wear dark suits and black ties with white gloves, and the reason for this is that we are in mourning for the death of Hiram Abif, so we dress as for a funeral. On the United Grand Lodge of England's website, it even stipulates that the tie must be black without decoration.

Many Grand Lodges require officers to wear black ties or bow ties and white gloves, but they do not do it, and even Grand Lodge Officers often do not bother. A few years ago, I attended the Annual Communication of a certain Grand Lodge where the Inner Guard was wearing a yellow suit! I'd like to think that, at least in England, that Brother would not have been allowed into the building let alone the Grand Lodge; but times change, and this relaxation of dress code may be a sign of those changes.

Is it important? I believe that it is. First, it is insulting to those that have taken the effort to change into formal attire and secondly, it gives a bad impression to visitors, who think that if members of the Lodge cannot be bothered to dress correctly, then they cannot be bothered to start on time, they cannot be bothered to learn their parts, they cannot be bothered to prepare a proper Festive Board, and the end result is that members cannot be bothered to attend.

The Worshipful Master of the Lodge sets the tone for the Lodge, if he attends wearing training shoes then everyone thinks that is acceptable. A Brother will find it difficult to ask the Master to dress appropriately, so what should be done? It is up to the Grand Lodge to impose the rules that it has drawn up, that's its job. It cannot expect to play "Monday-morning quarterback" by complaining about a lack of standards and decreasing membership. There need to be regular inspections by the Grand Lodge.

The way a Brother presents himself as a Mason is the public's opinion of what Masonry is about. Simply said: "A smart sailor makes a smart ship!"

Memory Work

Many Brethren find that learning the Ritual is not only difficult, but also that it takes a long time. Is it really necessary to learn the Ritual by heart? Isn't reading it the same thing?

This challenge has made some Brethren feel that they are just actors. Though it is important to impress on a new candidate the Ritual of Freemasonry, it is equally important for the Brother himself to internalize the teachings. I had been a Freemason for twenty years before I started to see a richer and deeper lesson within the Ritual.

The Scottish Schaw Statutes of 1598-9 required memorization of the ritual as most manual workers were illiterate, and it helped them remember large amounts of information at a time when printing was in its infancy.[350] Later, at the time of the Revival, memory work was important as there was no Monitor, the ritual was remembered by emulation. It is believed that a secondary motive was as a "great form of moral training," using a memory palace as a mnemonic device.[351]

Now, when Speculative Freemasons learn the Ritual to become familiar with it, they do not see the hints (Signposts) that have been put there purposely to open our minds to another lesson hidden *under* the text. Our eyes and mind normally just gloss over these without thinking about them, but when you learn the text by heart, then the Signposts start to raise questions and suddenly the hidden teachings float up to the surface of your mind. Secondly, concerning the moral lessons, we should contemplate on what the lessons mean and how should we apply them in our lives. This is the genius of the Ritual; it works on many levels at the same time.

For long passages of text, I apply the same technique I use to learn pieces of music. I start by memorizing the last bar, then add a bar at a time, until I get to the beginning of the piece. For the Ritual I also start learning from the end, a line at a time. This way, reciting it gets easier as you near the end, rather than having a strong start and faltering at the end.

The Ancient Landmarks

As we saw in the previous chapter, the Landmarks of Freemasonry are not consistent across the world. It is a pity that Anderson did not list the Landmarks in the *Constitutions* of 1723, it would have saved many people a lot of anxiety.

The term "landmark" is taken from the Book of Proverbs:[352] "Remove not the ancient landmark which thy fathers have set", referring to stone pillars set to mark boundaries of land. This is based on ancient Jewish property law: "Thou shalt not remove thy neighbours' landmark, which they of old time have set in thine inheritance."

In 1863 George Oliver listed forty Landmarks in *The Freemason's Treasury*, and seven years later, Robert Macoy made a list of nineteen Masonic Landmarks.[353] This was followed by Roscoe Pound (1870-1962), Dean of Harvard Law School, who reduced the number to just six:

1. A belief in a Supreme Being

2. A belief in the immortality of the soul

3. A "book of sacred law" as an indispensable part of the "furniture" (or furnishings) of the Lodge

4. The legend of the Third Degree

5. The secrets of Freemasonry: The modes of recognition and the symbolic ritual of the Lodge

6. That a Mason be a man, freeborn, and of lawful age.

Later, Pound in *Lectures on Masonic Jurisprudence*, 1920, recommended that "A belief in immortality" be replaced with "a belief in the persistence of personality," genuflecting to religious syncretism, "so that the doctrine of transmigration and ultimate Nirvana would meet Masonic requirements." [354]

In 1913 the United Grand Lodge of England recognised the Grande Loge Nationale Française (GLNF) as it adhered to monotheism and the precepts of regularity issued by the United Grand Lodge of England, which were:

1. While the Lodge is at work the Bible will always be open on the altar.

2. The ceremonies will be conducted in strict conformity with the Ritual of the "Regime Rectifié" which is followed by these Lodges, a Ritual which was drawn up in 1778 and sanctioned in 1782, and with which the Duke of Kent was initiated in 1792 (son of King George III and Queen Charlotte.)

3. The Lodge will always be opened and closed with invocation and in the name of the Great Architect of the Universe. All the summonses of the Order and of the Lodges will be printed with the symbols of the Great Architect of the Universe.

4. No religious or political discussion will be permitted in the Lodge.

5. The Lodge as such will never take part officially in any political affair but every individual Brother will preserve complete liberty of opinion and action.

6. Only those Brethren who are recognised as true Brethren by the Grand Lodge of England will be received in Lodge.

It is said that these "basic principles" were accepted by UGLE itself in 1929 and written into its constitutions.[355] A belief in immortality was missing, and the list did not specify that a belief in a Supreme Being was necessary to become a Freemason.

In 1914, Joseph Newton reduced the landmarks to five: "The fatherhood of God, the brotherhood of man, the moral law, the Golden Rule, and the hope of life everlasting." [356] At this point a belief in immortality was still a Landmark in America. But then in 1956, the Commission on Information for Recognition of the Conference of Grand Masters of Masons in North America upheld just three "ancient landmarks":[357]

1. Monotheism, an unalterable and continuing belief in God.

2. The Volume of The Sacred Law, an essential part of the furniture of the Lodge.

3. Prohibition of the discussion of Religion and Politics within the Lodge.

In the 2018 version of *Constitutions* of the "Antient Fraternity of Free and Accepted Masons under the United Grand Lodge of England," under the *General Laws and Regulations for the Government of the Craft*, paragraph 125 states that "any visitor must profess a belief in T.G.A.O.T.U. and acknowledge that this belief is an essential Landmark." However, it does not list up any actual Landmarks. Under the "Aims and Relationships of the Craft," the *Constitutions* set out "certain fundamental principles of the Order," to avoid "disintegration of the order," what may be termed Landmarks, of which only four would be deemed traditional Landmarks:

1. A belief in the Supreme Being. This is essential and admits of no compromise.

2. The Bible, referred to by Freemasons as the Volume of the Sacred Law, is always open in the Lodges. Every Candidate is required to take his Obligation on that book or on the Volume which is held by his particular creed to impart sanctity to an oath or promise taken upon it.

3. Everyone who enters Freemasonry is, at the outset, strictly forbidden to countenance any act which may have a tendency to subvert the peace and good order of society; he must pay due obedience to the law of any state in which he resides or which may afford him protection, and he must never be remiss in the allegiance due to the Sovereign of his native land.

4. While English Freemasonry thus inculcates in each of its members the duties of loyalty and citizenship, it reserves to

the individual the right to hold his own opinion with regard to public affairs. But neither in any Lodge, not at any time in his capacity as a Freemason, is he permitted to discuss or to advance his views on theological or political questions.

There is no mention of a belief in immortality. The Principles of Grand Lodge recognition also state the same.[358] As Freemasonry originated in England, one would hope that UGLE would lead the world in defining the Landmarks once and for all, calling them *Landmarks*, and including a belief in immortality. Several places in the *Constitutions* of the United Grand Lodge of England emphasize the importance of "always taking care that the antient Landmarks of the Order be preserved," which is a tall order if they are not specified as such.

One of the stated Landmarks of the Grand Lodge of Massachusetts is a "Belief in immortality, the ultimate lesson of Masonic philosophy." Conversely, this now poses a new problem – should candidates wanting to join a Lodge under the Grand Lodge of Massachusetts profess a belief in both a Supreme Being and immortality?

We can see that in many Grand Lodges the Landmarks have been left intentionally vague, perhaps to allow a broad interpretation in times of religious equality. However, there are two Landmarks that are essential to the Craft, besides a belief in the Supreme Being, and should be included in every Grand Lodge Constitution, though they seem to have been left out of many constitutions:

1. A belief in immortality is essential

2. The right of every Mason to appeal to the Grand Master if they believe a decision by their Lodge to be unfair - though this may be difficult to implement by some Grand Lodges, especially England (UGLE), as it has 200,000 members.

Anti-Masonry

When people do not understand something, they tend to believe the worst about it, as Cornelius Agrippa said in the introduction to *The Four Books of the Occult*, "dogs bark at what they don't know."[359]

The three chestnuts that keep circulating in controversy literature are that first, men are humiliated by being made to ride a goat during their initiation into a Lodge, secondly, that Freemasons worship the devil and lastly, that the pope excommunicates anyone associating with Freemasons.

Masons and the Goat.

Stories of Masons having a goat in the ritual and using it to haze new candidates by "riding the goat," have been circulating since the 1800s, and are nonsense. Associating Freemasonry with a goat has nothing to do with the Hebrew idea of a scapegoat either.[360] The background to the story is more mundane.

In 1813, when the Grand Lodge of England, the Moderns, amalgamated with the Grand Lodge of All England, the Antients, each had a different patron saint. The Antients had adopted the saint used by Operative Masons, St. John the Evangelist, and Operative Lodges were often called St. John's Lodges, based on the "Old Charges" of Freemasonry which speak of St. John the Evangelist, as a "Saint of the Craft." So, the Moderns adopted St. John the Baptist as their patron saint.

The summer solstice is when the sun is at its highest point in the heavens, known as the "triumphant sun," and is also when the sun rises over Stonehenge and hits the Altar Stone dead centre. The feast day of St. John the Baptist is the 24th of June, and is in the Zodiac house of Cancer, the crab; St. John the Evangelist's feast day is the 27th December in the House of Capricorn, which is represented by a goat. So, the sun in Cancer was revered by Speculative Masons and they scorned the "goat." This may also have to do with the backgrounds of the two Sts. John in the Bible, the Baptist was the son of an influential rabbi while the Evangelist was probably an illiterate fisherman.

The Premier Grand Lodge of England was established on the feast day of St. John the Baptist, June 24th in 1717, while St. John Lodges, including the Antients, were dedicated to St. John the Evangelist, whose feast day was December 27th. So, the story of Masons and the goat, is in fact the Masons of the Premier Grand Lodge deriding what they saw as the spurious Antients' Grand Lodge. The fact that the Antients also conferred the degrees very quickly, often giving the First and Second Degree together and the Third Degree the following month, as well as their connection with Jacobitism, were also seen in a poor light.[361]

The Working Tools in the Ritual are a recognition of the role of Operative Masonry in the Revival of Freemasonry, though I doubt that Speculative Masons would have encouraged their Operative colleagues to join a Lodge, as we saw in Masonry Dissected (1730), Operative Masons were "denied Admittance" to the Lodge at the Goose and Gridiron Tavern. A Lodge in the 1720s would have welcomed gentlemen, people who either did not work for a living, as they had unearned income, or they were professionals such as doctors or university professors.

In England there are still some pubs (taverns) called "The Goat and Compasses," but the name has nothing to do with "riding the goat." The origin of the phrase is from the words "God encompasses us,"[36] which degenerated into "Goat and Compasses." This refers to the fact that English inns and taverns inherited a tradition of hospitality from ancient monasteries.

Devil Worship!

Many people confuse the appendant degrees, such as the Scottish Rite and the York Rite, with Blue Lodge Freemasonry, that is to say "pure Antient Masonry consists of three degrees and no more, viz., those of the Entered Apprentice, the Fellow Craft and the Master Mason,

---

[36] St. Augustine, "We in God and God in us; with this difference, however: that *God encompasses us,* and that we are encompassed by him," in A. Fitzgerald ed., *Augustine Through the Ages*, 1999

including the Supreme Order of the Royal Arch." Admittedly, the Royal Arch Degree can be found in all three organizations, which alludes to the importance of its teachings. However, there is no Lucifer, Satan, Beelzebub or Prince of Darkness in Blue Lodge Masonry.

Blue Lodge Freemasonry is concerned with the transmission of "Light," and somehow this became associated with Lucifer. Lucifer is not the devil, he is the light-bringer from the Latin "lux" light, and "ferre" to bring or bear; the same as Christopher, Christo+ferre, means the bearer of Christ.

Several authors have taken Masonic texts, such as *Morals and Dogma* of Scottish Rite Freemasonry, out of context to support an anti-Masonic theory. In this book Albert Pike confirms that Lucifer is the "son of the morning" and the "Light-bearer." Though authors insist on regurgitating old Catholic dogma confusing Lucifer with "the Prince of Darkness," who spreads doubt, confusion and lies.[362] In the Bible the Prince of Darkness is an epithet for Satan.[363]

It is strange that the Church fathers would believe that light, be it literal or the light of wisdom, was an evil to be shunned.[364] The background is that ancient Babylonians worshipped the morning star, Venus, which they called Istar.[37] In Isaiah, the prophet refers to the king of Babylon as "light-bearer, son of the morning!" [365] In the Vulgate Bible, the Greek *"phosophoros"* (light bearer) was translated as *Lucifer*, meaning the morning star, and this was also copied in the King James Bible. In the New Testament the term Lucifer (morning star) is used in a positive sense[366] and, in the fourth century, there was even a Saint Lucifer of Cagliari, a supporter of Eastern Orthodoxy, who was celebrated on May 20th, though his status is said to be "controversial."

Augustine (354-430 AD), in lectures on the Gospel of John, was the first to associate Lucifer with evil when he mistakenly gave him as an example of an enlightened person joining the forces of darkness. Since then, this error has become Catholic doctrine; Augustine wrote:

> A certain one was named Lucifer, who fell; for he was an angel and became a devil; and concerning him the Scripture said, "Lucifer, who did arise in the morning, fell." Isaiah 14:27 And

---

[37] From where we get the word Easter.

why was he Lucifer? Because, being enlightened, he gave forth light. But for what reason did he become dark! Because he abode not in the truth. [367]

In Hogarth's etching *The Mystery of Masonry brought to Light by ye Gormogons* it shows Anderson, whose head is between the rungs of the ladder, kissing Desaguliers's (the joker's) buttocks. At the bottom of the etching is a ditty, of which two lines read:

But mark Free Masons! What a Farce is this?
How wild their Myst'ry! What a Bum they kiss![38]

This is an attempt to besmear the Speculative Freemasons with the claim of devil-worship. There is an ancient Satanic ceremony, blaspheming the Holy Ghost, called "Hieros Gamos" (Sacred Wedding), that usually involved the "Osculum Infamis" (Obscene Kiss), which was kissing a witch's, or the devil's, buttocks as a token of deference or homage. Again, Freemasonry was not, and is not, involved with devil-worship but, as everyone knows, "rumors are carried by haters, spread by fools, and accepted by idiots."[368]

Freemasonry's Relationship with Catholicism

The 1738 Papal Bull, *In Eminenti Apostolatus Specula*, banning Catholics from becoming Freemasons has been enforced over the centuries, and initially Catholics who became Freemasons were automatically excommunicated. This was reviewed in 1917 with the codification of Canon Law that stated Catholics even just associated with Freemasonry were automatically excommunicated, and were not able to receive the mass, nor marriage or funeral rites.

In 1974 the Catholic Bishops' Conference of England and Wales met to discuss how to interpret the 1917 canon, and stated that it applied only to those Catholics who were members of Masonic associations that "machinate against the Church." This was interpreted by the public as allowing Catholics to join Freemasonry as long as those Freemasons were not hostile to the Church.[369] The conference recommend-

---

[38] Notice how the word "kiss" is spelled with a German double "s" in the etching, Kiβ. This is an indication of the influence of the Hanoverian court on society.

ed that Catholics should discuss "the implications of such membership" with their parish priest.

The 1917 canon was updated again in 1983, stating that any person
who joins an association (not identifying Freemasonry per se) which
plots against the Church would be punished with an interdict, that is,
they would be prohibited from attending Mass or receiving rites,
though the Canon states that Catholics "who enrol in Masonic
associations are in a state of grave sin and may not receive Holy
Communion." This is the current situation, however, because of the
ambiguity of the language, Catholics, especially those in America,
thought that the Church's position on Freemasonry had changed, and
many joined the Craft as it does not machinate against the Church.
The fact that the position of the Catholic Church concerning Freemasonry seemed to be different in different countries, such as the
Philippines, has also led to some confusion, especially in light of the
liberalization of the Church after Vatican II.

One of the unusual outcomes of this situation was the founding of the
Knights of Columbus in 1882. This is a Catholic fraternal society,
named in honour of the explorer Christopher Columbus, set up to
serve as a mutual benefit society for immigrant and working-class
Catholics in the United States. It was seen as an alternative to Freemasonry, and has a select membership and a secret initiation, with the
intention of encouraging pride in a Catholic American heritage.

The outcome of the 1534 Act of Supremacy in England and Wales
meant that Britain has not been seen as a country friendly to Catholics.
As of the 2001 National Census, the number of Catholics as a percentage of the population of England and Wales was 8%, up from 4.8% in
1901;[370] part of this growth may be due to Irish and Spanish immigra-
tion into England. This can be compared to Europe where the Catholic
percentage of the population was 35%.[371]

The Spiritual Temple

The Working Tools lecture in the First Degree emphasizes the
importance of building a spiritual temple, "fitting us, as living stones,
for that spiritual building, that house not made with hands, eternal in

the heavens." How this should be done, is for each to discover by himself, but Light forms part of the answer.

Many understand "Light" as either "illumination" or "inspiration," or as Gould says, "opening to the Truth." However, we read in the ritual of the Knight of St. Andrew, the 29th degree of Scottish Rite, that this light changes:

> In every degree of Freemasonry, the Candidate seeks to attain Light. In the Philosophical Degrees [of Scottish Rite] you journeyed continually toward the east, in search of intellectual light. In the Chivalric Degrees you seek to be illuminated by the knightly and heroic virtues, which are the light of the soul.[372]

I believe that a Mason, who really understands the import of the three degrees as I have analysed them, will have no trouble in discovering his spiritual temple.

As an aside, in the Far East, spirituality has a long history, which can be seen in the national flags of many countries: China has stars, Japan and Taiwan the sun, and Korea displays the *YiJing* and *Yin-Yang*.

The Bible

The study of the Bible is indispensable for a Freemason as not only does it give God's blueprint for creation, with the Old Testament showing the preparation, which was manifested in the New Testament and concluded in the Book of Revelation, but also, the Bible is the "rule and guide of our faith," as well as the supreme arcane literature of the Western World.

One thing we can be sure of is that Freemasons in the late 17th and early 18th centuries knew the Bible very well, and this is now a new challenge for Freemasonry. As a consequence of Masonic syncretism, many members believe that the Bible is just for Christian Masons, and others need not concern themselves with it. This book has used over eighty quotations from the Bible in its interpretation of Spiritual Freemasonry, which is an indication of how deeply Freemasonry is entwined with the Bible. So, despite syncretism, the Bible has to be better understood by all Masons. This is not the same as Bible-thumping.

Hidden secrets

I started this book by giving a definition of "the secrets of Freemasonry" and now, after this long adventure, we find that there really
are other profound secrets hidden in the ritual. I often asked myself
why three educated gentlemen would spend eight years to draw up a
new three-part ritual to make "good men better." However, considering that the first three Grand Masters were all connected in some way
to alchemists and had knowledge of an important secret, that they also
wanted to share without devaluing it, their efforts now make better
sense.

We can now understand the meaning of "secrecy" in Freemasonry.
The obvious answer is that Freemasonry is not a secret society but
rather "a society with secrets," and the most important of these is to
understand how we can be resurrected in our own lifetimes and
experience immortality.

The words of Rev. George Oliver, nearly 130 years after the Revival,
still ring true:

> Masons... may be fifty years Masters of the Chair and yet not
> learn the secret of the Brotherhood. This secret is, in its own
> nature, invulnerable; for the Mason, to whom it has become
> known, can only have guessed it and certainly not have received
> it from any one; he has discovered it, because he has been in the
> Lodge, marked, learned and inwardly digested. When he arrives
> at the discovery, he unquestionably keeps it to himself, not com-
> municating it even to his most intimate Brother, because, should
> this person not have capability to discover it of himself, he
> would likewise be wanting in the capability to use it, if he
> received it verbally. For this reason, it will forever remain a
> secret. [373]

The Brotherhood of Man under the Fatherhood of God

Now that I have "elucidated" the facts behind the initiation, the
alchemical passing and the mystic Christian raising, how can the
experience for candidates entering Freemasonry, as well as member
retention, be improved? I believe that by understanding what detrac-
tors assume concerning the Craft, Freemasons can re-evaluate what

they are doing to improve the experience. Some improvements could be:

1. The insistence on wearing dark suits to show the seriousness of Freemasonry and the gloves for the sanctity. Based on Salomon's House in Bacon's *New Atlantis*, Lodges should be an ideal society, a centre of learning where "generosity and enlightenment, dignity and splendor, piety and public spirit" are the common traits.

2. Do not show the Lodge to anyone. Do not brag. The lecture says that the cable-tow is to take obstreperous candidates out of the Lodge "before they even know what it looks like." The Lodge is meant to be mysterious for a reason. Some Lodges may feel like "God's waiting room," but the festive board need not be sombre.[374]

3. The Transmission of Light in the First Degree has to be done perfectly, and the "thunder and lightning" have to be timed properly, for the utmost impression when the candidate first sees the Three Great Lights.

4. Are Masons really trying to make the third King Solomon's Temple in their hearts to receive the Lord? What does that actually mean? How is it done? Each Mason should deliberate on what immortality means to him. Does he believe in it? What would it be like? He needs to learn what the rituals show a Mason about how to experience it.

5. Freemasonry is a quest, not an exercise in collecting merit badges. There is no end to the quest – the Holy Grail is elusive. Masons must study. Confucius said, "Learn as if you could not reach your object and were always fearing also lest you should lose it."[375] Or, consider this Confucian riddle: "He who learns but does not think is lost. He who thinks but does not learn is in great danger."[376]

6. Business meetings should be kept as brief as possible. That could mean handing out minutes and reports in advance to be voted on later, without having to read the whole thing in Lodge,

and instead use the time for education, discussion, question time &c.

7. In Freemasonry, the new candidate must join "of his own free will and accord." People should look at Freemasons and say that they want to associate with upstanding people like Free-masons - and want to join for that reason alone.

8. Wear your Masonic lapel pin with pride! Don't hide your light "under a bushel." Explain to anyone who challenges you that there are six million Brethren worldwide, that Freemasonry is a syncretic organization that "conciliates true friendship among people that might have remained at a perpetual distance," with a history of over three hundred years. Also, we donate millions of dollars every week to charities around the world, without asking anything in return. There are few other organizations that can make that claim.

> In Lodge I wear my Square and Compasses with Pride,
> Though in public these symbols I have to hide.
> I pray that one day
> Men, being free, may
> Display their immortal Light hidden inside!

Masonic Light by C.J. Earnshaw

9. Do not focus on the money, focus on the Brother. Many Brethren are NPD (dropped for "non-payment of dues"). Why? Expulsion should not be automatic; no wonder membership numbers are down. A way around this could be to introduce a way to leave the Craft for a few years without paying dues and come back after being examined on the catechisms for the three degrees, without penalty. This would be especially useful for members of the military when they make a permanent change of station (PCS).

10. We meet on the level. This means that we are all equal in Lodge. Unfortunately, people with more wealth than others tend to believe that it can buy them preference and advancement. We need to make sure that all Brothers feel equally able to advance in Freemasonry, based on merit not advantage. I would rather

a Mason be impressed by respectability, courtesy, knowledge and kindness than by medals, titles and rank. Again, to quote Confucius, "The superior man is aware of righteousness, the inferior man is aware of advantage."

11. Masonry has to be a meritocracy. At present if a well-known person such as a celebrity or an ambassador joins Masonry, he will soon be elevated into a position of responsibility. He becomes an "attractor" so that non-Masons will be inspired to join. This does not happen so much in the large Masonic organizations such as the United Grand Lodge of England, but in smaller Grand Lodges it is very prevalent.

12. Many Masons are unfamiliar with not just the Constitution of their Grand Lodge, but also their own Lodge Bylaws, and skirt around the rules. There needs to be an examination system that is enforced for advancement in Freemasonry, such as the "Master Craftsman" examinations in Scottish Rite. There should be privileges for passing the exams, one of which would be eligibility to hold Grand Lodge rank. The Masonic exams should cover several areas such as ritual, the bylaws and the Constitution, history, conspiracy theories and knowledge of leading Masonic texts, such as those of Pike and Gould, and of course, the Bible.

13. The "genius" of the first three Grand Masters was that they realized that if their revived ritual was to succeed, they needed endorsements, and in those days in the England the best recommendation one could have was from the king. Even nowadays companies jealously guard their Royal Warrants of Appointment, which give a company the ability to use the monarch's coat of arms on their products and in advertising.

However, a king is not going to put his stamp of approval on just any scheme; so, the Grand Masters started by inviting lesser nobility to take the reins of the organization as figurehead Grand Masters, while controlling from behind. This strategy helped Freemasonry grow by a quantum leap.

The same thing has to be done again to make Freemasonry attractive to people. There has not been a U.S. president in

Freemasonry since Gerald Ford, and in the country of origin, few of the closest members of the Queen's family are Masons. This is a challenge for Freemasonry in the 21st century.

14. Quality vs Quantity. Due to declining memberships, many Lodges have tried to bolster the membership without taking time to check whether a candidate is a good fit for the Lodge. Finding the right candidate is not just about him being "a good man." His values should also be in line with those of the Lodge. More than just three investigators should be involved in the process and, because everyone is so busy nowadays, the process should be made as easy as possible, so rather than having three separate interviews, perhaps the candidate could attend just one.

15. It must be explained that there are requirements for membership, which needs to be understood by people who apply to join a Lodge. Freemasonry is not a networking organization (many people join only to quit after a year or two because the networking potential is low), there are responsibilities to membership. The *Constitutions* do not allow Masons to proselytize, but if we set a good example, people will come. We spend a lot of money on charitable events, and the public should be made aware of this.

16. Leadership: the future of Freemasonry relies on good leadership. Again, Brethren should not be elected Master of the Lodge just because they are "good men." They need experience in leading and planning. It comes down to the question of experience vs ability vs precedence. Experience is what comes of many years' attendance at the Lodge, ability may be found both in competence in the ritual and in a career outside of the Lodge. Precedence is from working through the positions in the Lodge and becoming "next in line." By appointing a Brother to a position in Lodge that has responsibilities, the Lodge can see if the Brother is up to the job. If, later, he should have made a good impression in overseeing the banquets and festivities as Junior Warden, then as Senior Warden, carried out his fiduciary responsibilities of budgeting and money management equally conscientiously, then the Brother should be ready to lead the

Lodge. Electioneering should have no place in the Lodge; if a Brother has not convinced the members by his actions that he is ready for responsibility, then the position should be filled by a more qualified Brother.

The Fourth Era of Freemasonry

There have been three eras of development in the history of Freemasonry:

1. The era of stonemasons, their guilds and trade secrets, from which developed Operative Masonry. This era emphasized the science of building that incorporated sacred geometry, and the importance of an apprenticeship and qualifications.

2. The second era was the Revival from 1717, marking the beginning of Speculative Freemasonry, until about 1837, and the beginning of the Victorian era. The Revival emphasized the spiritual quest for immortality, and how a man could be resurrected in his own lifetime to experience immortality.

3. The third era, which we are now in, started in the Victorian era around 1837 and emphasized propriety and "a peculiar system of morality." It is important that Freemasonry is done with decorum and dignity, however, this has led to many people feeling that Freemasonry is a religion for old men.

4. The fourth era is for us to build. It should continue the emphasis on morality and propriety, decorum and dignity, but we need to put back the soul that has been expunged. The sense of wonder and mystique needs to be preserved, like for example, replacing electric lights with candles, or (re)introducing the Chamber of Reflection as found in many European Lodges. We need to make Freemasonry something that is a privilege to join, not just another networking opportunity. Introducing new candidates should be thought of as a meritorious deed, as the Brother is supporting the awakening of another soul.

Yes, butters

The Mason who has read this far will perhaps discuss these findings with his Brethren, and unfortunately many will come across the "Yes, but..." default answer from some older Masons. Do not let this discourage you, the search is well worth a few cynical looks. I'm reminded of a Russian joke (Russian humour is very dry!), which you might like to tell such Brethren. An astronomer was on the deck of a ship one night and asked a sailor standing nearby if he could identify the stars in the night sky. When the sailor answered that he could not, the astronomer replied that the sailor had lost so much by not knowing. Later that evening the ship started to list and was obviously sinking. The astronomer clung for dear life to the railings on the deck, and as the sailor prepared to jump into the sea he asked the astronomer if he could swim, and when he answered that he could not, the sailor replied, "professor, you have lost everything!"

Conclusion

The three years I spent writing these four books have been both an education and an adventure. I now appreciate the Ritual even more than when I was first raised, for both its simplicity and profound complexity. The truth is that I cannot be sure that all the events I have written about actually happened, the story is more of an educated guess based on dozens of synchronicities and assumptions.

We will never know for sure the reason three intelligent men decided to spend eight years rewriting and expanding on a play (the ritual) that had been in existence for over a hundred years among the building trades, and none of the three men was a builder. Their intentions were not recorded, neither was the ritual in the early days. The ritual was learned by emulation so all we know is from exposés, often written by disgruntled members. Also, when George Payne was Grand Master in 1720 a large number of documents were destroyed.

This is not the end of the story. The alchemy of the "Transmission of Light" in the First Degree (explained in *Freemasonry: Initiation by Light*), together with the alchemy of "hidden dew" of the Second Degree (given in *Freemasonry: Spiritual Alchemy*) combine to produce a life-changing experience, once the Mason has understood what the Signposts are pointing to.

Am I holding anything back? Yes! First, the answer to the Twenty-fifth Signpost, which is explained in *Freemasonry: Royal Arch*. Secondly, Masons are on a quest. Why? Because the Third Degree does not complete anything. The Grand Master is dead, the Temple has not been completed, and we have not found the Lost Word, and that is how the Ritual ends. The Master Mason has been given the tools, so he now needs to complete the quest!

References

[1] A. Pike, *The Symbolism of the Blue Degrees of Freemasonry*, 1888

[2] M. Jacob, *The Origins of Freemasonry: Facts and Fictions*, 2007

[3] Extract from *Report of Board of General Purposes*, adopted 10 March 1999, UGLE, p27, accessed June 24th 2017 http://d3pl5apc7wn4y0.cloudfront.net/images/files/Information_Booklet_-_2016_-_Website_Edition_Secured.pdf

[4] *Merriam-Webster Dictionary*

[5] *Random House Unabridged Dictionary*

[6] Quoted from Grand Lodge of Scotland's website, *www.grandLodgescotland.com*, accessed June 24th 2017

[7] *What is Masonic Education*, midnightfreemasons.org, accessed June 24th, 2017.

[8] J. Anderson, *The Constitutions of the Free-Masons*, 1738

[9] A. Mackey, *Ethics and Masonry in Mackey's Revised Encyclopaedia of Freemasonry*, 1909

[10] W.Bro. Y. Yagi, Square and Compass Lodge, Tokyo, in conversation with the author, May 2017

[11] *Duncan's Masonic Ritual and Monitor*, by Malcom C. Duncan, 1866

[12] S. Shepherd, The Webb Ritual in the United States, in *Masonic Enlightenment*, 2006

[13] Proceedings of the Grand Lodge of Ancient, Free & Accepted Masons of Canada, 1892

[14] A. Mackey, *An Encyclopaedia of Freemasonry and Its Kindred Sciences*, 1874

[15] S. Shepherd, The Webb Ritual in the United States, in *Masonic Enlightenment*, 2006

[16] T. Webb, *The Freemason's Monitor*, 1859

[17] Siddhartha Gautama, The Buddha on Belief from the *Kalama Sutta*, 4th century BC

[18] F. Le Van Baumer, *The Early Tudor Theory of Kingship*, 1940

[19] N. Pasachoff, *Playwrights, Preachers and Politicians: A Study of Four Tudor Old Testament Dramas*, 1975

[20] J. Ure, *Pilgrimages: The Great Adventure of the Middle Ages*, 2006

[21] J. Tuck, *The Cambridge Parliament 1388*, 1969

[22] J. Ruskell, L Clark and C Rawcliffe ed., *The History of Parliament; The House of Commons1386-1421* ; 1993

[23] G. Trevelyan, *England in the Age of Wycliffe*, 1963

[24] J. Burton, *Monastic and Religious Orders in Britain 1000-1300*, 1994

[25] *Studies in the Early History of Shaftesbury Abbey*, Dorset County Council, 1999

[26] G. W. Bernard, The Dissolution of the Monasteries, in *History*, 2011

[27] C. Cross, *Church and People 1450-1660*, 1976

[28] T. Smith, English Guilds Oxford 1870 as quoted in *Piety, Fraternity and Power* by D. Crouch, 2000

[29] J. Tuck, The Cambridge Parliament 1388, as quoted in *Piety, Fraternity and Power* by David J.F. Crouch, 2000

[30] D. Crouch, *Piety, Fraternity and Power*, 2000

[31] A. Poole, *From Doomsday Book to Magna Carta*, 1993

236

[32] M. Prak, *Craft Guilds in the Early Modern Low Countries: Work, Power and Representation, 2006*

[33] D. Crouch, *Piety, Fraternity and Power*, 2000

[34] S. Ogilvie, Guilds, efficiency, and social capital: evidence from German proto-industry, in *Economic History Review*. 2004

[35] S. Ogilvie, Guilds, Efficiency, and Social Capital: Evidence from German Proto-industry, in *Economic History Review*. 2004

[36] I Tim iii, 16

[37] 2 Thess ii 7

[38] *The Harpers Book of Facts*, 1895

[39] A. Pollard, *English Miracle Plays, Moralities and Interludes*, 1978

[40] De Mandatis Divinis quoted in M. Aston *Lollards and Reformers: Images of Literacy in Late Medieval Religion*, 1984

[41] D. Sharpiro, *Oberammergau*, 2000

[42] *Ars Quatuor Coronatorum*, vol. XXIV

[43] R. Gould, *History of Freemasonry* Vol 1, 1883

[44] R. Gould, *History of Freemasonry* Vol 1, 1883

[45] J. Wormald, *Jenny Mary, Queen of Scots, 1988*

[46] P. *Croft, King James, 2003*

[47] M. Giuseppi ed., *Cecil Papers in Hatfield House*, 1883

[48] S. Lee, ed. *Brooke, George in Dictionary of National Biography,*1893

[49] *Charter to Sir Walter Raleigh: 1584, The Avalon Project, Yale Law School*

[50] R. Trevelyan, *Sir Walter Raleigh*, 2002

[51] A. *Fraser, The Gunpowder Plot, 1996*

[52] K. *Brice, The Early Stuarts 1603–40; 1994*

[53] I Samuel 16

[54] I Peter 2:13–20

[55] J. Sommerville, *Royalists and Patriots: Politics and Ideology in England 1603-1640*; 1999

[56] Romans 13: 4-6

[57] A. *Dickens, The English Reformation, 1978*

[58] J. Sommerville ed., *Patriarcha and Other Writings*, 1991

[59] James I King of England, *Basilikon Doron*, 1599

[60] Sir A. Weldon, *The Court and Character of King James I*, 1651

[61] C. Trueman, *James I and Witchcraft,* 2015

[62] M. *Gibson, Witchcraft and Society in England And America, 1550–1750; 2006*

[63] S. Mitchell, *Some Memoranda in Regard to William Harvey, M.D.*, 1907

[64] D'A. Power, *William Harvey: Masters of Medicine*; 1897

[65] *The Life of John Wesley* in the Library of Christian Biography, 1856

[66] R. Sherwood, *Oliver Cromwell: King in All but Name, 1653–1658*; 1997

[67] C. Atkinson, *Great Rebellion,* 1911

[68] A. Hughes, *The Causes of the English Civil War*, 1998

[69] S. Church, *Oliver Cromwell, a History: Comprising a Narrative of His Life*, 1895

[70] W. Sachse, *England's "Black Tribunal": An Analysis of the Regicide Court*, in The Journal of British Studies, 1973

[71] E. Poole, *An Alarum of War, given to the Army, and to their High Court of Justice (so called) by the will of God: revealed in Elizabeth Pooll, sometime a messenger of the Lord to the Generall Councell, concerning the cure of the land, and the manner thereof*, 1649.

[72] C. *Carlton, Charles I: The Personal Monarch; 1995*

[73] G. *Edwards, The Last Days of Charles I; 1999*

[74] G. *Edwards, The Last Days of Charles I; 1999*

[75] Daniel 2:44

[76] S. Newman, *The Real History of the End of the World;* 2010

[77] S. Skinner, *Millennium Prophecies,* 1994

[78] *Roundhead on the Pike,* Time Magazine, 1957

[79] J. Jones, *Country and Court: England 1658–1714;* 1979

[80] S. Newman, *The Real History of the End of the World;* 2010

[81] Ecclesiastes 3:19

[82] B. Worden, *Literature and Politics in Cromwellian England,* 2007

[83] C. Hill, *Milton and the English Revolution,* 1977

[84] R. *Hutton, Charles II: King of England, Scotland, and Ireland, 1989*

[85] C. Trueman, *Samuel Pepys and the Plague,* historylearningsite.co.uk., accessed July 24th, 2017

[86] J. *Miller, Charles II, 1991*

[87] C. Trueman, *Cures for the Plague,* historylearningsite.co.uk., accessed July 24th, 2017

[88] *G. Steventon; S. Mitchell, Molecules of Death, 2007*

[89] J. Anderson, E. Barnes, E. Shackleton, *The Art of Medicine: Over 2,000 Years of Images and Imagination,* 2012

[90] E. Anders, 'A Plea for the Lancet': Bloodletting, Therapeutic Epistemology, and Professional Identity in Late Nineteenth-century American Medicine, in *Social History of Medicine,* 2016

[91] A. Tinniswood, *By Permission of Heaven: The Story of the Great Fire of London,* 2003

[92] Estimated using www.measuringworth.com, 1666 values at 2017 values.

[93] R. Rideal, *1666: Plague, War and Hellfire,* 2016

[94] W. *Besant, London in the Time of the Stuarts, 1903*

[95] J. Christopher, *Wren's City of London Churches,* 2012

[96] A. *Fraser, King Charles II, 1979*

[97] G. Burnet, *History of His Own Time,* 1979

[98] J. Kenyon, *Stuart England,* 1978

[99] C. Earnshaw, フリーメイソン：真実の歴史、2017

[100] I. Newbould, *Whiggery and Reform, 1830–41;* 1990

[101] J. Miller, *James II,* 2000

[102] J. Henslowe, *Anne Hyde Duchess of York,* 1915

[103] J. Callow, *The Making of King James II: The Formative Years of a King, 2000*

[104] M. Haile, *Queen Mary of Modena: Her Life and Letters,* 1905

[105] E. Gregg, *Queen Anne,* 2001

[106] J. Van der Kiste, *William and Mary* 2003

[107] J. Miller, *James II,* 2000

[108] E. Gregg, *Queen Anne,* 2001

[109] Cassell's Illustrated History of England, Vol. 3, Ch.14

[110] M. McIntyre, Mary II (1662–1694), in Anne Commire ed., Women in World History, 2002

[111] D. Szechi; *The Jacobites: Britain and Europe, 1688-1788,* 1994

[112] J. Van der Kiste, *William and Mary,* 2003

[113] J. Aylward, *The English Master of Arms,* 1991

[114] N. Johnson et al., *Firearms Law and the Second Amendment: Regulation, Rights, and Policy,* 2017

[115] P. Mathias, The Brewing Industry in England 1700-1830; 1959

[116] K. *Chisholm, A Tonic for the Nation, 2002*

[117] H. Fielding, *An Enquiry into the Causes of the Late Increase of Robbers,* 1751

[118] W. Hogarth, in his etching *Gin Lane*, 1751

[119] R. *Schofield, Stephen Hales, Scientist and philanthropist, 1980*

[120] D. Defoe, On Conjugal Lewdness, 1727

[121] T. Scrubb, Desolation: Or, The Fall of Gin, 1736

[122] P. *Laslett, John Locke, Two Treatises of Government,* 1988

[123] P. des Maizeaux, Biography of John Toland, 1722

[124] S. *Schama, Britannia Incorporated. A History of Britain, BBC, 2001*

[125] E. Gregg, *Queen Anne*, 2001

[126] R. Parker, *Memoirs of the most remarkable Military Transactions from 1683 to 1718 in Ireland and Flanders*, 1746

[127] D. Oakleaf, *A Political Biography of Jonathan Swift*, 2015

[128] J. Plumb, *England in the Eighteenth Century*, 1950

[129] D. *Sobel, Longitude: The True Story of a Lone Genius Who Solved the Greatest Scientific Problem of His Time, 1989*

[130] S. Schaffer in D. Aubin et al. (ed), *The Heavens on Earth: Observatories and Astronomy in Nineteenth-Century Science and Culture*, 2010

[131] J. Boswell, *Life of Samuel Johnson*, 1759

[132] K. Lippincott, *A Guide to the Royal Observatory*, 2007

[133] E. Halley and N. Thrower, *The Three Voyages of Edmond Halley in the Paramore*, 1698–1701, 1982

[134] N. Goldsmith, *Alexander Pope: the evolution of a poet*, 2002

[135] P. Monod, *Jacobitism and the English People 1688-1788*; 1989

[136] J. Appleby, *The Relentless Revolution*, 2011

[137] Estimate. The first census in Britain was 1801.

[138] L. *Clopper, The History and Development of the Chester Cycle, 1978*

[139] A. *Baker, Fifteen Signs of Doomsday, 1897*

[140] E. *Forbes, Greenwich Observatory: Origins and Early History 1675–1835; 1975*

[141] G. Whiting, *Black Munday turn'd white: or, A Whip for Star-Gazers, &c.*, 1652

[142] Cicero, *De Natura Deorum*, 45 BC

[143] S. *Moss, Wild Hares and Hummingbirds. 2011*

[144] A. Geneva, *Astrology and the Seventeenth Century Mind, William Lilly and the Language of the Stars,* 1995

[145] L. *Kassell, Medicine and Magic in Elizabethan London, 2007*

[146] R. Renny, *An History of Jamaica*, 1807

[147] M. Wolfgang, *England Under George I. The Beginnings of the Hanoverian Dynasty*, 1981

[148] R. *Hatton, George I: Elector and King, 1978.*

[149] P. H. Brown, A History of Scotland to the Present Time, 1911

[150] R. *Hatton, George I: Elector and King, 1978.*

[151] F. McLynn, Charles Edward Stuart: a Tragedy in Many Acts, 1989

[152] L. Worsley, *Bad Blood: Stuarts to Hanoverians*, BBC, 2013

[153] A. Somerset, *Queen Anne: The Politics of Passion*, 2012

[154] MacKay, J. et al., *A history of Western society: from the Renaissance to 1815*, Vol 2, 1995

[155] *The Family Bible Encyclopedia*, 1972

[156] B. *Moynahan, God's Bestseller: William Tyndale, Thomas More, and the Writing of the English Bible, 2003*

[157] W. Tyndale, *The Obedience of a Christian Man*, 1528

[158] E. Knowles ed., James I in *The Oxford Dictionary of Quotations*, 2014

[159] I. H. *Hall, The Revised New Testament and History of Revisions, 1881*

[160] Lord Herbert of Cherbury, *De Veritate,* 1624

[161] W. G. Wilson, J.H. Templeton, *Anglican Teaching:* an Eexposition of the Thirty-Nine Articles, 1962

[162] C. *Joppke, Veil, 2013*

[163] K. Heussi, *Kompendium der Kirchengeschichte,* 1956

[164] P. Croft, *King James,* 2004

[165] J. Calvin, *Institutes of the Christian Religion,* 1536

[166] John 1:1–18

[167] W. Gibson, *The Church of England 1688–1832: Unity and Accord,* 2001

[168] S. Snobelen, *Isaac Newton, Socinianism and "the One Supreme God,"* 2005

[169] P. Johnson, *A History of the Jews,* 2013

[170] J. *Parkes, The Jew in the Medieval Community, 1976*

[171] Numbers 15:37-41

[172] *Medieval Sourcebook: Twelfth Ecumenical Council:* Lateran IV 1215, Canon 68

[173] R. Mundill, *England's Jewish Solution: Experiment and Expulsion, 1262-1290*; 2002

[174] R. O'Brien, *The Life of Charles Stewart Parnell, 1846-1891*; 1968

[175] S. Joy, *The IRA in Kerry 1916–1921*; 2005

[176] R. Davies, *British Slaves on the Barbary Coast,* 2003

[177] G. Milton, *White Gold,* 2012

[178] H. Milman, *Annals of S. Paul's Cathedral,* 1868

[179] D. Willson, *King James VI & I,* 1956

[180] Isaiah 66:2, Ezra 9:4

[181] F. Aveling, Antinomianism in *The Catholic Encyclopedia,* 1913

[182] S. Skinner, *Millennium Prophecies,* 1994

[183] C. *Firth, The Last Years of the Protectorate, 1656–58, 1909*

[184] H. *Campbell, The Britannica Guide to Political Science and Social Movements That Changed the Modern World, 2009*

[185] Acts 4:32

[186] M. Casaubon, *A Treatise Concerning Enthusiasme,* 1656

[187] S. Skinner, *Millennium Prophecies,* 1994

[188] R. Wallace, *Antitrinitarian Biography: or, Sketches of the lives and writings of distinguished Antitrinitarians,* 1850

[189] W. S. Palmer, *The Confessions of Jacob Boehme,* 1954

[190] H. Martensen, *Jacob Boehme: his life and teaching, or Studies in theosophy,* 1885

[191] C. Gribben. Millennialism, in M. Haykin and M. Jones, ed., *Drawn into Controversie: Reformed Theological Diversity and Debates Within Seventeenth Century British Puritanism,* 2011

[192] G. Bonet-Maury, *Early sources of English Unitarian Christianity,* 1884

[193] G. Blainey; *A Short History of Christianity,* 2011

[194] F. Thilly, *A History of Philosophy,* 1914

[195] J. Waldron; *God, Locke, and Equality: Christian Foundations in Locke's Political Thought,* 2002

[196] A. Collins, *A Discourse of Freethinking, Occasion'd by the Rise and Growth of a Sect called Freethinkers,* 1713

[197] J. *Orr, English Deism: Its Roots and Its Fruits, 1934*

[198] E. *Wilson, P. Reill, Deism, 2004*

[199] 1 John 5:7

[200] F. McGillion, *Blinded by Starlight,* 2002

[201] J. Hobson, *The Eastern Origins of Western Civilization,* 2004

[202] J. Parker, *Windows into China*, 1978

[203] J. Force, *Introduction in W. Stephens, An Account of the Growth of Deism in England (1696)*, 1990

[204] J. Orr, *English Deism: Its Roots and Its Fruits*, 1934

[205] Matthew 12:32

[206] I Corinthians 3:13-15

[207] Johann Tetzel (1465-1519) a Dominican preacher in Leipzig

[208] Ezekiel 18:4

[209] Matthew 10:28

[210] 1 Corinthians 15:51-54

[211] 1 Thessalonians 4:13–18

[212] Matthew 10:13

[213] 1 Timothy 6:15-16

[214] E. Brandon, *The coherence of Hobbes's Leviathan: civil and religious authority combined;* 2007

[215] 1 Corinthians 3:15, Matthew 12: 32, Rev 21:27 and Pope Gregory the Great (540–604), *The Dialogues Bk. IV*

[216] R.A. Morey, *Death and the Afterlife*, 1984

[217] 1 Samuel 28:3–25

[218] J. Donelley, *Calvinism and Scholasticism in Vermigli's Doctrine of Man and Grace*, 1976

[219] Noncanonical text, 1 Macc.2:29-38

[220] F. Bacon, *Essayes. Religious Meditations. Places of Perswasion and Disswasion. Seene and Allowed*, 1597

[221] H. King, "*An Exequy* [a funeral rite or ceremony] *to His Matchless Never to be Forgotten Friend*, c1624

[222] V. Rees, *Marsilio Ficino*, 2001

[223] II Corinthians 12:2

[224] J. Milton, *Paradise Lost*, 1667

[225] D. Edwards, *Christian England: From the Reformation to the 18th Century*, 1983

[226] W. Shakespeare, *Macbeth*, Act 4 Scene 3, 1606

[227] D. Dalrymple, *Annals of Scotland*, 1776

[228] H. Bradley, *Howard, A Handbook of Coins of the British Isles*, 1978

[229] P. Waring, *The Dictionary of Omens & Superstitions*, 1987

[230] W. MacNulty, *Freemasonry: A Journey Through Ritual and Symbol*, 1991

[231] E. Mueller, *A History of Jewish Mysticism*, 2008

[232] Fulcanelli, *The Mystery of the Cathedrals*, 1926

[233] A. De Hoyos, *Scottish Rite Ritual Monitor and Guide*, 2008

[234] E. Mueller, *A History of Jewish Mysticism*, 2008

[235] D. Cottrell, *Genesis 1: The Design and Plan for the Kingdom of Heaven*, 2010

[236] F. Bacon, *New Atlantis*, 1627

[237] A. Milborne, *New Atlantis and Freemasonry*, in *Masonic Enlightenment* ed. M. Poll, 2006

[238] B. Price ed., *Francis Bacon's New Atlantis: New Interdisciplinary Essays*, 2002

[239] J. Weinberger ed., *Francis Bacon, New Atlantis and The Great Instauration*, 1989

[240] Deuteronomy 27:5

[241] S. Baring-Gould, *Curious Tales of the Middle Ages*, 1866

[242] Proverbs 25:15

[243] John 3:3

[244] M.P. Hall, *The Secret Teachings of All Ages*; 1928

[245] A. Pike, *Morals & Dogma*, 1871

[246] A. Pike, *Morals & Dogma*, 1871

[247] A. Pike, *Morals & Dogma*, 1871

[248] R. Macoy, *General History, Cyclopedia and Dictionary of Freemasonry,* 1870

[249] P. Camporesi, *The Fear of Hell: Images of Damnation and Salvation in Early Modern Europe*, 1990.

[250] Luke 12:5

[251] 1 John 4:8

[252] Hebrews 10:31

[253] Matthew 6:1-4

[254] Matthew 10:13

[255] Ecclesiastes 9:5

[256] Isaiah 26:19

[257] Ezekiel 37:28

[258] Daniel 12:2

[259] Acts 13:22

[260] Acts 2:29

[261] 1 Corinthians 15:18

[262] 1 Corinthians 15:22

[263] 1 Corinthians 15:51-53

[264] J. Priestley, *History of the Corruptions of Christianity*, 1782

[265] Pope Gregory the Great, *The Dialogues bk. IV,* c.591

[266] *The New Catholic Encyclopedia*, 2nd ed., 2003

[267] I Corinthians 3:15, Matthew 12: 32, Rev 21:27 and Pope Gregory the Great, the Dialogues bk. IV, c.591

[268] D. Pieper, *Christian Dogmatics*, 1953

[269] J. Pelikan, H. Lehmann ed., Commentary on 1 Corinthians 15, in *Luther's Works*, 1973

[270] M. Luther, *An Exposition of Salomon's Booke, called Ecclesiastes or the Preacher*, 1553

[271] A. McGrath, *In the Beginning: The Story of the King James Bible and How It Changed a Nation, a Language, and a Culture*, 2002

[272] C. Butterworth, A. Chester, *George Joye. A Chapter in the History of the English Bible and the English Reformation*, 1962

[273] G. Juhasz, Some Neglected Aspects of the Debate between William Tyndale and George Joye (1534–1535), in *Reformation*, 2009

[274] W. Tyndale, *Tyndale's New Testament: Translated from the Greek*, 1534

[275] Matthew 12:32

[276] Psalm 119:161

[277] Luke 23:32

[278] A. Shamir, English Bibles on Trial: Bible burning and the desecration of Bibles, 1640–1800, 2016

[279] 1 Thessalonians 4:13–18

[280] N. Burns, *Christian Mortalism From Tyndale to Milton*, 1972

[281] I Timothy 6:15-16

[282] Luke 16:23-26

[283] Matthew 27:51-53

[284] B. Ball, *The Soul Sleepers: Christian Mortalism from Wycliffe to Priestley*, 2008

[285] B. Ball, *The Soul Sleepers: Christian Mortalism from Wycliffe to Priestley*, 2008

[286] E. Cardwell, ed., Article 40 of the Forty-Two Articles of Religion, in *Synodalia*, 1842

[287] Genesis 2:7

[288] R. Overton, *Man Wholly Mortal*, 1655

[289] R. Overton, *Man's Mortality*, 1644

[290] Of the State of Men After Death, and of the Resurrection of the Dead, Article 32 of the Westminster Confession of Faith, 1646

[291] Tim S. Gray, Hobbes, Thomas, in *The Oxford Companion to British History*, 1997

[292] Quoted on frontispiece of *Leviathan*, Job 41:24

[293] Victor Nuovo, ed., *John Locke, Writings on Religion*, 2002

[294] D. Wolfe, ed., *Treatise on Christian Doctrine, in The Complete Prose Works of John Milton, 1953–1982,* 1953

[295] 1 Corinthians 15 and 1 Thessalonians 4

[296] E. Law, *Considerations on the State of the World with Regard to the Theory of Religion*, 1745

[297] P. Peckard, *Observations on the Doctrine of an Intermediate State Between Death and the Resurrection*, 1756

[298] J. Priestley, *Disquisitions Relating to Matter and Spirit*, 1777

[299] E. Pagels, *Beyond Belief: The Secret Gospel of Thomas*, 2003

[300] A. Pike, *Morals and Dogma*, 1871

[301] Luke 24:39

[302] 1 Corinthians 15:42-44

[303] Ephesians 2:8-9

[304] John 3:16

[305] C. Ducasse, *The Belief in a Life after Death*, 1961

[306] I John 3:15

[307] Psalm 68:2

[308] Matthew 18:3

[309] 1 Corinthians 13:11

[310] M. Duncan, *Duncan's Masonic Ritual and Monitor, First Degree*, 1866

[311] H. Valborg, *Symbols of the Eternal Doctrine: From Shamballa to Paradise*, 2011

[312] Isaiah 41:19

[313] Exodus 25:23-30

[314] R. Cooper, *The Red Triangle: The History of the Persecution of Freemasons*, 2011

[315] Image of the scarlet pimpernel by Jean-Jacques MILAN, CC BY-SA 3.0

[316] D. Cordingly, *Under the Black Flag: The Romance and Reality of Life Among the Pirates*, 1995

[317] C. Johnson, *A General History of the Robberies and Murders of the Most Notorious Pyrates*, 1724

[318] S. Padget, *Wren's St. Paul's: Axis Mundi of the New Jerusalem*, paper read at Ball State University, 2000, www.scribd.com/document/86203892/Steve-Padget-Kabbalistic-Cathedral-Symbolism, accessed June 24th, 2017

[319] W. Wilmshurst, *The Ceremony of Initiation. Analysis and Commentary*, 2010, https://www.brad.ac.uk/webofhiram/?section=walter_leslie_wilmshurst&page=Initiation.html, accessed June 24th, 2017

[320] John 3:16

[321] John 8:32

[322] V. Nabokov, *Pale Fire,* 1962

[323] C. Leadbeater, *Glimpses of Masonic History*, 1926

[324] J. Phillips, C. Wetherell, *The Great Reform Act of 1832 and the political modernization of England*, American Historical Review, 1995

[325] J. Wallis, *Pennant's London: Being a Complete Guide to the British Capital*, 1814
[326] J. Westfall, W. Sheehan, *Celestial Shadows: Eclipses, Transits, and Occultations*, 2014
[327] Acts 17:24-25, Matthew 6:5-6, Revelation 3:20 and 1 Corinthian 3:16-17
[328] A. Johnston ed., *The Advancement of Learning and The New Atlantis*, 1974
[329] Proverbs 10:19
[330] J. Doelman, *King James I and the Religious Culture of England*, 2000
[331] T. Kirby, P. Stanwood, *Paul's Cross and the Culture of Persuasion in England 1520-1640*; 2013
[332] S. Padget, *Christopher Wren, Christian Cabala and the Tree of Life*, on www.acsforum.org, retrieved June 14th, 2017
[333] B. Holland, *The Masons are still at it after all these years!* 1998
[334] R. Lund, *The Hidden Code in Freemasonry: Finding Light Through Esoteric Interpretation of Masonic Ritual*, 2016
[335] Albert Pike, Chapter 30 The Knights Kadosh in *Morals and Dogma*, 1871
[336] A. de Hoyos, *Scottish Rite Ritual, Monitor and Guide*, 2008
[337] Rev G. Oliver, *History of Initiation*, 1855
[338] http://www.anglican.ink/article/freemasonry-and-doctrine-church-england, accessed 24th June 2017
[339] I. Gordon, *The Craft and the Cross*, 1989
[340] https://www.ugle.org.uk, accessed 24th June 2017
[341] A. Lusher, *Independent Newspaper*, Saturday 6 August 2016
[342] Masonic Service Association of North America, http://www.msana.com/msastats.asp, accessed 24th June 2017
[343] J. Harper, Freemasons grow in popularity in Asia, in *The Telegraph*, 10 Dec 2012
[344] R. Putnam, *Bowling Alone: The Collapse and Revival of American Community*, 2000
[345] Masonic Service Association of North America, http://www.msana.com/msastats.asp, accessed 24th June 2017
[346] A. Pike, *Morals and Dogma*, 1871
[347] UGLE, Dress code, http://d3pl5apc7wn4y0.cloudfront.net/images/files/Information_Booklet_-_2016_-_Website _Edition_Secured.pdf, accessed 24th June 2017
[348] GLS, Dress Code, http://www.pglrpss.co.uk/masonicetiquette.pdf, accessed 24th June 2017
[349] GLM, Dress Code: https://massmasons.org/mmdocs/gov/Grand_Lodge_Protocol_Manual_June_2010.pdf, accessed 24th June 2017
[350] F. Yates, *The Art of Memory*, 2011
[351] M. Faulkes, *A Mosaic Palace*, 2018
[352] Book of Proverbs 22:28
[353] R. Macoy, *General History, Cyclopedia and Dictionary of Freemasonry*, 1870
[354] T. Satchell, *A Modern Examination of the Landmarks of Freemasonry*, undated, on http://www.freemasons-freemasonry.com/landmarks-freemasonry.html, accessed 24th June 2017
[355] A. Bernheim, *My Approach to Masonic History, 2011* on http://www.freemasons-freemasonry.com/bernheim27.html#_ednref39 accessed 24th June 2017
[356] J. F. Newton, *The Builders*, 1914
[357] Grand Lodge Recognition: A Symposium on The Conditions of Grand Lodge Recognition, Compiled and Published by The Commission on Information for Recognition of the Conference of Grand Masters of Masons in North America, 1956
[358] *Constitutions of the Antient Fraternity of Free and Accepted under the United Grand Lodge of England*, 2016

[359] A. de Hoyos, S. Morris, *Is it True what They Say about Freemasonry? The Methods of Anti-Masons*, 2004

[360] Leviticus 16:7-10

[361] W. Hughan, Masonic Sketches and Reprints, 1871

[362] K. Bowers, *Hiding in Plain Sight*, 2001

[363] Ephesians 6:12

[364] K. Kay ed., Pharos, the Silas H. Shepherd Reader, *Esoterica*, 2014

[365] Isaiah 14:12

[366] 2Peter 1:19

[367] Tractate 3: 7

[368] Z. Abdelnour, H. Cain, *Economic Warfare: Secrets of Wealth Creation in the Age of Welfare Politics,* 2011

[369] W. Whalen, *Christianity and American Freemasonry*, 1958

[370] Census 2001 National Report for England and Wales, https://data.gov.uk/dataset/b8333b70-3498-4fd5-b9b2-5a9d463e5f15/census-2001-national-report-for-england-and-wales, accessed June 24th 2017

[371] *Global Christianity 2011*, Pew Research Center, http://www.pewforum.org/files/2011/12/Christianity-fullreport-web.pdf, accessed June 24th 2017

[372] A. de Hoyos, *Scottish Rite Ritual, Monitor and Guide*, 2008

[373] Rev. G. Oliver, *Historical Landmarks*, 1845

[374] A. Lusher, *Independent Newspaper*, Saturday 6 August 2016

[375] Analects 8:17

[376] Analects 2.15

Index

B

Introducing the Author

Christopher J. Earnshaw PhD 33°

Past Grand Historian, Grand Lodge of Japan.

Past Master of the Research Lodge, Grand Lodge of Japan.

Scottish Rite 33° IGH, Past-Chairman of Education Committee.

Recipient of the Order of Merit, Grand Lodge of Japan, for educational activities.

Past Master of Sinim Lodge, Grand Lodge of Massachusetts.

PhD in neuroscience and CEO of a Medical Device manufacturer, living in Tokyo, Japan - amateur cellist.

Other Books by C. Earnshaw:
>Freemasonry: Spiritual Alchemy (pub. September 2019)
>Freemasonry: Initiation by Light (pub. April 2020)
>Freemasonry: Royal Arch (pub. September 2020)
>The Tarot of the Revelation
>Sho: Japanese Calligraphy

FSC for feedback, suggestions and criticism, please email me at:
>freemasonrybook@gmail.com

Other Books in the **Spiritual Freemasonry** series

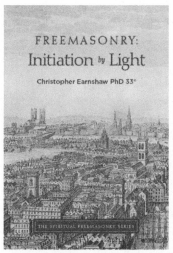

The First Degree
Freemasonry: Initiation by Light

The first three Grand Masters had changed the existing Operative Masons' rituals in some way to create modern Speculative Freemasonry. Did they use a scroll owned by a librarian at the University of Oxford that might hold the formula for alchemy's ultimate prize, the Philosophers' Stone? Who was the Chinese mandarin, who may hold the secret to one of the degrees? Why did a rival "Chinese" secret society try to bring down Freemasonry?

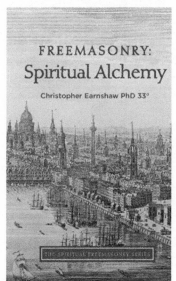

The Second Degree
Freemasonry: Spiritual Alchemy

In 1716 four Lodges of Operative Masons met at the Apple Tree Tavern in London and decided to create a "Grand Lodge" to reorganize Freemasonry, which was slowly dying out. After the establishment of the Premier Grand Lodge the next year, 1717, one of the Lodges, the Rummer and Grapes, took a decidedly new direction that resulted in the creation of what would later become known as "Speculative Freemasonry," the basis of modern Freemasonry, and the invention of an alchemical transformation.